Watching in Tongues

Multilingualism on American Television
in the 21st Century

James G. Mitchell, Ph.D.
Salve Regina University, USA

Series in Language and Linguistics

 VERNON PRESS

www.vernonpress.com

In the Americas:
Vernon Press
1000 N West Street,
Suite 1200, Wilmington,
Delaware 19801
United States

In the rest of the world:
Vernon Press
C/Sancti Espiritu 17,
Malaga, 29006
Spain

Series in Language and Linguistics

Library of Congress Control Number: 2020932715

ISBN: 978-1-64889-072-7

Also available: 978-1-62273-609-6 [Hardback]; 978-1-64889-008-6 [PDF, E-Book]

For my mother, MaryAnn.

Since I first started watching TV, you have always been with me

offering love, support and encouragement, challenging me to do my best.

For my father, Malcolm.

Although you left us before this work was finished,

your love and support were keenly felt throughout this process.

I love and thank you both.

Table of contents

List of Tables

Acknowledgments

I have many people to thank for helping me to get to the point of putting my research into this form. First and foremost, I must thank my good friend Leigh Edwards. It was Leigh who first encouraged me to begin investigating issues of language in popular media. She realized well before I did that, although I love the study of second language acquisition in the classroom, my passion for television could be harnessed into a viable direction for second language research. Without Leigh, this book would never exist.

I would like to offer a hearty thanks to my editors. Carolina Sanchez was the first to see value in this manuscript, which may have remained unpublished without her. To Argiris Legatos, I thank you for the push I needed to finalize this project. Thank you both for your extreme patience, generosity and support.

I must also thank an anonymous reviewer who provided important feedback that helped me to improve this text. The reviewer's perspective and comments allowed me to re-evaluate aspects of my work so that I could better explain my approach and analysis. I am grateful for the time they took reading my work. Any errors or remaining moments of obscurity are fully my responsibility.

I have a number of friends and colleagues who've offered encouragement and support throughout this long journey. Esther Alarcón-Arana and Emily Colbert Cairns always had a kind word or offered an ear to hear about my struggles to complete this work. Jennifer McClagnahan told me the exact words I needed to hear at a crucial moment in the process of finishing this work. Laura O'Toole kept me focused on the goal of completing this project even as she had so much of her own work to accomplish. Karen Abbondanza helped keep me sane. I owe them all my gratitude. The Writing Cohort at Salve Regina University offered me a venue to develop this project. Salve Regina Univesity also helped support this work by funding my sabbatical in the fall of 2015. I am indebted to both.

I am grateful to my colleagues farther afield as well. From the Popular Culture Association, Language Attitudes and Popular Linguistics area: Agnes Ragone, Deb Schaffer, Rachel Schaffer, Seth Katz, and more recently Justin Paz—over the years, I have been inspired many times by your work to continue my own. And, gone far too soon, I owe more than I can say to Patricia Donaher, who first welcomed me into the field of popular linguistics and encouraged me to pursue my interests in language and television. Through the many students she trained and her years helming the Language Attitudes and Popular Linguistics area, her indelible influence still remains strong.

I need to thank the people and places where I've presented aspects of this research in the past. Allen Antone invited me to speak about my scholarship at Salve Regina University's McKillop Library in March 2012. Agnes Ragone gave me a platform as the keynote speaker at the 4th Biennial Foreign Languages Conference at Shippensburg University of that same year. Agnes passed away as I was finishing this manuscript. Her kindness was unmatched and her goodness beyond belief, as the tributes by friends, colleagues, and students attest on her Facebook page. Her impact on this world will live on through the good works of those she touched. Kevin Sandler arranged for me to give a talk in February 2013 at Arizona State University's Institute for Humanities Research. All of these opportunities propelled my research forward. Without these experiences and the people who made them possible, I doubt that this book would have reached fruition.

Of course, I want to thank my parents. My mother and father who have never really understood what I do, but have always supported and loved me unconditionally. My father died in the summer of 2018, when I was first trying to finish this work. His loss delayed completion of this book, but I hope the time that I needed to recover helped make this work better. I'm sorry that he will never see it. My mother has become a daily part of my life since then. I am glad to have her in my corner. The book is finally done!

Last but not least, I thank my partner, Jason Crocker. This project was the third wheel in our relationship for many years. He tolerated my distraction for all that time and supported me throughout. I also want to thank our feline kittos, Thor, Hunter, and Cooper (and Ichabod, whom we miss every day), who provided needed diversions and never let me lose sight of what's most important in life.

As I stated above, I am uniquely responsible for any errors and/or omissions in this work. Please note, as a part of this book, I discuss the plots of many TV shows to greater or lesser degrees. There are times when I necessarily reveal important aspects of a given episode. Be warned!

Preface

The last decade or so has witnessed an enormous increase in linguistic studies of film and television. A recent bibliography compiled by the author with Raffaele Zago (University of Catania) is now 23 pages long![1] Yet, few of these studies focus on multilingualism as depicted in contemporary US television series. Having just this specific focus makes this book a unique contribution to this emerging sub-field of linguistics. James Mitchell focuses on the representation of second language speakers and second language use as well as language learning in US network TV series, drawing from his vast collection of examples from the first two decades of the 21st century (2003 to 2019). In most cases, the second language spoken is English, although cases where L1 English characters speak or learn a second language such as Spanish or French are also covered. A variety of languages are discussed in the book, including Spanish, Italian, Chinese, German, and French.

When examining fictional television series, two main approaches to coverage are possible: you can focus on one TV series in depth, or you can discuss a particular theme in a variety of programs; this book usefully does both. On the one hand, there are individual chapters that focus mainly on in-depth analyses of one or more scenes from a particular program – such as the crime series *Psych* in Chapter 2, the children's animated series *Xiaolin Showdown* in Chapter 4, the (telenovela-based) comedy-drama *Ugly Betty* in Chapter 5, and the sitcom *How I met Your Mother* in Chapter 8. On the other hand, these chapters are complemented by chapters that take a broader view. For instance, Chapter 3 discusses eight examples from *Monk*, *Bones*, *The Closer*, *Castle*, *White Collar*, and the *Law & Order* franchise, while Chapter 6 covers episodes from *American Housewife*, *Brooklyn Nine-Nine*, *The Middle*, *Modern Family*, *Schooled*, *Speechless*, *One Tree Hill*, *Pretty Little Liars*, *The Simpsons*, *10 Things I Hate About You* and *Ben 10: Ultimate Alien*. All in all, the book references over 50 different TV series. The author's focus on network television will enable future comparison with depictions in programming from premium cable (HBO, etc.) and streaming outlets (Netflix, Hulu, Amazon, etc.), which have different business models.

The author uses a broadly defined, applied linguistics framework to categorize and discuss the various ways in which L2 speakers, L2 use, and L2

---

[1] http://unico.academia.edu/RaffaeleZago/Bibliography

acquisition are represented on television. The book's 12 chapters focus on a wide variety of issues, ranging from humor, stereotyping, and crime solving to depictions of language learning and language attitudes. The diversity of issues covered in the book means that there will be much to interest different readers. Mitchell also draws on the use of subtitling, where relevant, and considers the many functions of TV dialogue and its aim to create believable stories and characters, as well as entertain viewers. To give just two of many examples, Chapter 7 shows how language plays a role in amplifying stereotypes for comedic effects, while Chapter 3 discusses how second language use can function to drive crime-solving plots. In that respect, Mitchell hypothesizes that "the next big TV show could popularize linguistics in the American imagination" (p. 81). Indeed, an announcement was made in November 2019 that CBS is developing a forensic linguistic procedural crime drama called *Fighting Words*, which will feature a forensic linguistics professor as the main character![2]

The book's many examples show that there is not only one way in which second language acquisition and use are depicted in contemporary network television, and it uncovers both negative and positive trends. While some televisual representations of L2 speakers can be negative, stereotypical, and even racist, others are more sympathetic in their depiction of linguistic diversity in the US. They illustrate the characters' *language resistance* to the subordination of their language or dialect, challenging other characters' prejudices and assumptions. The representation of L1 English speakers with poor command of other languages can embody a critique of US American monolingualism, and knowledge of a second language can even be depicted as key to solving a crime! In some instances, the way in which televisual representations are interpreted and evaluated also depends on viewers, showcasing the ambiguity of contemporary television.

The US is arguably a perfect context for this exploration. While there are other 'Anglo'-countries that feature multilingualism in relation to immigration, the global impact of US-American pop culture in the realm of fictional TV series is unparalleled. Many successful programs are exported overseas, including to countries where English is spoken as a second or foreign language. Even though Mitchell's book mainly addresses a US audience, it would seem there is potential for a much wider reach. Many of the TV series discussed would also be familiar to non-US audiences, and many of those viewers would be speakers of English as a second or foreign language with a clear interest in this topic.

---

[2] https://deadline.com/2019/11/cbs-fighting-words-crime-drama-jeffrey-kramers-juni per-place-prods-1202787251/

Furthermore, the author hopes his book will inspire others to investigate similar issues on US television, but, in connection with language-specific and locally-relevant research, it could similarly be used as a springboard for investigations of such issues in other countries.

Mitchell's qualitative approach means that many scenes are individually described and discussed concerning what is taking place in them. This approach lends itself well to a linguistic classroom setting, where many of the scenes could easily be turned into activities (e.g., in terms of language learning theories, and to contrast televisual depictions of outdated grammar-translation or audiolingual methods with more recent language pedagogies). The conversational style, accessible use of theory, and personal reflections that occur throughout also make this book ideal for use in teaching. As depictions on television also reflect contemporary issues in US-American society (such as political polarization and anti-immigrant sentiment) and because Mitchell makes concrete connections to real-world issues such as language and immigration policy (e.g., the Deferred Action for Childhood Arrivals/DACA program; official English state legislation), the book can also be used in the teaching of US culture. For example, Chapter 11 introduces readers to depictions of child *language brokers*, the bilingual children of immigrant parents who mediate between their parents and monolingual speakers and institutions in the US. Interesting facts about historical developments in television are also presented. For example, the Puerto Rican grandmother in the sitcom *Freddie* (discussed in Chapter 8) was the first character to speak only in Spanish on a US-American TV series. This invites comparison with *Abuela* (the character of Alba Gloriana Villanueva) in the more recent comedy-drama *Jane the Virgin*, which furthermore invites comparisons to *Ugly Betty*, discussed by Mitchell in Chapter 5.

Analyzing and critiquing televisual representations of multilingualism is important, not least because of the potential impact of such representations. As Mitchell puts it, "The globalization of our world finds a mimetic outlet on the small screen, reinforcing the need to look beyond our own borders, beyond our own language" (p. 109). As Mitchell also notes, the increasing diversity in writers' rooms has already given us new depictions of multilingualism in the 2019-2020 TV season. There is no doubt, then, that the theme of multilingualism will remain significant and that representations will continue to evolve, with much scope for future analysis of the television-society debate through the prism of linguistics.

Prof Monika Bednarek
Department of Linguistics
SLAM, Faculty of Arts and Social Sciences, The University of Sydney

Introduction

Popular media have long shaped societal views in America on a variety of issues. They have been responsible for both perpetuating stereotypes on the one hand, and presenting evidence to contradict, and sometimes even tear them down, on the other. Television has, perhaps, the most pervasive power in this domain, given its ubiquity in American society. A negative portrayal of a given minority group, be they a linguistic, racial, or ethnic minority, can do great damage to that group's image in the collective American psyche. Whereas a positive storyline revolving around a minority character can help mainstream that minority group by erasing or softening linguistic, racial, ethnic, and cultural differences, essentially presenting the message that *they* are just like *us*. In the end, we are all the same—we all express the same concerns and face the same challenges in the complex world that we live in today. Of course, the questions surrounding who the *they* and the *us* might be are ever evolving depending upon the expected target audience of a given program. Nevertheless, the power of television to impact American attitudes toward a given language, group, or culture is undeniable.

As a television junkie from a young age and a second language learner from almost as early, I have always been interested in when and why languages other than English were being used in real life and, of course, on the television that I'd watch growing up in a suburb of New York City. As a grown-up who became an applied linguist and second language acquisition researcher, I finally had the tools to understand and analyze these portrayals from a linguistic perspective. My hope for this book is to explore a number of issues and ideas raised by these depictions of second language speakers and second language use on television.

Of course, my work is not exhaustive in any way, nor is it meant to be. It would be nearly impossible to find and cite every example of second language (L2)[1] use on television today, especially with the proliferation of channels, streaming services, and original network and non-network programming. I do, however, try to investigate issues that have not received much attention to date in an

---

[1] In this book, I deliberately use the term second language or L2 and not terms like LX, where X is 2, 3, 4, etc., to represent multilinguals, because the U.S. is primarily a monolingual context.

effort to provide answers that shed light not only on issues of the representation of language learning and language use, but also provide an optic through which American society as a whole might be understood. As Queen (2015) tells us, "we can consider the scripted media to be fundamentally interesting precisely because of the ways in which they are of the culture of which they are a part, even as they play a role in shaping that culture" (p. 20).

The bulk of my data comes from shows on the five major U.S. broadcast networks (ABC, CBS, Fox, NBC, and the CW) that most American viewers would be able to access quite easily. I also include some data from shows on basic cable networks (ABC Family [now Freeform], Cartoon Network, TNT, USA), as well as a single show from a premium cable channel (Cinemax). My research spans the first two decades of the 21st century. I principally analyze episodes from 2003-2019, with the exception of a single, very relevant episode of *The Simpsons* from 1990. I recognize that, since I began looking at how second language speakers and second language use are portrayed on television, the very nature television itself has changed. With options like Netflix, Hulu, and Amazon, as well as streaming platforms from networks themselves (e.g., CBS All Access), how people watch television and what they watch is undergoing significant disruption. As much as the landscape of content delivery for television has changed from the turn of the 21st century until today, I imagine that in another five or ten years, things will be even more dramatically different. These changes notwithstanding, the fundamental questions that I explore in the chapters ahead remain relevant, especially in light of the current political climate and partisan divisions in the U.S. Our divisions are often keenly felt by immigrants who speak other languages and often have a second-language (L2) accent in English.

II. Theoretical & Methodological Approach

I am certainly not the first person to apply linguistic analysis to television. Queen (2015) provides an excellent guidebook for exploring linguistic variation, including dialect and language differences, in narrative media such as films and television. Through the lens of corpus linguistics, Bednarek (2018) analyzes TV dialogue and its many functions, from moving the narrative forward and aiding character development to capturing audience emotions and fostering linguistic innovations. I am also not the first to look at multilingualism in media. Bleichenbacher (2008, 2012) considers the role of multilingualism in film, providing important insights that can translate to the context of television as well. Although Pandey (2016) looks at the use of multilingualism and monolingualism in prize-winning literary fiction, her work is relevant to my own exploration of these issues on television.

Broadly speaking, I employ an applied linguistics framework to the analyses that I present in the chapters below. I borrow theories and ideas from the texts that I've just mentioned, as well as others from the fields of second language acquisition (SLA), sociolinguistics, and bilingualism to explore various topics in the text. I also employ close reading techniques used by my colleagues in literary studies. My approach is necessarily interdisciplinary because of the breadth and variety of phenomena related to L2 use. In some sense, my goal in this book is to catalogue the diversity of ways in which L2 speakers and L2 use are depicted on TV, meeting those phenomena where they are instead of trying to impose a one-size-fits-all approach. Rather than being limited by a specific methodological approach, I see the variety of perspectives that I make use of as offering those in fields beyond linguistics, such as television studies, sociology, or intercultural communication, a way to approach this text to suit their needs and the needs of their students. It must also be said that there has not been much research done that links television and L2 use. It may seem to the reader that my approach is somewhat disjointed—in some ways it is—but this choice results from a desire to look at the phenomena themselves, to try to make connections among different shows and from those shows to the real world.

The analytic approach I take in this book is decidedly qualitative. I do very little counting of tokens; I don't compare the numbers of episodes in which I find certain languages or incidences in which a given language is used to accomplish a specific task. Rather, I am interested in trying to understand the contexts in which languages other than English are used or in which L2 English speakers are found. I am not a media critic nor am I a television expert. Without doubt, scholars from those fields would be able to add a great deal to my analysis. That being said, I do try to reach out beyond television to other happenings in our popular culture (e.g., plays, news, etc.) that support the points I seek to make in an effort to demonstrate the interconnectedness of our TV lives with our real ones.

III. Structure

Over the last decade and a half, I have collected many examples of television depictions of L2 speakers and L2 use that I include in the chapters to come, and many others that I have had to leave out for the sake of brevity. I have noticed some trends in terms of the ways in which these examples are employed to achieve specific ends. These trends have shaped the structure of my book in the form of four sections, each containing three chapters: Humor and Homicide; Language Learning; Subtitles and Stereotypes; and Language Attitudes and Mediation.

In the first section, Humor and Homicide, I look at two disparate aspects of the inclusion of L2 speakers and L2 use on television. On the one hand, L2 use or L2 speakers are often depicted to create humor in various ways, especially through miscommunication or misunderstanding. I evaluate the reasons behind such portrayals, both positive and negative. On the other hand, I analyze the use of L2 knowledge or the ability to speak a second language to solve crimes in the detective/police procedural genre. I describe how this phenomenon works and also what messages it might convey to viewers.

In Language Learning, I include three chapters on how language acquisition is represented, or misrepresented, on American television. These chapters cover aspects of adult acquisition of a second language as well as child acquisition of vocabulary and metaphor in a new language. Additionally, a more general chapter on realistic and non-realistic language-learning depictions rounds out this section.

Subtitles and Stereotypes explores the ways in which L2 speakers are often negatively depicted on television based on stereotypes. Two chapters in this section specifically investigate the role that subtitles play in leading viewers to such conclusions, employing the idea of language subordination, a process that devalues non-standard language while validating the norms and beliefs of the dominant group (Lippi-Green, 2012). A third chapter in this section analyzes other ways in which stereotypes are used, sometimes to undermine negative perspectives on L2 speakers. In this section, we will see how various groups are targeted by stereotyping, including Italian-Americans, Asian-Americans, and newcomers to the U.S. who speak English as a second language. Sometimes the stereotypes utlilized in the television shows I cite are related to language use, sometimes not. In some cases, the stereotypes depicted have much in common with prejudical attitudes toward minority groups. In these chapters, such negative attitudes are directed at Asian and Latinx characters. Certainly, these groups are not the only ones subject to stereotyping and negative portrayals on television. Other racial, ethnic, religious, and minority groups, such as Arabs, Muslims, African-Americans, and LGBTQ Americans, for example, are far from immune to such treatments on television. The chapters in this section focus on what I found in the data I collected and analyzed. In no way is it my intent that my analysis should discount discrimination faced by other minority groups in the U.S., on television or in real life.

Finally, in the fourth section of the book, Language Attitudes and Mediation, I present and evaluate depictions of second languages used as tools of mediation. I look at this process in both historical and satirical terms. I conclude with a chapter focused on attitudes toward those who speak English with non-standard accents, including not only varieties of L2 English but regional varieties of American English. I consider how those with non-standard accents engage in language resistance (based on Worth's (2006, 2008) idea of foreign language resistance) to combat linguistic prejudice.

Overall, there are both positive and negative depictions of L2 speakers and L2 use. However, this patchwork of portrayals is complex, with multiple valences and interpretations possible from the same scene. For instance, comedic depictions of L2 speakers/use can lead us to conclude that L2 speakers are just like us and can lessen the sense of otherness. But, such depictions can also undercut the agency or intelligence of L2 speakers, leaving viewers to think of them in a negative light (cf. Queen, 2015, pp. 31-33 for a discussion of how variational use of languages can be used to show similarity/solidarity or difference/otherness). It is precisely the ambiguity of these portrayals that I hope to highlight. Subtitles can also play a role in this process as Queen (2015) demonstrates in her analysis of a scene from the movie *Crash* (2009). By drawing attention to the perhaps unintended negative aspects of these portrayals, we can hopefully develop more sophisticated ways of representing L2 speakers as more like us than not.

I view this book as a first step. Certainly, there may be perspectives to add and other analyses possible, but I hope to inspire others to investigate issues of L2 language use or L2 language speakers on American television. If any of the episodes I cite intrigues you, I invite you to find them and watch!—most are readily available on Amazon, Netflix, Hulu, or via some other service, if not available on DVD. Now, sit back, and enjoy the show!

Part I:
Humor & Homicide

Chapter 1

I Will Not Sugar-Jacket How Much of a Cheapsteak You Are! Second Language Use at the Crossroads of Humor and Social Commentary

I. Introduction

In this chapter, I consider the ways in which second languages (L2s) and second language speakers (L2 speakers) are used on television to create ethnic humor. Mintz (1996) describes ethnic humor as "the construction of caricatures based on familiar ethnic stereotypes and linguistic humor—puns, malapropisms, double entendres, and accent play, including broad exaggeration and misunderstandings, which result from faulty pronunciation" (p. 20). Ethnic humor is a fundamental way in which L2 English speakers are used to get laughs, often in a cheap manner, but sometimes in more sophisticated ways that cause us to question our assumptions and beliefs about non-native speakers. Native English speakers using languages other than English, in general poorly, are also a source of humor. We will see examples of this trope below as well. Before we look at any data, let's consider some research perspectives on L2 use in television.

II. Background research

Bednarek (2018) proposes a new functional approach to television series (FATS) consisting of five main functions related to the following areas: 1) communication of the narrative, 2) aesthetic/interpersonal effect and commercial appeal, 3) thematic messages and ideology, 4) realism, and 5) the serial nature of TV narratives (p. 37). Three of these functions, the aesthetic/interpersonal (2), the narrative communication (1), and the thematic (3), are relevant to the discussion below. In the aesthetic/interpersonal function, Bednarek locates jokes and humor, the most widely used way in which L2 speakers and L2 use serve the shows in which they are included. In the narrative communication function, the development of the narrative and the anchoring of characters are considered. This function of TV dialogue is often used in concert with the aesthetic function to tell us more about characters or to move the dialogue forward while making us laugh. Finally, it is important to consider the ideological function. Often scenes with L2 speakers/use convey messages about language, whether subtle and implicit or explicitly named by other characters, we must consider these in our analysis. "There are many cases where it is not clear if aspects of the dialogue have been designed to create an explicit/implicit message, but where the dialogue nevertheless challenges, reinforces, or negotiates hegemonic ideologies" (Bednarek, 2018, p. 69).

Queen (2015) discusses code-shifting, a process encompassing changing between different dialects or languages.

> Code-shifting minimally involves people who have more or less fluent command of the codes being used; thus code-switching is a phenomenon that involves either bi- (or multi-) lingualism and/or bi- (or multi-) dialectalism. This means that code-switching can be a part of the linguistic repertoire used to do various kinds of speech acts, and this includes being part of the repertoire available for moving the plot of the narrative along within the fictional media. (p. 197)

Queen goes on to discuss examples in which code-shifting is part of the action, and how that shift from one code to another accomplishes some discursive end or serves a specific discursive purpose. Queen uses the catch-all term code-shifting to encompass what others have termed style-shifting (from one dialect or register to another) and code-switching (from one language to another). Inherent in the idea of code-switching is the idea of changing from the grammar of one language to the grammar of another language, i.e., the grammars of the languages in question are viewed as separate, self-contained systems. Translanguaging[1] (Otheguy et al., 2015), on the other hand, holds that speakers have only one mental grammar, that comprises in a structured but unitary way the features of any/all languages that the bilingual speaks. In education, a translanguaging perspective suggests that bilingual students

---

[1] I choose the term translanguaging from among many other proposed theories of code mixing because both languages are seen as a single unitary system in the user's mind and because many times, L2 language use has resonance with the L2 classroom, where translanguaging has become a popular idea when working with bilinguals. Among other post-structuralist views on language, Shin (2018) cites "**code-meshing** (Canagarajah, 2013), **crossing** (Rampton, 2005), **languaging** (Blommaert & Rampton, 2011; Shohamy, 2006), **translanguaging** (García & Li, 2015), **heteroglossia** (Bailey, 2007), **flexible bilingualism** (Creese & Blackledge, 2011), **polylanguaging** (Jørgensen et al., 2011), **polylingualism** (Møllet, 2008), and **metrolingualism** (Pennycook & Otsuji, 2014)" (p. 127, emphasis in original).

should be able to use all linguistic resources available to them in both languages (not one language at a time) to learn and interact in the classroom. Watching how bilingualism is represented on TV may provide support for this idea and the related idea of transidentitying (Richards & Wilson, 2019), "how different identities or identity characteristics are often created and negotiated within a single or series of related interactions" (p. 179). The notions of translanguaging and code-switching in bilinguals are certainly relevant to the ways in which L2 speakers are depicted on television.

Finally, Pandey (2016, 2019) identifies two competing forces affecting the landscape of prize-winning literary fiction: 1) increased visual prominence of nationally-bounded languages (i.e., languages like English and French that have countries associated with them) and 2) linguistic monolingualism in which languages vie for value. The first of these ideas she calls linguistic exhibitionism, which she defines as the "use of shallow multilingualism— lexically oriented, rather than deeply discoursal-discursive; ... an ornamentalized incorporation of linguistic difference hearkening towards complete semiotic equivalency, and semantic transparency; the deliberate use of modern multilingualism for cosmetic effect" (Pandey 2016, p. 83). For example, moments in fiction where a character is said to be speaking Bengali, for instance, but the dialogue on the page is rendered in English. With respect to how languages vie for value, they are subject to market forces. Books in languages with larger markets and in which the "interruptive force of multilingualism is kept to a minimum by paratextual marginalization (e.g., to a glossary at the end)" (Pandey, 2019) garner more prestige and renown, therefore value. We will see if these concepts from the literary world find corollaries in the fiction of episodic TV.

With these ideas in mind, let's consider some data.

III. Data

a. Missed Metaphors, Imprecise Idioms, Parsing & Pronunciation

One of the more difficult aspects of a new language for L2 learners is metaphor and idiomatic language. There are various reasons that make this type of language a challenge for learners. Metaphorical and idiomatic language is difficult to learn because it is low frequency, employed only at specific moments under the correct situational constraints. Also, its use is not always clearly connected to the actual meanings of the words involved or the direct connection that may have existed at one time has been lost to history and evolution of the language. In addition, metaphorical and idiomatic language changes with the times. That being said, it is crucially important for L2 speakers to master idiomatic and metaphorical language to some extent in order to truly understand the L2 culture and to integrate more seamlessly into L2 society.

In popular television, misuse of metaphor is often used to evoke the audience's laughter. Perhaps there is no better L2 example of this than the character of Gloria on the very popular series *Modern Family* (2009-2020). Gloria, a native Spanish speaker from Colombia, learned English it appears in a largely naturalistic way—not in a classroom, but rather through living her life in the English-speaking environment of the U.S. Perhaps because of this method of learning English, she is more aware of the importance of metaphorical language in everyday interaction. At the very least, the writers certainly are and have created many situations in which Gloria misses the target ever so slightly to create humor. In the example below, Gloria is trying to express the idea that Claire is giving her the cold shoulder, but she pluralizes it, ending up with "cold shoulders."

(1.1)
Claire: I'm going to yoga.
Gloria: Ay! That sounds like so much fun.
Cam: Oh, you should go with her, Gloria!
Claire: Oh, we should definitely do that sometime. I would love it. Bye!
Gloria: Do you see how she gives me the **cold shoulders**? I don't even know why I try. [Puts an icepack on Cam's back] Ay. Sorry.
Cam: Oh, well, that's just Claire, you know? She's a Pritchett.[2]
(Ko & Winer, 2012)

In an episode from earlier in the series, Jay gives Gloria's new friend Guillermo some advice about a business proposal involving a revolutionary new system for training dogs. The dog-training system fails to impress. Jay is very blunt in expressing his thoughts to Guillermo, which Guillermo takes badly. He pretends to put his dog Stella back in the car, but ultimately drives off leaving Stella behind.

---

[2] For languages other than English, the English subtitles have been added when provided onscreen. When no English subtitles were present, speech in a language other than English that is not subtitled has been added by the author whenever possible.

(1.2)

Guillermo:	I go put Stella in the car. I don't want to ruin any more of your beautiful things. Gracias. Bad dog.
Gloria:	Why were you so tough with him? He's very sensitive.
Jay:	Did you think that was a good idea?
Gloria:	Of course not, but I'm nice and **I put on the sugar jacket.**
Jay:	Sugarcoating is not gonna help him. He needed to hear what I said to him, even if it hurt a little bit. He's gonna thank me one day.

(Higginbotham et al., 2011)

Here, Gloria extends the idea that "coat" and "jacket" are often synonyms in English. Moreover, since one puts on a jacket, she logically assumes that one puts on a "sugar jacket." Jay immediately responds with the correct term, "sugarcoat" providing implicit correction or recast (cf. Ellis, 2006, pp. 228-31) of Gloria's error by restating the term, much as a teacher might do in a foreign language classroom.

Gloria is not the only character on TV misusing metaphors in English. The French-speaking character Luc in the ABC series *Brothers & Sisters* (Monreal et al., 2011) also provides an example of this phenomenon.

(1.3)

Justin:	Could you have picked a more difficult dinner to make?
Luc:	Of course it's difficult. It's Cassoulet D'Artagnan, a French stew with lamb, duck, veal. Justin, you don't promise your fiancée a beautiful, romantic, home-cooked meal and then serve up a plate of spaghetti. Sarah's been working hard. I want to do something special for her. Something out of the ordinary.
Justin:	Well, barnyard soup is definitely out of the ordinary.
Luc:	All right, you call it what you want. But it's complex, extravagant. Women love the big grand gesture.
Justin:	You know, Luc, I think I'm gonna disagree with you there. I think women like something a little more personal to them. Like Sarah, you know what she would like? Chilidogs.
Luc:	I know. But if I do something like that, for Sarah, I would look like a **cheap steak**.
Justin:	It's cheapskate. But a cheap steak is what I'm talking about.
Luc:	Okay, Dr. Valentine's. What are you doing tonight?

(Monreal, et al., 2011)

In this conversation with his soon-to-be brother-in-law, Justin, Luc explains why he is making a very complicated and special dinner for his fiancée, Sarah, Justin's sister. When Justin suggests something simpler might be better, Luc expresses his fear of being perceived as a "cheap steak." Justin explicitly corrects him and makes a something of a pun based on Luc's malapropism, "But a cheap steak is what I'm talking about."

These slightly incorrect uses of idiomatic language are designed to make us laugh and often hit the mark. They fall squarely in Bednarek's (2018) aesthetic/interpersonal function, as they do not really move the narrative forward, but serve rather as humor. Beyond mistakes using L2 English metaphors, miscommunications that arise from problems of accent or parsing result in humor as well. Parsing refers to the ability of a speaker to determine where one word ends and the next begins. Even native speakers can have trouble with parsing; consider, for example, the following phrase: **For all intents and purposes**. Often we hear the related phrase, **For all intensive purposes**. The fact that these two phrases exist is the result of a parsing problem by English native speakers.

Again, we can look to *Modern Family* for clear examples of issues with parsing. Early in season two of the show, a scene between Gloria and her husband Jay very explicitly addresses the difficulties that non-native speakers of English can have with parsing. Prior to this scene, Gloria has been corrected for pronouncing gargoyle like gargle. She is feeling sensitive about her L2 English in this scene, but nonetheless asks Jay to correct some of her linguistic mistakes so that she can learn.

(1.4)

Gloria:	Jay! This came for you.
Jay:	Oh, hi, honey. What is it?
Gloria:	I called your secretary and told her to order you some crackers and those cheeses that you like. The tiny little ones.
Jay:	Thanks. Did you pick up my gargle costume too?
Gloria:	Are you making fun of me?
Jay:	No.
Gloria:	First Manny correcting me, and now you? If I have a problem, I want to know, Jay.
Jay:	Honey, look. English is your second language. You're doin' great.
Gloria:	Yeah, you're not helping by protecting my feelings. I want you to be honest with me.

Jay:	Okay, well, I may have noticed some tiny little mistakes you might want to take a look at.
Gloria:	Like what?
Jay:	Just little mispronunciations. Like, for example, last night you said we live in a "doggy-dog" world.
Gloria:	So?
Jay:	It's "dog-eat-dog" world.
Gloria:	Yeah, but that doesn't make any sense. Who wants to live in a world where dogs eat each other? Doggy-dog world is a beautiful world full of little puppies. What else do I say wrong?
Jay:	Well, it's not "blessings in the skies." It's "blessings in disguise."
Gloria:	What else?
Jay:	"Carpal tunnel syndrome" is not "carpool tunnel syndrome."
Gloria:	And what else?
Jay:	It's not "vo-lump-tuous."
Gloria:	Okay, enough. I know that I have an accent, but people understand me just fine.
Jay:	[Opening the box, looking inside] What the hell is this?
Gloria:	I told you, Jay. I called your secretary and told her to order you a box of baby cheeses. [Jay pulls out a little baby Jesus.]
Gloria:	Oh, so now that is my fault too.

(Richman & Spiller, 2010)

Jay characterizes what Gloria calls "mistakes" as "little mispronunciations." That does not stop him from having a series of corrections to offer his wife: her "doggy-dog" should be "dog-eat-dog," "blessings in the skies" should be "blessings in disguise," and "carpool tunnel syndrome" is really "carpal tunnel syndrome." She recognizes that she has an accent but after so much explicit correction, she finally stops Jay with, "people understand me just fine."

The humor in this scene derives from the explicit comparison of what Gloria says to the actual English phrases—in her own ability to parse the English that she hears and, subsequently, to reproduce what she thinks she hears. However, the humor is layered. Despite the mis-parsed phrases, there is Gloria's contradictory understanding of what dog-eat-dog world, or in her parlance doggy-dog world, means. She thinks this idiom refers to something positive and sweet, while the actual meaning is quite the opposite. Moreover, the scene makes clear that parsing is not the only aspect of language that can be an issue for non-native speakers. The way others understand and parse what the L2 speaker is saying can also cause issues. This point is brought home when Jay opens up the gift that Gloria had his secretary order for him. Gloria believes she ordered little baby cheeses that Jay likes to have with crackers. However, Jay opens the box perplexed when he pulls out a little baby Jesus figurine. Although Gloria knows she said "little baby cheeses," Jay's secretary clearly misunderstood and ordered little baby Jesuses. This problem is likely the result of Gloria's accent or her pronunciation in her L2, English.

In an early Christmas episode in the series, because she is afraid of spiders Gloria enlists her young step-grandchild Luke to look for a beloved family Christmas angel that is stored in the attic at her and Jay's home. In the scene below, there is explicit discussion of the way "Luke and "look" sound the same to Gloria and, consequently, how she is unable to realize the difference between the vowels /u/ and /ʌ/.

(1.5)
Gloria: Luke!
Luke: At what?
Gloria: What do you mean, "at what"? I said "Luke."
Luke: I am looking.
Gloria: I know you are. Stay on the beams. Maybe it's here. [Uncovers a dog-faced butler] Ay, dios mio! El diablo! It's back! [descends the ladder] What is so special about that angel, anyways?
Luke: I don't know. I guess Nana made it for mom and Uncle Mitchell when they were kids.
Gloria: Ay, that's nice. Look where you're going!
Luke: To open more boxes. [Foot falls through ceiling] Oh, you said "look where you're going," didn't you?
Gloria: Yes.
Luke: Every time you say "Luke," I think you're saying "look."
Gloria: I don't hear the difference.
Luke: It's not that hard. One is my name.
Gloria: Juan is not your name! Stop kidding around and look, Luke! Ay, I get it. "look" sounds like "Luke."
Luke: Yes. Thank god. I've been carrying that one around for three years.
(Chupack & Spiller, 2011)

This interaction between Gloria and a young member of her family (Luke is a pre-teen in this scene) is interesting because Luke doesn't really understand what the difficulty is in pronouncing his name correctly. This speaks to some segments of the American public that don't understand what it is to speak a second language, that may not understand that learning an L2 in adulthood almost always results in some degree of accent. On the other hand, he demonstrates some tolerance in the way he has been "carrying that one around for years" without demonstrating any overt frustration with Gloria. There is also the related joke in the scene relating the sound of "one" with the name "Juan." In fact, it is that confusion, which Gloria figures out on her own, that causes her to realize that, although "look" and "Luke" sound the same, there is a significant difference that is important to Luke.

These episodes along with the metaphor difficulties can be characterized as examples of ethnic humor (Mintz, 1996). Thus, one of the main functions of L2 English speakers on American TV, especially their mistakes, is to add levity. All of the examples thus are fit into Bednarek's aesthetic/interpersonal function precisely because they are jokes/humor. In addition, however, the two most recent examples, involving pronunciation difficulties can also categorized as part of the narrative communication function because they help to anchor a significant feature of the character of Gloria, her non-native accent in English. The metaphor examples do not mark her clearly as a non-native speaker, because even native speakers of English can make errors when using metaphorical language.

In these examples, the audience seems to be laughing with Gloria and Luc, who are rather proficient English speakers that make the occasional error. The characters themselves, especially Gloria, seem to recognize that their English is imperfect and constantly improving, but as Gloria says, people understand her just fine. There is a more problematic portrayal of L2 English speakers that is meant to be funny, but the humor seems to come at the expense of the L2 English character.

In a 2017 *Modern Family* episode entitled, "All Things Being Equal," Phil and Jay decide to go into business together by buying a parking lot in a busy downtown area. They need to hire a parking attendant, so they interview an L1 English woman named Joan and an L2 English man named Tibor. Below I excerpt only the portion of the interview with Tibor:

(1.6)
Phil: So, Tibor, tell us why you're excited about a career in parking.
Tibor: Is good.
...
Phil: Tibor, what are your favorite kinds of music?
Tibor: Tibor. Is good?
(Straton et al., 2017)

It seems that Tibor is incapable of truly understanding or speaking English. The fact that Tibor can only say his own name and "is good" may evoke laughter, especially because the character also speaks with a strange L2 accent, and even though Jay wants to hire him over Joan, the whole interaction comes off as making fun of a non-native speaker. Tibor seems to be the butt of the joke. This inclusion of an L2 English character, certainly an example of ethnic humor, strikes me as mean-spirited. The writers of this episode picked the lowest hanging fruit on the humor branch. This example demonstrates one of the dangers of employing ethnic humor using L2 English or non-English-speaking characters.

Bednarek (2018), in her survey of style manuals, finds that some writers acknowledge that "foreign accents may be exploited for humor" (p. 214) but also seem aware that this could lead to stereotyping and negative portrayals. In interviews with European American scriptwriters, she found some reluctance to write dialects that they did not speak (i.e., African American Vernacular English). In fact, Bednarek notes that, "in general, they…wanted to avoid stereotypes and would often leave it up the actors to provide the necessary authenticity through dialect or accent" (p. 214). Tibor is reminiscent of Bleichenbacher's (2008, 2012) study of a corpus of 28 English-language Hollywood films from 1984-2003 in which he found a high proportion of negative depictions of speakers whose L1 was not English. This result echoed Lippi-Green's (1997) study of the accents of Disney characters where she found that L2 accents in English were often associated with negative characters in the films she analyzed. Whatever the specific case may be for Tibor, presenting the character in this ways leaves a great deal to be desired.

b. Americans as Bad Language Learners

Humor is also achieved when native speakers of English, usually Americans, attempt to deploy their knowledge of a foreign language. Often, in these cases, part of the joke is that Americans are not good at speaking languages other than English, trading on Americans' reputation for being resistant to language learning, or worse, for attempting to imperialistically impose (American) English on other nations and peoples. In the first example, below, from *How I Met Your Mother* (Lloyd & Fryman, 2011), main character Ted accompanies his friend Lily to the airport to pick up an academic who is speaking at a dinner hosted by Lily's husband. To convince Ted to come, Lily tells Ted that Professor Rodriguez speaks only Spanish and that she is relying on Ted to communicate with the professor. In this case, we hear Ted speak in Spanish, badly, and see a faithfully bad English translation on screen.

(1.7)

Ted:	There he is. Here we go. [Speaking Spanish subtitled in English] Professor Rodriguez, I are Ted. This am Lily. We'd like to get inside you and go forward.[3]
Professor:	I'm sorry. I don't speak whatever it is you're speaking.
Ted:	Um, he speaks perfect English.
Lily:	Yeah, I-I know.
Ted:	Then why did you ask me to come?
Lily:	So you can drive him to the fund-raiser. Supporting Marshall this much is driving me crazy. I'm going to Spain. My flight leaves in 45 minutes. *Adios, muchacho.*

(Lloyd & Fryman, 2011)

It's interesting to note that Professor Rodriguez, potentially a Spanish speaker, is utterly unable to decipher what Ted is saying in Spanish. Ironically, Lily, who recruited Ted for his help speaking Spanish, leaves for Spain with a well-executed "adios muchacho."

A similarly comic situation arises in the Big Bang Theory episode called, "The Gates Excitation" (Kaplan et al., 2018). In the last scene of the episode, Stuart, who owns the comic book store and becomes the nanny (or *manny*, if you prefer) to Howard and Bernadette's baby, ventures to the park with his charge. He addresses two nannies sitting on a bench in Spanish. The nannies, speaking in Spanish to each other, express suspicion of him and his efforts to use Spanish. He begins with an enthusiastic, "¡Hola!" In reaction, one nanny says to the other in Spanish that is subtitled in English, "Ay, este hombre otra vez," ('Oh, this guy again.'). As they look at Stuart, who clearly does not understand, smiling at them strangely, the second nanny says to the first, ¿Qué le pasa?" ('What's wrong with him?'). Stuart continues in English, "How you ladies, doing? Raise your hands if you're *bueno.*" The second nanny continues speaking to the first nanny, "¿Quien le dejaría cuidar a sus niños?" ('Who would let him watch their kids?'). Her friend responds, "A lo mejor, se los robó," ('Maybe he stole them.'). Stuart, continuing to try to make friends with them, offers, "Me llamo Stuart Bloom," (this line is not subtitled in English). The second nanny counsels the first, "Apúntalo. A lo mejor tenemos que dar a la policía," ('Write that down. We may have to give it to the cops.') (Kaplan et al., 2018). In this case, the humor is achieved, not so much by the fact that Stuart's Spanish is bad, but rather because his Spanish is simplistic

---

[3] *"Yo eres Ted. Este soy Lily. Queremos entrarte y ir delantero."*

and he is not proficient enough to understand the conversation between the two nannies, who find him strange and fear his intentions.

In the next example, from *Modern Family* again, through a series of unfortunate mishaps, Phil and Claire risk missing their daughter Alex's valedictory speech at her graduation. Phil and Claire are desperate when Phil spots an opportunity that can help them arrive on time.

(1.8)

Phil:	I'm not missing that speech! [Runs into the street and stops a landscaping truck] Hello! Hello!
Claire:	What's the plan, Phil?
Phil:	Mi nombre es Felipe. Yo voy a la escuela.
Landscaper:	You need a ride to the school?
Phil:	Yes, please.
Claire:	"Felipe"!
Phil:	¡Vámonos, muchachos!

(Zuker & Levitan, 2011)

The interesting thing about examples 1.7 and 1.8 is the assumption that characters who look Latino or have Latino names will speak Spanish—with the caveat that Lily lied to Ted about Professor Rodriguez. Even so, I doubt the audience would question that assumption on its face. Here we find television writers playing with our expectations about identity in a not-so-subtle way that problematizes the conclusions we make simply based on stereotypes. Perhaps both the landscaper that Phil stops and Professor Rodriguez do speak Spanish, but should that be our first thought? Why couldn't they be bilingual or even monolingual English speakers? In this way, the expectations associated with ethnic humor are sometimes undermined in ways that create humor. Not only is it funny that Phil and Ted speak Spanish—Ted's Spanish is funny because it is so poor; Phil's is funny because it is simplistic and childlike—but it is also funny and subversive that their interlocutors reply in perfect American English with no trace of L2 accent. Bednarek (2018) is hopeful after speaking with scriptwriters that perhaps they are keenly aware of stereotyping and wish to avoid it. These examples would support that notion.

In a related way, sometimes writers use the lack of knowledge of an L2 as a way to create humor. In the scene below from *Modern Family*, Phil is celebrating his 50th birthday with his family, which he uses as an opportunity to list all of the things he wants to do in the upcoming year: take piano lessons, learn to ride a unicycle, and learn Spanish.

(1.9)
Phil: Also, I'm gonna learn how to speak Spanish.
Gloria: Excelente!
Phil: [Blank expression] Uh, I haven't started yet.
(Levitan, 2019)

Gloria is excited that Phil has set learning Spanish as a goal for his fiftieth year. She expresses her approval with "excelente," a cognate to English 'excellent'. The humor comes from Phil's blank expression, indicating a total inability to recognize "excelente" as a cognate. Hopes for his acquisition of Spanish are lessened by this moment. Later in the scene, Jay, Phil's father-in-law re-gifts a book to Phil that another family had given Jay on his birthday. The ruse is discovered because the book is inscribed to Jay. This leads Gloria to become so upset that she can only express her anger in her native tongue, Spanish.

(1.10)
Gloria: [Speaking Spanish subtitled in English] Why are you so
               thoughtless to this desperate man-child who craves your
               love?[4]
Phil: A year from now, I'm gonna know what that means.
(Levitan, 2019)

This moment is part of the payoff for the earlier moment in the scene. Phil will know what Gloria has said by next year after he studies Spanish. And, finally, a full year later at the end of the episode, on the day when Phil's first grandchildren are born, we do get to hear how Phil's Spanish has progressed. Looking lovingly at his newborn grandchildren, Phil expresses his contentment, "Mi ano fue hermoso...My year was beautiful." Gloria offers a minor correction, "Año means 'year'. Ano means 'anus'." Undaunted, Phil retorts, "Still works" (Levitan, 2019). Here the set-up from the beginning of the episode has its ultimate payoff with the joke about Phil learning Spanish reaching its inevitable conclusion. He did learn some Spanish, but not as well as he should have.

This more sophisticated use of ethnic humor, or perhaps reverse ethnic humor, demonstrates a more evolved way of weaving L2 language use into the fabric of the episode. It represents an evolution in the storytelling of *Modern*

---

[4] *"¿Por qué tiene que ser tan desconsiderado con este pobre hombre inmaduro y ridiculo que anhela su amor?"*

Family, which has been using ethnic humor since it was first broadcast over a decade ago. Instead of an isolated moment, as we see in earlier examples from the show, here we have the set-up for the joke in the opening moments of the episode and the punchline at the very end of the episode.

Other instances of reverse ethnic humor occur in shows such as *Superstore* and *Cougar Town.* In the *Superstore* episode, "Local Vendors Day" (Malmuth & Patel, 2018), principal character Amy doesn't feel Latina enough when the soda delivery guy flirts with her in Spanish, which she can't speak. Similarly, the *Cougar Town* episode, "Damaged by Love" (Ho & McDonald, 2011), finds the Cuban character Andy upset by the fact that all the other characters speak Spanish to some degree except for him. In both of these instances, the writers play with our expectations that the Latinx characters should know Spanish. Since they do not, the humor comes from the reversal of what we would typically expect in ethnic humor.

Returning to Spanish use in the *Modern Family* episode, we might ask ourselves are these merely incidents of linguistic exhibitionism (Pandey, 2016), the tokenization of Spanish in this episode? I would argue that the picture is more complicated than that. On the surface, the use of "excelente" and Phil's line about his anus would seem to be so. However, Gloria's line at the end of the first scene, "Why are you so thoughtless to this desperate man-child who craves your love?" realized in Spanish with English subtitles does double duty. On the one hand, it is another example of linguistic exhibitionism in that the audience doesn't have to know what she is saying because the subtitles are provided—a bit of token exoticism. On the other hand, she delivers the line at the rate of speed that one might expect if she were speaking to other native speakers of Spanish and, given the premise of the episode, that Phil will learn Spanish, there does seem to be some positivity directed toward the idea of speaking Spanish. Again Gloria's use of Spanish in this scene seems to be primarily focused on the narrative communication function per Bednarek (2018) as her Spanish L1 is a major feature of her character. While the learning of Spanish is clearly related to the plot of the episode, also a narrative communication function. There could be some ideological work occurring as well, related to the thematic function, in terms of the positive valence directed toward the learning of Spanish.

c. Americans as Good Language Learners

There are also humorous instances of American characters speaking L2s quite well, or at the very least being depicted in such a way as to convince the audience that that is the case. In fact, in some ways, these examples turn the idea of ethnic humor on its head, because it is not the expected "ethnic" character using an L2, but rather the Anglo character. Of course, as I said, these examples provide moments of humor as the proficient use of an L2 by an Anglo character is often unexpected. This humor often arises from the mismatch between the aesthetic/interpersonal and the thematic functions. The ethnic humor that we expect in the aesthetic/interpersonal function is undermined by the thematic function of upending our expectations, presenting an alternative to the prevailing American ideology of monolingualism. In addition, by having the character using the L2 make slight mistakes in their deployment of the L2, as we'll see in some examples, we get more sophisticated and complex moments that elicit laughter. In both instances, writers are playing with our expectations. First, because we don't expect Anglo characters to speak an L2 well. Then, in some examples, because once they seem to be doing well, the rug is pulled out from under them with an egregious mistake to make the audience laugh.

Here is an example from *The Big Bang Theory* (Holland et al., 2017) in which Sheldon speaks Hindi. The four main male characters (Sheldon, Leonard, Howard, and Raj) are at their favorite comic book shop, perusing comics when Sheldon brings up the idea of super-aging as a way to combat getting beaten by teenagers in online videogames, as happened to them earlier in the episode. A discussion ensues around that topic:

(1.11)

Leonard: How is super-aging any different than, like, doing crossword puzzles?

Sheldon: Well, it's not just doing simple cognitive tasks. You need to push your brain out of its comfort zone and reach mental exhaustion.

Leonard: I drive you to work every day, my brain must look like the Hulk's.

Raj: If you really want to challenge yourself, you could learn to speak Hindi.

Sheldon: [Speaking Hindi, subtitled in English] Did that when I was eight.[5]

Raj: Could you say that in English? I actually, I never learned Hindi.

(Holland et al., 2017)

---

[5] As best I can discern using Google translate, Sheldon says: *"Jab mein aat saal ka tha Maine seekha tha"* (क्या जब मैं आठ साल का था; Pronunciation: kya jab main aath saal ka tha).

Here, when Raj suggests that Sheldon learn Hindi to increase his brain power, he (and the audience) does not expect Sheldon to respond with Hindi. Sheldon's response completely undermines the audience's expectations, making them laugh. The humor is extended by the idea that Raj, who is Indian, grew up in India, and speaks with an Indian English accent, does not speak Hindi. This revelation further undermines what the audience expects. Again, both of these jokes are a sort of reverse ethnic humor, because they flip the expectations associated with ethnic humor on their head.

In a less subversive, but more convincing way, the *Speechless* episode "D-I—DIMEO A-C—ACADEMY" (Chun et al., 2018), surprises us when principal character Maya speaks French.[6] In the episode, disabled son JJ's mainstream school will not let him graduate because he has not met the requirements to do so. JJ's mother Maya decides to pull JJ from his school and set up Dimeo Academy, to homeschool JJ so that he can catch up with his studies enough to graduate. One of the courses JJ is behind in is French, which explains this next exchange:

(1.12)

Maya:	I did my research. If we follow a registered online curriculum, you can get enough credits to graduate this year. Boom! Victory marshmallow is a thing now.
JJ:	[Looks skeptical and shakes his head][7]
Maya	No? All right.
JJ:	[Spelling out on his board, Maya reads] They said I couldn't do it.
Maya:	Yeah. So now we fight. Did you just meet me?
JJ:	You can't be my teacher. You don't know C-H-E chemistry or French.
Maya:	Well, that's where you're wrong. See, Mrs. Dimeo doesn't need to know everything. She just needs to know one chapter more than you. And as of last night, she does. Alors. Si tu as fini de déconner, il faut que nous nous mettions au travail. Allons-freakin'-sy.[8]

(Chun et al., 2018)

---

[6] I recognize that Maya is not American per se, but as an Anglophone character in an American sitcom, I think she fits into the spirit of my argument.

[7] JJ is non-verbal so he uses a board to spell out his lines, which others speak for him.

[8] "So, if you're finished messing around, we have to get to work. Let's freakin' go!"

Later in the episode, Maya and her husband Jimmy fight about Maya's homeschooling plan.

(1.13)
Jimmy: You can't teach him stuff that you just learned yesterday.
Maya: Ecoutez-moi bien, mon petit mec. Tais-toi, sinon je vais
            te faire désolé. Désolé vraiment![9]
Jimmy: I will give you that your French has gotten very good.
(Chun et al., 2018)

In both instances, Maya's French is extraordinarily good. It is clear to me that Minnie Driver, the actress who plays Maya, speaks French rather well. By extension, then, so does her character. The idea that a British woman (and Driver does use a native British accent for the character of Maya), who we discover in a later episode comes from a well-off family, speaks French is not so unusual. However, what is striking is, 1) her exceptional skill and native-like deployment of French, and 2) the fact that the French in these episodes is not subtitled in any way. The humor, therefore, is the surprise (and the conceit in the episode) that Maya speaks French well enough to speak fluently even though she is just learning enough material to be ahead of JJ, who is only in high school after all. In this case, the French that Maya uses does not seem to fit Pandey's (2016) idea of linguistic exhibitionism. What Maya says in French is not subtitled in any way and not so easily determined from the context of the episode, especially what she says to her husband. Admittedly, if you did not understand what she said in French, you could still follow what happens in the episode, but it is more reminiscent of Gloria's line in Spanish above. It is discursive, not semantically transparent, and interrupts the flow of the scene, running counter to the idea of linguistic exhibitionism. So, even in the U.S., we can find moments in which TV places a premium of sorts on a language other the English, making it stand out.

In contrast to the earlier Modern Family episode in which Phil utters only one line in Spanish that is not correct, the episode "Blasts From the Past" (Chandrasekaran et al., 2019) finds Phil and Clare speaking Italian rather well. They are gearing up for a four-week bike tour of the vineyards of Italy. In this scene, as the episode opens, they are riding their bikes in their living room following a road that wends its way through a landscape of Italy displayed on a projector screen.

---

[9] "Listen up, little man. Shut up, otherwise I'm going to make you sorry. Very sorry."

(1.14)
Phil: [Speaking Italian, English subtitles] Italy is truly the most
                 beautiful country, no?
Claire: [Speaking Italian, English subtitles] Yes. The food is
                 delicious and the people are nice.
Phil: [Speaking Italian, English subtitles] Let's stop. And kill that
                 old man for directions.
Claire: [Speaking Italian, English subtitles] Our Italian has gotten
                 very big. [10]
(Chandrasekaran et al., 2019)

Phil and Claire speak Italian well in this scene; their pronunciation (although Phil's *fermiamoci* sound more like *fermioci*) and grammar are generally good. The humor arises in the juxtaposition of their good pronunciation and grammar with some faulty lexical choices. For instance, the confusion of the verb "to ask" '*chiedere*' with the verb "to kill" '*uccidere*'. Also present is the funny translation "our Italian has gotten very big." Strangely, in Claire's spoken Italian, it does sound as if she says the correct verb, "*migliorare*" 'to get better' so it may be that they chose to insert this joke after the filming of the episode by simply changing the subtitles. Subtitles themselves are a complicated issue that I cover in Chapters 7 and 9.

At the end of the episode, Claire and Phil decide to give up their trip to Italy because of how crazy their lives have become. Their pregnant daughter and son-in-law move in with them as well as their son-in-law's mother, who is currently visiting from out of town, and his step-children—they have a full house and many concerns. While giving up on Italy for now, they share a final brief exchange of love in Italian:

(1.15)
Phil: [Speaking Italian, English subtitles] To that adventure that
                 is life.
Claire: [Speaking Italian, English subtitles] With you, every day is
                 a lawnmower.

---

[10] Phil: L'Italia è davvero il paese più bello del mondo, no?
Claire: Sì.. Il cibo è delizioso e le persone simpatiche.
Phil: Ah, fermiamoci. Uccidiamo quel vecchio per le direzioni.
Claire: Nostro italiano migliorato molto.

Phil: [Speaking Italian, English subtitles] I must be the tallest
             man in the world.[11]
(Chandrasekaran et al., 2019)

Again, the humor comes from the misuse of lexicon, not necessarily grammar
or pronunciation, although Claire's pronunciation of *felciatrice* 'lawnmower'
could be improved. In fact, that lexical item seems an obscure choice in this
particular scene, as if the writers were simply looking for an odd word to throw
in. It lacks the sophistication of other jokes that make use of a foreign language.
Nonetheless, this is an example of what even strong L2 learners often do, make
small but significant lexical errors. It's another example of ethnic humor and
serves as part of the narrative story arc of the episode.

There are two last examples of English-speakers using a foreign language
well that I think are worth mentioning. The first from the "Graham D'Amato:
Hot Lunch Mentalist" episode (McCormick & O'Malley, 2019) of *Single Parents*
tells the story of single father Will, whose ex-wife returns to reveal that their
divorce was never finalized because of a missing signature on the paperwork.
Will's ex-wife Mia, played by Vanessa Bayer, is an international aid worker. As a
part of her job, she must communicate by phone with colleagues in different
locales around the world who speak languages other than English. In the
episode, Mia speaks both French and Spanish. Although Will knows that Mia
is too focused on saving the world to be a good partner, each time he hears
her speak French, he is overcome with sexual desire. In the first scene, Will is
telling his friends that he knows Mia is not good for him, but he acknowledges
that when she speaks another language, he is enthralled. There is a cut to Mia
ordering food in French in Will's kitchen. As he enters, he waits in the
background not wanting to disturb her, but when he realizes that she is
speaking in French he shudders with longing.

(1.16)
Will: No. But Mia's got a hold on me. Like, when she speaks in a
             foreign language, it's so hot. [Cut to Will's kitchen, Mia
             ordering food on the phone, Will listening intently in the
             background]

---

[11] Phil: L'avventura che è la vita.
Claire: Con te, mio caro, ogni giorno è un falciatrice.
Phil: Io sono il uomo più alto tutto del mondo.

Mia: Je voudrais trois crêpes. Une avec les bananes et du miel.
            Une avec les bleuets.[12]
Will: [Shudders] Cold shower, anyone? [Chuckles]
(McCormick & O'Malley, 2019)

Later in the episode, the desire that Mia sparks in Will when she speaks a foreign language is ignited again. Even as he tries to finalize their divorce by signing the papers and giving them to his friend Angie to mail, he cannot ignore his more basic instincts. In the scene that follows, Will and Mia talk about their relationship, how they've both changed, and how their relationship can perhaps work if they give it another chance. Will is skeptical until he hears Mia speak in French:

(1.17)
Mia: You know, Will, um [Clears throat] I've been thinking about us.
Will: The couple so dysfunctional, they couldn't even get
            divorced right?
Mia: [Chuckles] I've been thinking about, you know, how much
            you've changed. You're so happy and confident, and I even
            detect a little more bass in your voice. [Grunts deeply] Do
            you think those papers were maybe a sign?
Will: [Exhales sharply] Look, Mia
Mia: I've changed, too. I know that I haven't been there for you
            and Sophie, but I want to be. Maybe I could cut back a little
            at work so that we could spend more time together as a
            family, and - [Jungle noises as cell phone rings] It's my
            mosquito-nets guy. But I can call him back.
Will: No. Take it.
Mia: Okay. [Cellphone beeps] **Salut, Manuel.** [Speaking French]
            **Y a-t-il des nouveaux[13] sur les filets. Désolée. Quoi? La
            livraison est retardée?** [Will sighs] [Shouting in French] **Je
            sais que c'est plus cher. Je sais que c'est plus cher. Oui, je
            sais.** [Cellphone thuds as Mia drops it to kiss Will][14]
(McCormick & O'Malley, 2019)

---

[12] "I would like three crepes. One with bananas and honey. One with blueberries…"
[13] This is an error, the French word for 'news' should be the feminine *nouvelles*.
[14] "Is there any news on the nets? Sorry. What? The delivery is delayed? I know it's more expensive. I know it's more expensive. Yes, I know."

Immediately following this exchange, Will runs to Angie's to stop her from sending the divorce papers, but, in the end, Will and Mia realize their differences are too great, agreeing to finalize their divorce.

This example does not involve ethnic humor. The humor arises from the idea that speaking a foreign language can be sexy, irresistibly so. Of interest is the stereotypical use of French, often considered the language of love in the U.S. Although Mia does use some Spanish in the episode, that scene takes place with Angie, Will's friend. Although Will says speaking in a foreign language is hot, the question remains if that language has to be French or not. Thinking of Pandey (2016), one might wonder if this has something to do with the way French is valued in American culture.[15] Nonetheless, this integration of French, as an important element of the storyline does not seem as contrived as some language use in the examples of ethnic humor or reverse ethnic humor above. This lack of contrivance could be the result of French (and other languages) being viewed as an integral part of the character. Bednarek's (2018) communication of the narrative function encompasses character traits as well as relationships between the characters. The relationship between Will and Mia is the central focus of this episode. Or, the use of French might not seem contrived because language is not the main focus of the joke. Either way, it gives us a different perspective on how language use can be integrated into a television episode.

Additionally, this use of French is not subtitled in any way, which is somewhat unusual for a comedy. However, the audience doesn't really need to understand what is said in French to understand the function of French in the episode. Although integral to the storyline of Will considering a reunion with Mia, the French use seems rather ornamental in keeping with the idea of linguistic exhibitionism. On the other hand, even having a bilingual character represented combats the prevailing idea that Americans are monolingual.

d. Language as an Element of Character

There are some examples that demonstrate the use of a language other than English as an integral part of a character's identity (again, Bednarek's (2018) narrative communication function of TV dialogue). A very definite example of use of a language other than English to add credence to a character's identity

---

[15] French is also used to represent love and desire in the *Suburgatory* episode, "Les Lucioles" (Kapnek & Hardcastle, 2014). Meanwhile in *Trophy Wife*'s "Back to School" (Seidell & Sohn, 2014) and the *Partners* episode "The Key" (Kohan et al., 2012) French signifies sophistication or cachet.

comes from the sitcom *Schooled.* In the episode "CB Likes Lainey" (Howard et al., 2019), two teachers have differing views regarding connecting the school to the Internet in the early 1990s. The Spanish teacher Ms. Taraborelli and the gym teacher Coach Mellor are forced by Principal Glascott to design the school's website together in order to work out their differences. However, tensions flair again when Coach Mellor declares that he will design the school's website himself, without Taraborelli's input. In the ensuing fight, unsurprisingly, the Spanish teacher uses Spanish to attack and insult her colleague.

(1.18)

Mellor:	John, our website on the information superhighway is going to be the face of our school. Would you rather it be this face [Frames his own face] or this face [Frames Taraborelli's face]?
Taraborelli:	Okay. [Speaking Spanish, English subtitles] How about I smack the teeth out of your face, you donkey ass![16]
Mellor:	Hey, that's not fair!
Glascott:	And it's not appropriate, either. I speak a little Spanish.
Taraborelli:	[Speaking Spanish, English subtitles] Gym teacher Rick is infuriating![17]
Mellor:	What's she saying? Is she agreeing with you?
Glascott:	[Speaking Spanish, English subtitles] He try you make friend. But whistle make weird yes.[18]
Mellor:	Is she insulting me? Tell me her words!
Taraborelli:	You want to know what I'm saying? I will never work with you for as long as I live, Gym Teacher Rick!

(Howard et al., 2019)

As in the *Single Parents* example above, this is not ethnic humor. The language use is tied to Taraborelli's identity as a Spanish teacher. However, Glascott's line in Spanish would qualify as the type of reverse ethnic humor I cite above, since his language skills are so poor, he definitely represents the American-as-poor-language-learner trope. Here, the use of Spanish contributes to the *authenticity* (Lopez & Bucholtz, 2017) of the Taraborelli

---

[16] ¡Qué tal si te golpeo los dientes, culo de burro!

[17] ¡Gym teacher Rico me enfurece!

[18] El intente que hacer amigo. Pero siblar es raro que sí.

character—she is a Spanish teacher and using Spanish confirms the character's role on the show.

Within roughly a six-month period in 2013, Hebrew and Yiddish were present in episodes of the sitcoms *Raising Hope* (March 28), *Trophy Wife* (October 8), and *New Girl* (October 15). Because Yiddish and Hebrew are associated with very specific occasions and a very specific group of people, those who are Jewish, the contexts for finding and using these languages are more restrictive and characters who make use of these languages are often Jewish or associated with places like New York City that has a large Jewish population (cf. Newman's (2014) Yiddishisms). I'll start with a more traditional portrayal of ethnic humor from the *New Girl* episode "The Box" (Rosell & Fleming, 2013).

In this episode, the character Schmidt is undergoing a crisis of conscience. After dating two women at the same time while lying to both, saying each is the only woman in his life, he gets caught in the lie. Because of this incident, he begins to question what it means to be a good person. He believes he is a good person, but wonders how he could do something so awful if that's true. This leads him to seek spiritual guidance. As Schmidt is Jewish, he seeks the counsel of a rabbi. The use of Hebrew/Yiddish finds contextualization in the fact that the character is Jewish and he seeks advice from a rabbi at a synagogue. Correspondingly, the use of Hebrew/Yiddish adds authenticity to Schmidt's character. Although the rabbi doesn't offer much solace, Schmidt finds what he seeks by performing a good deed. After witnessing a biker crash, Schmidt saves the man, who is choking on his gum, by performing the Heimlich maneuver on him. After, he celebrates with a song in Hebrew. I myself do not speak Hebrew but I maintain (as I will in other instances throughout this book) that it is not necessary to understand this particular usage. The use of Hebrew in the scene with the biker and the use of Yiddish in a later scene ("Gut yontif" meaning 'good holiday') and Hebrew ("tzedakah" meaning 'justice/righteousness' or more commonly 'charity' and "mitzvah" meaning 'good deed done from religious duty') (Rosell & Fleming, 2013) in a scene with his friend Nick (who is struggling to decide what to do with newly inherited money) are clear examples of Mintz's ethnic humor. The language use is based on stereotypical expectations—Schmidt is Jewish, thus he will use Hebrew and/or Yiddish. The situations in which these languages are used are attempts to add humor. The use of Hebrew/Yiddish also pushes the story forward as Schmidt seeks affirmation that he is a good person for having saved the biker's life. Later in the episode, he visits the biker in the hospital, revisits the rabbi during a Hebrew school lesson and, ultimately, after a conversation with his friend Winston, finds a way to live with himself. Winston points out that doing one bad act does not make you a bad person. That's enough for Schmidt to move beyond his existential crisis. Here again, the use of Hebrew/Yiddish is both fundamental to the character of Schmidt and it moves the story forward, recalling Bednarek's (2018) communication of narrative function of dialogue. As the L2 language use is normally deployed to achieve comedic ends, it falls in the aesthetic/interpersonal category as well.

In "Burt Mitzvah—The Musical," (Kaplan et al., 2013), the second-to-last episode of season three of the sitcom *Raising Hope*, the character Burt is told by his parents that he is really Jewish. This revelation utterly astonishes Burt. His mother expects him to embrace his Judaism and to have a *bar mitzvah*. A *bar mitzvah* (or *bat mitzvah* for young women) is an important religious ceremony, normally occurring at 13 years of age for boys (12 or 13 for girls), that signifies reaching the age of adulthood for young people in the Jewish community. Burt's newly revealed religious denomination and the impending "Burt mitzvah" sets up a frame to play with the idea of ethnic humor. Because the character is now Jewish, we expect Hebrew, and potentially Yiddish, to play a part and they do. Throughout the episode, we see mostly stereotypical uses of ethnic humor involving these languages, though there are a few non-stereotypical uses.

In terms of stereotypical uses, Burt, knowing nothing about being Jewish, seeks the council of a kosher deli owner. Keeping kosher means following Jewish dietary laws. To aid in that pursuit, many Jewish-Americans have established delicatessans to serve their fellow Jews' culinary needs. Burt's questions result in a roughly three-minute musical number full of stereotypes, including the usage of Hebrew/Yiddish (Kaplan et al., 2013). As with the New Girl example, we have ethnic humor in its classic sense. The one way in which this episode attempts to push the boundary is by having Burt himself attempt to adopt his new heritage. Burt is excited to use the word *kibitz* (from Yiddish), showing off to his wife that he knows that it means 'to talk' (Kaplan et al., 2013). This is perhaps doubly funny since the word has entered the standard lexicon in many varieties of English. It has an entry in Miriam Webster's online dictionary, for example. Thus even his attempt to be "ethnic" is woefully not so.

In another scene in Hebrew school studying for his *bar mitzvah*, Burt is flummoxed by the pronunciation of Hebrew (Kaplan et al., 2013). It is questionable whether this scene is truly humorous. By making the Hebrew seem overly foreign—difficult to pronounce, different alphabet written on the board in the background—this creates distance between American Jews who learn Hebrew growing up for their own *bar/bat mizvahs* and non-Jews. Burt even threatens violence to the boy sitting next to him for laughing at him. It seems at odds with the idea of the episode, which seems to be attempting to mainstream/explain Judaism.

In subsequent scenes, there are more stereotypes and songs. First, Shirley Jones' character, Burt's newly Jewish mother, demonstrates the trope par excellence of the Jewish mother, guilt, as she and Virginia, Burt's wife, shop for items at the grocery store to prepare a traditional *Seder* or 'ceremonial meal.' Not only does Burt's mother lay on the guilt when she offers to wait in the hot car, but she also does so with some appropriate linguistic panache: the originally Yiddish, now English "shvitzing" is used (Kaplan et al., 2013). The scene continues as Virginia, must learn what it means to prepare a *Seder*. Once more, a song based on ethnic humor and stereotypes is used to cover the basics of what observant Jews can and can't eat as well as the origin of the *Seder*, including the imprisonment of the Jews by the pharaoh and their subsequent escape with Moses, shopping aisles parted like the Red Sea and all.

The most unusual of the songs, the one that, perhaps, in some way does take the stereotypes and humor in another direction is the final song, "Rock the *Torah*,"[19] sung to the melody of the rock song *St. Elmo's Fire (Man in Motion)* (1984) from the 1985 film *St. Elmo's Fire*. Burt's son Jimmy exhorts Burt to be a man. The rock-n-roll sensibility of the song, including the rabbi singing like a hair-band frontman from the 1980s, finally seems to transcend the stayed nature of the other examples of ethnic humor in the episode, challenging the stereotypes somewhat and creating another level of humor (Kaplan et al., 2013). In this case, it's not just the stereotypes that create the humor but playing against the expectations that elevates this number.

At the end of the episode, the truth comes out at the synagogue as Burt is about to have his *bar mitzvah*: Burt was never Jewish. It was all a ruse. Burt's parents invented the whole scheme to bilk money out of their friends so they could go on a cruise. Despite this, Burt decides he must go forward and complete his *bar mitzvah*. These final moments of the episode provide one last opportunity to throw in some Yiddish. Virginia, the non-Jew, uses *schmendrick* 'a contemptible person' to describe her in-laws and *meshugganah* 'crazy' to characterize their scheme (Kaplan et al., 2013). Once more, all of the Yiddish used in the episode is also fairly common in several dialects of American English.

Overall, in this episode, there is an attempt to play with expectations. After all, *Raising Hope* seems to take place in a non-descript Southern location. The characters are generally portrayed as good-natured hicks or rednecks. In that sense the premise that Burt is Jewish would challenge the audience's expectations, however most of the usage of Hebrew/Yiddish happens in

---

[19] The *Torah* is the holy text of the Jewish religion.

locations where such usages would be expected (Jewish deli, Hebrew school, synagogue) and the Yiddish used is common in a number of American English dialects, where it may or may not be marked as Jewish. The only exception could be "Rock the *Torah*" which does go beyond expected situations/stereotypes.

The *Trophy Wife* episode "The Social Network" (Chun & Moore, 2013) does a better job of using Yiddish to play against expectations—not ethnic humor per se, but reverse ethnic humor. In this episode, the adopted child character Bert (not to be confused with adult Burt from *Raising Hope*), presumably of Chinese origins (he is Asian, speaks Chinese, and takes a Chinese class in a later episode) uses Yiddish. While the other examples of Hebrew/Yiddish use in *New Girl* and *Raising Hope* took place for the most part in expected contents, e.g., a synagogue or by a Jewish character, Bert's usage is wholly decontextualized.

In a variety of moments throughout the episode, Bert uses Yiddish, mostly as isolated lexical items, and always correctly. At various points, he uses, "shalom,"[20] "nosh," "tuchus," "oy vey," "schmutz," and "shayna punim"[21] (Chun & Moore, 2013). The storyline is unrelated to Bert's language use and otherwise unimportant to my argument. What is interesting, though, is the lack of explanation for where Bert has picked up his Yiddish—perhaps from his adopted mother, but that is never demonstrated or explained. Malin Akerman's character, the eponymous "trophy wife" and Bert's stepmother, even remarks that she has no idea where he's picking it up, but it must continue because it is adorable (Chun & Moore, 2013). It is adorable, but more than that, it pushes beyond ethnic humor in that it's funny exactly because it subverts the stereotypes associated with those who use Yiddish. In many ways, this example attempts to rewrite expectations for ethnic humor in terms of language usage in the ways that *Modern Family* (Levitan & Lloyd, 2009) or *The New Normal* (Di Loreto et al., 2012) (or even *Trophy Wife* (Halpern et al., 2013) itself for that matter) do for the American family. Sadly, of these shows, only *Modern Family* has lasted more than one season.

By playing against the expectations, Bert's use of Yiddish is perhaps funnier than some of the other examples I have cited. More than that, the humor loses some of the derisive quality that comes from laughing at the "other". In this example, otherness cannot be specifically located onto one group or ethnicity

---

[20] Shalom is the one Hebrew word Burt employs.
[21] *Shalom* literally means 'peace' but is used to mean 'hello/goodbye'; nosh means 'a snack' or 'to eat a snack'; *tuchus* refers to 'buttocks'; *oy vey* is an exclamation indicating dismay or grief; *schmutz* means 'dirt'; and *shayna punim* means 'beautiful face'.

as multiple groups/ethnicities are at play and the humor comes from this interaction. I would submit that this type of humor transcends ethnic humor because it challenges the expectations of ethnic humor. Queen (2015) discusses how language variation is used to show similarity/solidarity or difference/otherness on TV. With Bert's use of Yiddish, it is unclear who he might be trying to emulate or demonstrate solidarity with in the TV episode (perhaps his adopted mother, but she never uses any Yiddish in the episode). The lack of target leaves the reason behind Bert's variation particularly uncertain. This unmooring of the linguistic behavior from any clear reason intensifies the humorous effect, the idea that Bert, on his own, simply wants to have fun with language.

e. Foreign Language Just For Fun

There are additional examples where a foreign language is used on American television simply for the fun of it. The next two examples illustrate incongruous uses of Spanish language songs in ways that have little relevance to the storylines of the episodes in which they appear. Their inclusion seems almost to mirror popular culture in America, in which, from time to time, songs in languages other than English become popular. There is some implicit (and sometimes explicit) commentary on this phenomenon in these examples.

In the *Single Parents* episode, "The Elusive Zazz" (Rosenstock et al., 2019), stay-at-home dad Will gets an offer to go on air as a local weatherman. He makes an audition tape, soliciting feedback from his friends. They are unanimous in telling him that his audition tape is terrible. It is at this point that his friend Poppy compares Will's tape to their other friend Miggy's music video, "But and I don't know how to put this nicely, that audition is one of the worst things I've ever seen, and I've seen Miggy's music video" (Rosenstock et al., 2019). No sooner has she uttered this statement than the viewers are also treated to Miggy's video, called "Mystery Señorita." In the video, a woman is seated in the back of a car that Miggy is driving. Like a real music video, as the video begins, the bottom left-hand corner of the screen displays:

> Miggy Park
> "Mystery Señorita"
> Dir: Dwayne
> Miggy Park Records
> (Rosenstock et al., 2019)

The Miggy driving the car sings, "Mystery señorita. Señorita, chiquitita, mamacita ¿Quién eres?" Meanwhile, a picture-in-picture image of Miggy replaces the music video information and rhythmically speaks a translation, "Young woman, young woman, young woman, who are you?" (Rosenstock et al., 2019). This continues for the following turns:

(1.19)

Miggy in car:	Mystery señorita. Su nombre puede ser mi querida o tal vez Sandy?
Miggy translator:	Her name could be anything. It could be Sandy
Miggy in car:	Mystery señorita. Ella ya estaba cuando llegué al auto.
Miggy translator:	She was here when I got in this car. Who are you?

(Rosenstock et al., 2019)

It seems as if the point of the song is to satirize songs in Spanish like *The Macarena* (1993) and others that have simplistic lyrics. The song is also vaguely reminiscent of Madonna's song *Who's That Girl* (1987). Ultimately, it is simply a fun, if incongruous moment in the episode, rendered more silly by the fact that the song is partially in Spanish.

Great News's "Love is Dead" episode (Carlock et al., 2017). also features a song and a more explicit critique of the American listening audience. In the opening scene of the episode, one of the newsroom characters, Justin, who is portrayed in the episode as bilingual, is singing his favorite new Spanish song, "Rapido."

(1.20)

[Elevator dings, Justing exits]

Justin:	[Singing in Spanish] Rapido, rapido. Mejor nos damos prisa.[22]
Carol:	[Laughs] Oh, that's fun. I feel like I'm at Epcot. What is that song?
Justin:	It's the follow up to Luis Fonsi's "Despacito." It's even filthier. White people have no idea. They play it at kids' birthday parties. [Singing in Spanish subtitled in English] We have to do it quickly because you're my stepmother.[23]
Carol:	Oh, Justin, that's beautiful! [Chuckles] Rapido, rapido…
…	

---

[22] Quickly, quickly. Better that we hurry.
[23] "Tenemos que hacerlo rapido porque tu eres mi madrastra."

Carol: Oh, Justin, I downloaded the song.
["Rapido" playing over Carol's phone, lyrics subtitled in English:
"In a threesome with you and your dog that is sick"]
Carol: I'm gonna sing it at our church talent show.
(Carlock et al., 2017)

As can be seen from the English subtitles provided, the song is, as Justin says, "filthy". He makes the direct comparison of this song with Luis Fonsi's hit *Despacito* (2017), which enjoyed great commercial success in the U.S. and which many Americans loved, but far fewer understood the song's sexual message. Carol exemplifies this idea by stating that she is going to sing the song "Rapido" at her church talent show. She does not know what the lyrics mean, nor does she seem to care since the tune is so catchy. Thus, there is more overt social commentary in this example than in the previous one.

The song comes back in two later scenes. It is playing at a club where the main character Katie goes to pick up men, and, at the end of the episode, in another storyline that involves the character Porsche dancing where no one can see her, in this case at the retirement home. In that final scene, we hear more of "Rapido"[24] while everyone dances:

(1.21)
Rapido, rápido
Tengo el hombro dislocado
Solamente con tus senos, tu puedes areglarlo[25]
(Hay ratas, hay ratas en el rincón teniendo sexo
Sería una fiesta sexual
Si nos venimos al mismo tiempo, Mami.)[26]
(Carlock et al., 2017)

In this final scene, the dancing senior citizens emphasize that for many Americans the meaning of the lyrics in a foreign language is irrelevant if the song has a good beat. This could be equally true for the Korean band BTS, which has many fans in the U.S., but I would venture to guess that very few of them actually know or understand the lyrics to many of their songs. The question remains: is it a critique of popular culture in the U.S. or a critique of

---

[24] The full Spanish text of the song can be found in Appendix A.
[25] Quickly, quickly. I have a dislocated shoulder. Only with your breasts can you fix it.
[26] This portion is subtitled in English: "There are rats, there are rats in the corner having sex. It would be a sexual fiesta if we finished at the same time, Mami."

lack of inquisitiveness in Americans in general? In either case, the scenes involving the song in *Great News* and, to a lesser degree, the music video in *Single Parents*, seem to convey a fairly clear ideological message, Bednarek's (2018) thematic/ideological function, about Americans' relationship to Spanish specifically and other foreign languages more generally.

f. Foreign Languages for Concealment

Before I conclude, I want to analyze two final examples from my data, two diametrically opposed ways in which second languages play a pivotal role on today's television programs. Second language knowledge is used to solve crimes and to conceal things or dissemble. More and more popular television programs are making use of second languages as integral components of narrative and plot structures. This device has become increasingly evident in the police procedural and detective genre [more on this in Chapter 3]. To demonstrate this tendency of L2 use as an aid in crime solving, let us consider the "Paxton Petty" episode from the Fox drama *Alcatraz* (Lilien et al., 2012), in which knowledge of Chinese is key to discovering the suspect's hideout.

In this scene in question, government agents are trying to stop a suspect from bombing targets in San Francisco. They go to a shop for medicinal herbs in Chinatown, the proprietor of which only speaks Chinese.[27] Luckily, one of the agents is able to have a conversation with him in Chinese, which presumably he speaks well enough to communicate effectively, that is, convey his questions and understand the shopkeeper's answers. In fact, he successfully learns crucial information about the suspect. The conversation is not subtitled so the viewing public (who does not speak Chinese) must rely on the agent's translation of the conversation to his colleagues. Certainly, this usage of Chinese is part of the narrative function of the dialogue, both as it moves the story forward and as it tells us something about one of the main characters, i.e., he speaks Chinese.[28]

---

[27] Here I am using the generic "Chinese" because I am not sure whether the language being used is Mandarin or Cantonese.
[28] Of course, in Chinatown, one might expect to find Chinese speakers. This is a type of L2 use that I do not cover—when, based on the context, we expect characters to speak an L2. For instance, if the action of a particular episode takes place in France, and characters (either main characters or peripheral ones) speak in French, the expected language of the environment. I don't explore such examples in this work. Bleichenbacher (2008, 2012), however, does look at such examples in his corpus of Hollywood movies. This may also be a fruitful area of research for others in the future.

Let us also consider the positive effects that the depiction of such linguistic diversity may have on the American public. Using different languages represents not only the globalized world, but also something positive about the U.S. itself, a nation of immigrants with diverse communities where different languages are still maintained. Such representations may lessen our fears of the other, whom we may not always readily understand. This seems especially important with immigration a serious issue now in the U.S. (Dickerson & Kanno-Youngs, 2019; Sacchetti, 2019), especially in light of the 2020 presidential election in the offing. Not to mention the Trump administration's efforts to add a citizenship question to the 2020 census (Rogers & Liptak, 2019), a move even the Supreme Court's Chief Justice viewed as a pretext for not counting significant numbers of U.S. residents (Barnes & Marimow, 2019). The effects of the sort of window that television provides onto a multicultural and multilingual U.S. may make more humane immigration policies and acceptance of one's L2 English-speaking or non-English speaking neighbors more palatable.

In contrast to the positive message that using L2s to solve crimes provides, the funny yet potentially subversive or negative valence associated with using a second language to hide information may run counter to this trend. Although far less prevalent (I have come across far fewer examples), there is some depiction of this use on television. As an example, consider the *Rules of Engagement* episode "Anniversary Chicken" (Haukom & Mancuso, 2011).

In this episode, the character Russell takes an Italian-speaking woman, Sophia, out on a date; unfortunately, he does not know Italian. Thus, he coerces his assistant (who luckily happens to speak Italian) into translating for him. During the date, his assistant is forced to convey messages he finds in poor taste. The scene that I will discuss takes place at the end of the episode after Russell has bedded his Italian conquest with Timmy, who spent his night on the couch in case of emergency translating needs, as an unwilling accomplice.

(1.22)

Russell:	Timmy? Timmy. I need you.
Timmy:	Oh, again? Sir, at a certain point, I really don't think this is about the translating.
Russell:	No, no, no. You got to help me eject her from the cockpit. At some point during the night, she got a little clingy and annoying.
Timmy:	Well, you know, sir, that's your problem, because my translating duties are over.
Russell:	Oh, that's funny, 'cause my paying you duties are over.

Timmy:	What?
Sophia:	(Entering from bedroom) Buon giorno.
Russell:	All right, tell her, uh, you know, I had fun, but we both know the score.
Timmy:	Fine. (Speaking Italian, subtitled in English) I would love to see you again as soon as possible.[29]
Russell:	Uh, you know, I wish her the best, but I gots [sic] to move on.
Timmy:	Okay. If you need to marry for a green card, I will do it.[30]
Sophia:	Oh, grazie! (hugging Russell)
Russell:	Well, she's taking it like a real trooper.

(Haukom & Mancuso, 2011)

In this scene, the dialogue in Italian serves both narrative and aesthetic functions. We see how Timmy gets his revenge for being forced to participate in the previous evening. This scene demonstrates how speaking a second language can be very useful in keeping information from those who cannot understand (thus the joke). As is typical, this function is used to elicit laughter from the audience. Unlike in *Alcatraz*, the subtitles are used to convey meaning. At the same time, however, we see how the concealed information is potentially harmful to David Spade's character, Russell—he may end up married to an Italian green-card seeker, if he's not lucky.

This negative valence, although coupled with humor, could put some viewers ill at ease. When confronted with speakers of other languages, we sometimes think that they may be talking about us without our understanding. As Queen (2015) puts it, "a common American ideology about bilingualism...assumes when people are speaking a language you don't understand, they are talking about you in a problematic way or they are discussing something illegal or otherwise sinister" (p. 203). Many English-speakers work with speakers of Spanish, for instance, who may have occasion to speak Spanish with one another, much to the dismay of those who cannot understand, even if their conversations are about mundane matters that have nothing to do with their English-speaking co-workers.

---

[29] "Vorrei vederti di nuovo al piu presto possibile."
[30] "Se vuoi sposarti per la carta di soggiorno, io sono disponibile."

IV. Conclusion

We've seen a number of occasions in which second languages or second language speakers have been featured, often to humorous effect. Paz (2017, 2018, 2019) looks at how issues of dubbing or subtitling of languages other than English are handled when U.S. content is exported abroad.[31] Working independently, he also identifies humor and jokes (Paz, 2018, 2019) as one of the six functions of these language uses. The other functions he cites are: to signal otherness, in-group/out-group (cf. Queen 2015, pp. 31-33); to denote heritage (cf. Lopez & Bucholtz's (2017) *authenticity*); to lend authenticity to setting/location; as an obstacle for characters to overcome (the flip side of the example with Russell, Timmy, and Sophia above); and to signal stereotypes/associations. We will see most of these other functions in the chapters to come.

As I said at the outset, we cannot deny the power that television and other media have in shaping popular views on all sorts of matters. If we look beyond the humor, we see a host of other effects that result from these depictions, many of those outlined by Paz (2018, 2019) above. I would like to think that the powers behind the popular television shows I've cited, and many others that I have not discussed, seek to send a positive message about L2 English speakers, that they are trying to focus on the ways in which we are all alike. Humor is a great equalizer that allows us to take the first step toward seeing past our differences. People who speak English as a second language are just like native English speakers in the end.

Finally, as a second language educator, I like to think that second language use by English speakers is being featured to show the importance of learning another language, how useful it can be—not only in solving crimes, but in communicating with others. I imagine Hollywood writers and producers who've learned another language wanting to share the worth of their discovery with their viewers, or still other writers and producers who now realize they should have paid better attention and put more of an effort into Spanish or French class in high school and college. Such is the power of learning another language: it allows us to dream of a world in which TV supports the learning of foreign tongues to lead to us toward a harmonious world in which a cacophony of different languages sounds like the most beautiful of melodies.

---

[31] Queen (2004) looks at similar issues regarding how African-American English is dubbed into German, and the ways in which considerations of social status/associations affect how German dubbings are rendered.

Chapter 2

Psych!

You Thought This Show Was in English!

I. Introduction

In the USA Network series *Psych* (2006-2014), private investigator Shawn
Spencer, played by James Roday, solved crimes using his keen powers of
observation while pretending to be psychic. In the second season episode,
"Lights, Camera…Homicidio," (Berman & Shakman, 2008b) Shawn and his
sidekick, pharmaceutical salesman Burton 'Gus' Guster (actor Dulé Hill),
investigate a murder on the set of a popular Spanish-language *telenovela*. The
plot unfolds to include a show within the show as Shawn joins the cast of
Explosión Gigantesca de Romance ('Gigantic Explosion of Romance') to solve
the crime. His joining the cast provides opportunities for meta-analysis of the
telenovela genre. Moreover, this episode of *Psych* is itself framed as a meta-
analysis of the *telenovela* phenomenon, including the idea that this popular
form of entertainment is not in English.

II. Rewriting Reality

The first point that is made in "Lights, Camera…Homocidio" concerns the
importance and power of the *telenovela* genre, even in the United States, where
it did not originate. In a very early exchange in this episode, Gus tries to insist
that Shawn find a way for them to be involved in the case, as *Explosión
Gigantesca de Romance* is one of Gus' favorite shows. In the exchange, one can
observe Gus' enthusiasm as he knows all the actors' names, the location
represented by the set, as well as the most up-to-date details of the storyline.
Shawn resists, "It's all in Spanish!" But, undeterred, Gus points out that everyone
watches this *telenovela*. He goes so far as to call the *telenovela* "a craze."

(2.1)
Gus: This is Corrine's living room.
Shawn: Who the hell is Corrine?
Gus: It's the living room from Explosión Gigantesca de
          Romance.
Shawn: What are you saying?

Gus:	It's a Spanish soap opera, Shawn.
Shawn:	How do you know that? Who are you? What happened to my best friend?
Gus:	My gosh! And Lassiter is talking to Jorge Gama-Lobo. He plays Vicente on the show. He's my favorite. He slept with Mariana at his own mother's funeral, Shawn.
Shawn:	What the--
Gus:	It's on in every doctor's office I visit. I had no choice but to get sucked in.
Shawn:	You had a choice. You still have a choice. Who's the dead guy?
Gus:	That's Rinaldo Nuñez. He played Ernesto on the show. He used to be married to Corrine.
Shawn:	I'm sorry, dude. I can't believe you actually watch this show. It's in Spanish.
Gus:	Everyone in Santa Barbara is watching it, Shawn. The telenovela is a craze.[1]

(Berman & Shakman, 2008b)

Turns out, he's right. All the other main characters watch the *telenovela*, including the police chief, one of the detectives assigned to the case and Shawn's own father, who is clearly addicted to the show, as we will see in a later scene.

Bielby and Harrington (2005) looked at whether the traditionally closed landscape of the American TV marketplace was changing in response to new demographics in the U.S. (i.e., the growth of the Latinx population). They considered how U.S. soap operas were adapting practices common in *telenovelas*, such as shorter story arcs and increased presence of Latinx characters, concluding that while still very putative, the innovative techniques of the *telenovela* genre were being employed with success in the U.S. market. Of course, their research predates the coming of *Ugly Betty* (Hayek et al., 2006), the most straightforward adaptation of a Colombian telenovela, *Betty la Fea*. We must also mention *Jane the Virgin* (Snyder Urman et al., 2014), finishing its five-season run in 2019. Still, their results tell us that the U.S. market has been primed for this sort of programming, thus supporting Gus'

---

[1] For languages other than English, the English subtitles have been added when provided onscreen. When no English subtitles were present, speech in a language other than English that is not subtitled has been added by the author whenever possible.

argument. Moreover, the success of *Ugly Betty* and *Jane the Virgin*, provides further proof of his assertion.

Bielby and Harrington (2005) also point to the ways in which the soap opera genre and its kin, such as *telenovelas*, are universal. Many countries have their own versions of soap operas, which are widely available in the globalized marketplace. The storytelling conventions are similar enough the world over to consider this genre universal. *Psych* gives a nod to this idea of universality in another exchange between Shawn and Gus.

(2.2)

Gus: Let's get to work, Shawn. That's lance Rothstein. Let's start with him. He's the head writer on the show. I saw his picture once in *Soap Diary* magazine.

Shawn: Head writer? He's not even Spanish.

Gus: No, he was a Hollywood guy. Used to write on Blossom. Decided Spanish soap operas were a better reflection of the human condition.

(Berman & Shakman, 2008b)

Here, Gus points out Lance Rothstein, the head writer of the *Explosión Gigantesca de Romance*, as a place to begin their investigation. Shawn immediately remarks that he is "not even Spanish." Gus counters that Lance had worked in Hollywood but "decided that Spanish soap operas were a better reflection of the human condition." This exchange highlights a sense of universality that is represented in the *telenovela* genre. Despite the clearly humorous overtones inherent in having a seemingly Jewish-American head writer for a Spanish-language soap, there is a sort of ecumenical sensibility to the idea that the *telenovela* genre does not discriminate. In fact, it allows Lance to connect on a primal level with real human concerns and issues, according to Gus. This linking of the human condition and the *telenovela* evokes a powerful meta-analysis of the genre as a cultural product capable of communicating to a universal audience and crossing cultural divides.

Inherent in this episode is also a meta-commentary on the stylistics of the *telenovela* as a genre. This commentary focuses on such elements as the actual production of the *telenovela* (*e.g.*, acting, use of music) and the blurring of the lines between fact and fiction in the drama. With respect to the production itself, one characteristic element of the *telenovela* genre is clearly present: melodrama. Not only is melodrama clearly demonstrated in the show-within-a-show, *Explosión Gigantesca de Romance*, but it is clearly woven into the fabric of *Pysch* itself for this episode.

The strongest example of the over-the-top integration of melodrama in the episode occurs in another exchange between Shawn and Gus as they work to determine who killed the original victim and, then, put another victim into a coma. This particular dialogue takes place over the coma-stricken Jorge Gama-Lobo, Gus' favorite actor from the first dialogue.

(2.3)

Gus:	I get that Jorge was depressed about being off the show, but murder-slash-suicide-slash-coma? This whole thing is starting to feel like a real soap opera to me. I can't believe he would take his own life.
Shawn:	[Camera zooms between Shawn's eyes and Gama-Lobo's hairline] Unless he was wearing a wig he didn't. Someone else did.
Gus:	What? I don't get it.
Shawn:	Really? I thought I wrapped it up so nicely for you just now. It felt really good. It was organic. Synthetic hair. Just like the one found on the knife.
Gus:	So?
Shawn:	Dude. It means the same person was there when Jorge tried "to kill himself." He wasn't alone.
Gus:	So wait you're saying - he didn't try to kill himself?
Shawn:	I can't do this.
Gus:	You're not being clear, Shawn.
Shawn:	Come on, dude. I gave it to you three different ways.
Gus:	Did he or did he not try to kill himself?

(Berman & Shakman, 2008b)

Several aspects of this scene merit our attention. First, the acting style is reminiscent of a *telenovela*. Slade and Beckenham (2005) state that, "In production, there is an emphasis on the close-up shot of the face—of the emotional suspense of watching a face" (p. 338). This style, which accentuates the face, is clearly used in this scene. Every time Shawn suggests that Jorge has been framed by someone else (Unless he was wearing a wig, he didn't; Someone else did; Synthetic hair, just like the one found on the knife), mini-cliffhangers, the camera shot tightens to reveal an exaggeratedly knowing look on his face as he glances toward the body, the camera following his gaze. Moreover, the music comes in and builds to a crescendo emphasizing what he has just said as a key plot point, before Gus breaks in to question it.

In fact, in the audio commentary track about this episode, the creator, Steve Franks, says that the team that scored the episode "went full on with the *telenovela* music" (Berman & Shakman 2008a, audio commentary). Clearly, there is an awareness of the music as well as the acting in building the melodrama. In addition to James Roday's (the actor who plays Shawn) overacting in this scene, recalling the acting seen in the *telenovela* they are investigating, and the use of the music to accent this portrayal, Gus' explicit comparison of their case with a soap opera, "murder-slash-suicide-slash-coma, this whole thing is starting to feel like a real soap opera to me," provides compelling evidence for the *mise en abîme* structure of the episode. This structure further highlights the ways in which the producers of *Psych* are trading on the tropes of the *telenovela* genre to tell their story to greater effect and take advantage of the humorous aspects that such parody engenders. This choice would not have so powerful an effect if the components of the *telenovela* as a genre were not so marked and universally recognized, even by American audiences.

"Lights, Camera...Homocidio" also features a blurring of the lines between fantasy and reality, another aspect of the *telenovela*, in which artifice and fact are combined for an enhanced effect. Pearson (2005) talks about telenovelas "offering a *constructed reality* or a *reflection* of real life" having a "loose connection to *the* world we recognize" (p. 402, emphasis in original). She goes on, "The relation between the fictional and real worlds is necessarily complicated, as complicated as defining realism" (p. 404). On the show, even Shawn's father, Henry, a retired police officer used to teasing apart fact from fiction, becomes enmeshed in the crisscrossing threads that this episode brings forth. He engages Shawn in a dialogue in which he faults Shawn for his character Chad's shortcomings.

(2.4)

Henry:	How do you have fans? This is asinine. You started on the show five days ago.
Shawn:	Look, I have something.
Henry:	Did you ever think that maybe this is embarrassing for me?
Shawn:	Embarrassing for you?
Henry:	First off, your accent is terrible. It's disgraceful, really. You sound like that *El Pollo Loco* guy. And then, there you go, turning your back on Rinaldo, even after he defended you when you were accused of Maria's kidnapping. Come on.
Shawn:	First of all, I am trying to sound like the *El Pollo Loco* guy. And secondly, Rinaldo turned his back on me when he slept with Maria in the first place.

Henry:	Oh, come on, he would have given you half the reward money! Where's your integrity? It makes you look like such a bad person.
Shawn:	I'm Shawn. Those are things that my character Chad did. I play him on TV. It's Shawn. Shawny. Look into your boy's eyes. It's me, papa.
Henry:	Don't be an idiot. I'm not one of your fans. I barely even like you.
Shawn:	That's it. If my own father can blur the lines between the show and reality, why couldn't someone else? We've been looking in the wrong place. It's fans.

(Berman & Shakman, 2008b)

Here again, the *mise en abîme* structure is employed. The "*El Pollo Loco* Guy" is a real actor who does commercials as *El Caliente* for a Mexican chain restaurant found mostly in the Western U.S. In fact, the actor who plays El Caliente, the "*El Pollo Loco* Guy," is Matt Cedeño, who plays Jorge in this episode. Thus, the character Shawn is making reference to a real-world actor, who is appearing as a character in this episode with the actor James Roday who plays Shawn. In this dialogue, Shawn's dad is confusing him with his character Chad, while at the same time bringing up Matt Cedeño, a real actor who is concurrently a participant in the constructed realities of the telenovela *Explosión Gigantesca de Romance* as Vicente and the show *Psych* as Jorge. But, because we recognize this real-word reference to other characters Matt Cedeño has played, we are left with the question of who is really having this dialogue: Shawn and his dad *or* the actors James Roday and Corbin Bernsen. Which reality are we in?

In a moment just before this dialogue, there is another blurring of the reality between actor and character. Shawn and his dad are discussing Shawn's new job on the soap opera playing Chad. His father states that, "Acting in not a real job."

(2.5)

Henry:	Why am I here? This isn't lunch.
Shawn:	This is turkey with stuffing and cranberry. It's like Thanksgiving between two slices of bread. This whole place is like *Leaving Las Vegas* with food.
Henry:	Shawn, why'd you ask me here?
Shawn:	I thought you'd enjoy it. You said you never had the opportunity to visit me when I was working a real job, and now I have a real job!

Henry:	Shawn, this is not a real job.
Shawn:	Sure it is. Oh no, I think I got make-up on this t-shirt. Has anyone seen Ivan?
Henry:	Acting is not a real job, Shawn. I mean, how much attention do you need?
Shawn:	I'm not doing this for the attention. [Photo bombs the picture of a family of tourists] I happen to be solving a case. A murder. This is serious business.

(Berman & Shakman, 2008b)

The irony in this last line is clear. However, its irony is heightened by the fact that this particular episode focuses on the very essence of what makes this line humorous, the acknowledgment of the reality that exists beyond the boundaries of the fictitious constructed reality of the *Pysch* world.

Pearson explains, "The need for cultural verisimilitude is something that roots *telenovela* narratives in *the* world, a world separate from fiction but identifiable immediately with what is real" (2005, p. 405, emphasis in original). Given this perspective, and our own cultural landscape filled with reality television and its "stars" who share primetime with actors creating true artifice, it's no wonder there is confusion. By using the *telenovela's* surrealistic exaggeration of reality, which is firmly grounded in reality, in addition to the *mise en abîme* structure suggesting multiple levels of reality, this episode provides a strong meta-analysis of our own media culture. What is reality these days? Should it give us pause that telling the difference between shows that purport to be reality and those of pure fiction is not always as easy as it should be? This, too, would be characteristic of the *telenovela* genre. For example, Slade and Beckenham (2005) discuss Mexican *telenovelas* as having "taken on the role of offering criticism of and reflection on social issues" (p. 340). Bielby and Harrington (2005) cite Brazilian and Colombian serials for explicitly engaging in the treatment of political and social issues as well (p. 385).

This episode pushes the question of reality and fantasy further, by asking which is more important. At one point, Lance Rothstein, the head writer, finds himself behind bars accused of the murder. Shawn and Gus visit him in jail so that Shawn can reveal to him that he believes that it's a fan committing the murders to protect Corrine, the principal character of *Explosión Gigantesca de Romance*. Rothstein asks, what's the end of the story? Or, how do we write an ending to *this* story?

(2.6)

Shawn:	Look, we need to talk about Corrine.

Lance:	Corrine?
Shawn:	Corrine.
Lance:	Oh, Corrine.
Shawn:	Yes, it came to me in a vision. The murderer is doing this to protect her. Think about it. First, Ernesto cheated on her. And was stabbed and killed. Then you wrote that Vicente betrayed her and went missing. Someone took it into their own hands and tried to kill him.
Gus:	Well, not Vicente, but Jorge.
Shawn:	That's my point. They can't tell the difference. It's a fan.
Lance:	That's interesting. I'm not disagreeing, but what's act two? I mean, let's say it is just one fan. How you gonna find one fan among thousands?
Shwan:	Easy. That's where you come in. You just write me a storyline where I put Corrine's life in Jeopardy. Then we won't have to go looking for the murderer. The murderer will come looking for *me*.

(Berman & Shakman, 2008b)

We are left asking, which story? Is it the story on the soap opera? Is it the story being told in this episode of *Psych*? Regardless, the message to us, the spectators, is that it's the *story*, the fiction, that counts. Shawn's suggestion that Rothstein write him a storyline in which he puts Corrine's life in jeopardy to flush out the killer seems to echo this idea. It's the story on the soap opera that will lead to the resolution of the case, and thus the story of the episode. Even the fact that a fan is doing it, conflating reality with the *telenovela*, calls into question our notion of reality.

These connections between our reality and the realities created in the *telenovela* genre are also explicitly addressed in this episode of *Psych* by purposefully breaking through the fourth wall, openly conceding that what we are viewing, though verisimilar, is a fiction, not reality. The fourth wall is established throughout the show as various characters, ranging from Shawn's dad to the Police Chief are shown watching *Explosión Gigantesca de Romance* on television, a furtherance of the *mise en abîme* structure discussed earlier. Interestingly, *Ugly Betty* (Hayek et al., 2006) uses a similar device. The character of Ignacio, Betty's father, often watches a *telenovela* in the background of his scenes. Usually, the action in the Spanish-language soap opera visible on the small TV screen in the frame reinterprets emotions or actions in the actual storyline, creating a comparable mirroring effect.

In the course of this episode of *Pysch*, however, there are several moments when the fantasy of the *telenovela* is shattered, causing us to ponder the relationship between fantasy and reality in the *Psych* world itself. In one scene, before Rothstein, is arrested, Gus and Shawn appear to be visiting him in jail. However, as the camera pans out, it becomes clear that the jail is merely a set. They are still on the soundstage of the soap opera merely discussing the murders in a fake jail. In addition to calling into question the fourth wall, this scene creates an internal doubling of the image as Gus and Shawn later visit Rothstein in a "real" jail.

At the end of the episode, reality and fantasy come together once more and the fourth wall tumbles again. In the midst of a live broadcast of the *telenovela*, Shawn reveals the identity of the murderer from the set, on camera. When the murderer is revealed to be Kelly, the production assistant, the reality-conflating moment occurs as the director orders the camera to pan from the set to the murderess standing offstage. The artificial reality of the *telenovela*, its fourth wall, crumbles with this action. Moreover, it should be noted that the original murder of Reynaldo occurred on camera when the prop knife was replaced with a real one. Shawn also barely escapes his own assassination with a *pistola de clavos* ('nail gun') when the prop is replaced with a real one to punish his character, Chad, for breaking Corrine's heart. This transfer of "real" objects to the "fantasy" environment also demonstrates a rupture of the barrier between the two worlds.

Additionally, in the audio commentary that accompanies the episode on the DVD set (Berman & Shakman, 2008a), the producers and actors discuss how the studio lot that Gus and Shawn pass through in the beginning of the episode is indeed the studio lot where *Psych* itself is produced. The mentioning of Matt Cedeño as the "*El Pollo Loco* Guy" is yet another example of how this episode makes very clear the fact that there is a reality that exists beyond the *reflection* of reality found on the show.

III. The Role of Language

The breaking of the fourth wall, conflating fantasy and reality or multiple realities, if you will, furnishes an elegant counterpoint to the *mise en abîme* created by other aspects of this episode. One of those aspects, to this point not discussed, is the use of language by *Psych* characters and by characters of the fictitious *telenovela*. All the actors demonstrate different levels of proficiency in English and Spanish. For example, the characters in the telenovela are all able to communicate in English, although all three, Quintessa (Corrine), Jorge (Vicente), and Anita, have accents in English. The two women speak flawless English despite the accent, whereas Jorge speaks with a very thick accent and uses unusual expressions that mark him as foreign, such as, "music to my earlobes" and claims to "hunger for meatballs the way a jackal salivates for an injured possum" (Berman & Shakman, 2008b). All of the actors are American and presumably speak English as a native language, so we must assume these accents are merely an exaggerated performance reflecting the performances one would expect to see in Spanish on a *telenovela*.

Shawn, too, takes on such a persona when acting in the *telenovela*, although he admits he is "getting by with the Spanish [he] learned from Charo on *Love Boat*" (Berman & Shakman, 2008b). Even off the set, he adopts Spanish pronunciations. He begins to say characters' names, such as Corrine, Vicente, and Ernesto, with a strong Spanish accent that is not always understandable.

(2.7)
Shawn: Look, we need to talk about Corrine.
Lance: Corrine?
Shawn: Corrine.
Lance: Oh, Corrine.
(Berman & Shakman, 2008b)

In the jailhouse scene above (example 2.7) with Lance, Shawn introduces the topic of Corrine, attempting to say her name with the phoneme /R/ that we would find in a word with double "r", not the flap that would be found in this name with only one "r", and pronouncing the second syllable with the high front tense vowel /i/ as it would be in Spanish. Lance is unable to understand, thinking he said "Colleen". It is only once Shawn repeats that he understands who Shawn is talking about: "Oh, Corrine," which he pronounces /korIn/. Again, we have an occurrence of doubling, this time between Spanish and English. Is it /koRin/ or /korIn/? By virtue of her own bilingualism, does she herself have two linguistic identities as indicated by the two distinct pronunciations of her name? In this way, we have a problematizing of the reality of the bilingual. Which is real, English or Spanish, or do these linguistic worlds intersect and bleed into one another like the realities in this episode of *Psych*?

Continuing with our focus on Shawn's use of Spanish, in his conversation with his father, Shawn's pronunciation of *El Pollo Loco* is Spanish. He exaggerates his accent, of course, prompting his father's criticism, calling his accent "embarrassing" and "disgraceful" (see example 2.4 above). In his conversation with Rothstein, as well, he ups the ante by throwing in a personal pronoun in Spanish, *me*, instead of English "me" at the end of the conversation.

The final dénouement of the episode is arguably the most linguistically complex moment. The live broadcast begins with Shawn (as Chad) and Quintessa (as Corrine) on camera acting out a scene in which Shawn is reading Spanish from cue cards. He, once more, uses an exaggerated pronunciation and what the characters say in Spanish is subtitled in English on the episode of

Psych. In the scene, the two characters are preparing to attend a charity ball hosted by Corrine's sister. Shawn's character, Chad, goes offstage to change for the ball, but as he does so, Corrine asks him to bring her the nail gun ('*pistola de clavos*') from the garage so that she can fix a loose shelf. There is some dramatic repetition around the 'pistola de clavos' when it is first mentioned (--*Pistola de clavos? –Sí, el pistola de clavos*), but Chad/Shawn agrees and leaves the stage to change costumes (Berman & Shakman, 2008b).

Once Chad/Shawn returns and Corrine/Quintessa asks for the nail gun, his use of Spanish language devolves significantly. He begins speaking in English with a Spanish accent, mixing English with Spanish, and saying words in English with Spanish endings (e.g., "*es mucho dangerioso;*" "*you could muerte me with this thing*"), eventually devolving into a series of words in Spanish adding up to unintelligible gibberish, but ends with an improvisational accusation of the murderess in English with a heavy Spanish accent (Berman & Shakman, 2008b). At this point, Shawn/Chad is no longer subtitled in English, but Corrine's dialogue, still in Spanish, remains subtitled. Shawn asks Quintessa to translate his accusation into Spanish, whispering it into her ear, only for Quintessa to point to the murderer, saying "She did it!" dramatically in English. Just as Shawn struggles to get out his accusation in Spanish, we cut to his father watching at home, who comments, "High school Spanish comes back to haunt him" (Berman & Shakman, 2008b).

One further note on the Spanish language use in the episode involves the theme song, typically sung in English. A Spanish translation of lyrics was written for this episode and at the opening and closing of the episode, the theme song is performed in Spanish. This element adds to the sense that this episode is more than simple pandering to a Latinx audience but rather something more like an homage or genuine interest in exploring the telenovela genre for what it can offer to the show.

IV. Conclusion

Beyond the comedy of the final scene, the linguistic hybridization, perhaps even the type of translanguaging[2] (Otheguy et al., 2015) we might find in an L2 classroom, that Shawn enacts recalls Charo, whom Shawn evokes earlier in

---

[2] Leone-Pizzighella (2016) proposes an interesting type of translanguaging for the former Prime Minister of Italy Matteo Renzi called *inglaliano*, proposing how it could be a form of "language ideological metacommentary." Given the telenovela structure and focus of the episode, there could be metacommentary about Spanish/English use, but I would see it in a positive light, i.e., if you don't speak Spanish, maybe you should consider learning some.

the episode. In fact, Shawn's adaptation to aspects of Spanish language use, to which he was completely resistant initially (recall from example 2.1: "It's in Spanish.") taken with the reference to Charo says something about where Americans are in their own acceptance of cultural difference. The use of the *telenovela* as the vehicle to tell this story as compared to the tokenism of Charo's appearance on *Love Boat* allows us a historical vantage point by which we can evaluate our national progress. Charo is reminiscent of the idea of linguistic exhibitionism (Pandey, 2016)—having a native-speaker of Spanish operate in a principally monolingual English environment as a representative token of difference. On the contrary, framing the storyline in this *Psych* episode within the *telenovela* and adopting the tropes and the Spanish language (to some extent) of the genre, do not feel tokenizing. While the invocation of Charo brings to the fore ideas connected to "mock Spanish" (Hill, 1998) and its negative and racializing messages associated with the "elevation of whiteness" (p. 684), I believe that the message here is quite the reverse: an attempt to valorize the telenovela and Spanish.

The hybridity in language use, including the code-mixing, or potentially translanguaging, at the end of the episode, speaks to the confluence of American and Latinx languages and cultures as they mix in the space of globalized pop culture. Shawn's code-mixing in the spirit of translanguaging represents the experience of many Spanish-English bilinguals (although he is not one himself), using both codes together as one. A clear tolerance for cultural and linguistic difference is evident, although the fact that this message is delivered in a somewhat inept way given Shawn's lack of Spanish-language skills would be a valid critique.

Language use in this episode, the actors' and their characters' interaction as they pass from one frame to another, one language to another, one accent to another, recapitulates the *mise en abîme* structure of the episode itself. The multiple realities constructed in the intersecting levels of the story told in the *telenovela* style reflect the embodiment of multiple identities that each actor/character incarnates on screen. In short, these personages come to represent the viewer, as they surmount the fourth wall and challenge us to investigate the hybrid identities in each of us.

Chapter 3

Second-language Sleuths Solve Mysteries: Decoding Foreign Language Use in Popular Crime and Detective Television

I. Introduction

With greater consciousness of the multiethnic composition of the U.S. and a keen awareness of the shrinking globe in the early part of the 21st century, more and more popular television programs made use (and continue to make use) of second languages as integral components of narrative and plot structures. In addition to programs like *Lost* (Abrams et al., 2004) and *Heroes* (Kring et al., 2006), which prominently feature characters who speak first languages other than English, this device became increasingly evident in the police procedural and detective genre. In less than a year, from April 2009 through February 2010, *Bones* (Lin & Liddi-Brown, 2010), *Castle* (Molina & Barrett, 2010), *Law & Order* (Sweren et al., 2009), *Law & Order: Criminal Intent* (Chernuchin & Coles, 2009), *Law & Order: Special Victims Unit* (Greene & Leto, 2009), *Monk* (Breckman et al., 2009), *The Closer* (Baldwin et al., 2009), and *White Collar* (Campolongo et al., 2009) all featured knowledge of a second language as a key element in understanding and eventually solving a crime. In the sci-fi genre, both *Fringe* (Abrams et al., 2008) and *Dollhouse* (Whedon et al., 2009) also took part in this trend, featuring characters that speak a second language and whose interaction with the protagonist is crucial over the storytelling arc of an episode. Including second-language use is not necessarily new to television nor to the popular detective or mystery-solving genre writ large (e.g., Dan Brown's *The DaVinci Code* (2003), for instance), but why this profusion of examples within a single calendar year? Why such focus on the crucial importance of understanding languages other than English in order to accomplish the job, solve the crime, and put the criminal behind bars? Although little if any formal research exists linking these types of broadcasts to second language use, through the exploration of this area, I will attempt to make more concrete associations between L2 use and this genre. Thus, in this chapter, we will analyze examples from the series cited above in an effort to decode the patterns behind this trend in order to provide some meaning behind this inclination on the part of writers and show creators.

II. Data Analysis

a. Law & Order

To begin, let us consider the nature of the second language episodes in each of the series I mentioned above. In the *Law & Order* episode entitled "Promote This!" (Sweren et al., 2009) a Honduran day-laborer, Oswaldo Morales, an illegal immigrant to the United States, is found dead not far from a bridge underpass. Detectives work to discover how the man was killed. Their search eventually leads them to find out that three Long Island teenagers had picked up the man, promising him a paying job, but ultimately murdering him. In order to uncover this information, however, Detectives Lupo and Bernard must question other illegal day-laborers, promising upfront, "*No somos la migra*" ('We're not immigration'). In a first encounter, with Oswaldo's friend and roommate Tomás, a dishwasher at a local restaurant, Detective Bernard, after declaring he is not from Immigration, asks, "*¿Lo conoces?*" ('Do you know him?') while Detective Lupo brandishes a photo of the deceased. Tomás responds, "*Sí, es mi amgio Oswaldo. He okay?*" Interestingly, although the detectives begin the interaction in Spanish, it is the native speaker, Tomás, who switches to English. He tells the detectives where Oswaldo typically looks for work, "Under the highway 155. He wait for the cars to come, they give him a job" (Sweren et al., 2009).

In the next scene, Detective Bernard makes more extensive use of Spanish to ask questions of the group of laborers found waiting at the pick-up site. The detectives bring breakfast (coffee, pineapple pastries, cheese) for the workers, hoping to entice them into helping with the investigation. The workers are skeptical, one even saying, "*Es un truco, chavos*" ('It's a trick, guys'). Here, a key moment of L2 Spanish use occurs: picking up on the use of the word "*truco*," Detective Bernard explains, "*El truco es nosotros les damos desayuno y ustedes nos ayudan a busca[r] [a] las personas que hirieron a su amigo Oswaldo Morales*" ('The trick is we give you breakfast and you help us find the people who hurt your friend Oswaldo Morales') (Sweren et al., 2009). This use of Spanish sets the workers at ease and one does step forward when asked, in English, if anyone had seen Oswaldo. This interaction leads to the discovery of the teenagers and their eventual arrest.

b. Law & Order: Special Victims Unit (SVU)

A similar interaction occurs in the *Law & Order: SVU* (Greene & Leto, 2009) episode entitled, "Spooked". This episode centers on the killing of two drug dealers and the FBI's involvement with the perpetrator of said murders. The murderer, an FBI analyst on the Bureau's Cuba intelligence service, kills to protect the interests of the United States and the identities of American spies in Cuba. This information had been hidden on a data storage device within the silicone breast implants of one of the murder victims who was supposed to deliver them to resistance operatives in Cuba. Without delving much more deeply into the complexities of this episode's plot, the crucial moment that leads investigators to find the breast implants and unravel the thread of the FBI's involvement, including, ultimately, the true motives behind the killings, occurs in Spanish at a local grocery store. Here, the murderer, Terri Banes, exchanges grocery carts with another customer asking in Spanish for his help to reach something high on a shelf. Detective Benson, one of the series regulars, recognizes this act as a "drop," a handoff of the important merchandise (in this case, a paper bag containing the heretofore unrecovered breast implants containing the data storage device and the list of American spies) to a co-conspirator. Detective Benson tries to stop the murderer, but she flees, leaving the detective no other option but to stop the man with whom she exchanged grocery carts and question him in Spanish.

She begins the exchange in English, saying, "Excuse me." The man responds, "*No hablo inglés*" ('I don't speak English'). Without missing a beat, Detective Benson makes it clear she will not be deterred, "*Es tuya la bolsa*?" ('Is the bag yours?'). He replies negatively, pretending to realize only then that he "*accidentalmente*" took the wrong shopping cart. She continues, "*Entonces, no te importas si miro adentro*?" ('So you don't mind if I look inside?') (Greene & Leto, 2009). He agrees reluctantly by nodding his head. At this moment, Detective Benson finds the breast implants and the first piece of the larger puzzle falls into place. She arrests the suspect using Spanish, and in a subsequent scene interrogates him in Spanish to no avail, as he will not provide any information.

c. Law & Order: Criminal Intent

In "Revolution" (Chernuchin & Coles, 2009), a season finale episode of the drama *Law & Order: Criminal Intent*, knowledge of a second language plays a somewhat different role. After the botched kidnapping of a bank C.E.O., which results in his death and that of his driver, the Major Case Squad is called in to solve the crime. In the wake of the murders, those responsible send a letter to the *New York Times* claiming responsibility. Detective Zach Nichols, a savant of the crime-fighting arts, upon reading the letter and noticing the phrase, "We have started the revolution last night," posits that, "It could be a native Spanish speaker, or German. Some language where the present perfect is the same as the simple past" (Chernuchin & Coles, 2009). Indeed, in the end, we find out the ringleader of the group responsible for the crime is a German who emigrated to the U.S. after committing arson and killing a family in Germany two decades earlier. In fact, not all members of that family were killed. The man saved the one-year-old daughter of the family and raised her as his own in the U.S.

In the final scene of the episode, Detective Nichols must prevent the grown daughter, now converted to her adoptive father's revolutionary ideology, from blowing up a bank with innocent civilians in it. Again, knowledge of a second language, this time German, is important. To convince her that she is not really the daughter of the man who murdered her parents in Germany, Detective Nichols unearths old German newspaper articles about the crime, which he brings with him into the hostage situation (Chernuchin & Coles, 2009). Without reading knowledge of German, he may never have uncovered these facts, which prove just convincing enough to destabilize the girl, allowing a sniper's bullet to end her life before she can enact her plan to blow up the building. Once again, a second language plays a role as an integral plot device.

c. Monk

In the *Monk* episode "Mr. Monk and the Foreign Man" (Breckman et al., 2009), knowledge of French leads the title character to identify the killer. In this episode, a young Nigerian woman is run over and killed by a speeding van. Two weeks after the event, Monk comes across her grieving husband, intent on determining the circumstances of his wife's death. Monk, having lost his own wife under mysterious, unsolved circumstances, is moved to help in the investigation. While trying to track down the van, Monk, his assistant Natalie, and Samuel (the husband) speak with two men who spend their days sitting on a bench at a gas station near the crime scene, drinking beer and slacking off. One of the two men recalls the van, believing it to have been an exterminator's van since it had the word "poison" written on the side. In the next scene, Monk and Samuel are in a Laundromat doing laundry, when Samuel, seeing a poster of two men fishing, realizes that the word on the side of the van was "*poisson,*" French for 'fish' (Breckman et al., 2009). This leads the two men to discover the van involved in the accident, which they eventually link to its owner, the proprietor of a local restaurant and the man responsible for the death of Samuel's wife. Without Samuel's knowledge of French, the critically important identifying feature of the van, the word *poisson,* would have remained obscure, foiling the resolution of the crime.

c. Bones

"The X in the File" (Lin & Liddi-Brown, 2010), an episode of the series *Bones* that takes place in the New Mexican desert, finds our intrepid stars, Agent Booth and Dr. Brenan, trying to debunk supposed extraterrestrial activity while simultaneously working to solve a murder. The body of the victim is encased in a shell of her own melted fat tissue, giving her the appearance of something otherworldly, or that of a casualty of some extraterrestrial device or treatment. Dr. Brenan discovers various clues upon examining the body, one of which, a digital photo card reveals a video taken by the deceased. This video, a bizarre film of tanker trucks unloading a glowing bile of hazardous waste while people in full white hazmat suits look on, explains to some extent the confusion with extraterrestrials. In the end, however, it is knowledge of Spanish that leads to the unraveling of the case and the discovery of the murderer.

Angela, the lab's technical guru, uncovers an audio track on the video. However, the audio is in Spanish: "*Yo estoy encargada. Y si no lo terminas antes del amanecer te arrepentirás.*" Cam, the head of the lab, a former cop and coroner in New York City, discerns the meaning of the Spanish: "I'm in charge. If you don't get this done before sunrise, you'll regret it." She also goes on to state, "The way she says "*estoy*" and "*arrepentirás*". The Puerto Rican cops used to make fun of me when I pronounced my "T"s and "P"s like that... The speaker is definitely American" (Lin & Liddi-Brown, 2010). This is a central factor in helping Booth and Brenan narrow down the suspect pool and make the arrest. It is also a second example, along with the one from *Law & Order: Criminal Intent*, where explicit metalinguistic information is cited.

f. The Closer

In a similar vein, *The Closer* episode "The Life" (Baldwin et al., 2009) relies on an understanding of Spanish to uncover the genesis of several murders. A teenage boy is drawn into a scheme to kidnap and rape a young woman by several adult gang members. Although the boy does nothing but watch the woman while the others leave their hideout, the woman kills the boy in her desperate bid to escape. The adult gang members are subsequently murdered. The detectives discover that the teenage boy's father is responsible, ordered to do so by his other son, a gang kingpin already in jail. The key evidence comes in the form of a phone call recorded between the jailed son and his father. The phone call is entirely in English, until the moment when the critical order is given, "*Deseo ir al funeral,*" translated quickly by Detective Sanchez, one of several Spanish-speaking members of the squad, "I wish I could get out for the funeral" (Baldwin et al., 2009). The exchange continues in Spanish with various members of the team translating for Deputy Chief Brenda Leigh Johnson, their superior officer. But it is this first remark, followed by, "*Asegúrate que le[s] de[s] un funeral*" ('Make sure there's a funeral'), which cements the murderous intent being communicated between the jailed son and his father (Baldwin et al., 2009). This evidence guides the detectives back to the father, who is arrested for the crimes.

g. Castle

The final two examples come from the shows *Castle* and *White Collar*. Both examples involve a process similar to what we just observed in *The Closer*. Foreign speech is interpreted into English for the benefit of the agents or detectives solving the crime. In "Suicide Squeeze" (Molina & Barrett, 2010), title character Castle and Detective Beckett investigate the death of a professional baseball player, Cano Vega, who defected to the U.S. from Cuba at the outset of his career. Recently, he had returned to visit Cuba, after hearing rumors that his former fiancée, the woman he had planned to defect with, had given birth to a daughter he never knew he had. After confirming the rumors, he works to secure his daughter's safe passage from Cuba to the U.S. The night of Vega's death, she finally arrives. It is his daughter who, at the end of the episode, reveals the identity of the true killer, having seen him the night of her father's death. This revelation occurs mostly in Spanish with the interpreting to English by Detective Esposito. Without Detective Esposito's interpreting, this revelation of how Vega came to know about his daughter and about the history of Vega's relationship with her mother would not have been understood by the main characters, Castle and Beckett, but perhaps more importantly, the audience would not have had the full story. Interestingly, however, when Castle and Beckett ask questions, they are in English without interpreting to Spanish. Moreover, at the end of the revelation, Vega's daughter switches back to English when it concerns the actual identity of the murderer. So, in this case, although Spanish serves an important function to explain the story, fleshing out the details, it is not necessary for the actual identification of the killer.

h. White Collar

In *White Collar*'s "All In" (Campolongo et al., 2009), Neal Caffrey and Agent Burke are pursuing a Chinese money launderer named Lao in order to find a missing FBI agent. Neal goes undercover as a businessman seeking to launder funds with the target of their investigation. While trying to meet Lao at an underground gambling parlor to set up an illicit business arrangement, the gambling parlor is raided by the NYPD on a tip from a woman posing as the money launderer's concubine. Once Agent Burke discovers who tipped off the police and interrupted his plans, he is determined to discover why. This leads him to a hostess parlor in lower Manhattan where Agent Burke approaches several female employees smoking outside. He questions the group explicitly in English making sure to highlight the fact that he can't understand Chinese[1], to which he receives a cacophony of responses, in Chinese. He slyly records the interaction and seeks a translator upon return to his headquarters to discover what was said while the Chinese speakers believed him to be unable to understand, "Amazing what someone will say when they don't think that you can speak their language" (Campolongo et al., 2009). Problematically, the translator is delayed and a Chinese-American bilingual child, whose father is working with the bureau, happens in upon a playback of the recording and is drafted to write down what she hears. She produces a transcript of the conversation, which leads to further information about Lao's concubine and the location of a warehouse for an import-export business where the body of the missing agent is discovered. In the end, Lao is brought to justice for his crimes, important evidence of which, that is, the body of the missing FBI agent, is found because of the translation of the Chinese conversation by the child bilingual (see Chapter 11 for more on child language brokers).

As I mentioned in my introduction to this topic, television serials in the science fiction genre also support this trend of second language use as an integral part of storytelling. While this chapter focuses on the crime genre, suffice it to say such shows as *Fringe* and *Dollhouse* and even the third and most recent season of *Stranger Things* (Duffer et al., 2019) provide robust evidence. Episodes of each series featured second language use as a key element for understanding the events that unfold and, similar to the examples above from the police procedural/detective genre, lead to the unraveling of mysteries in some way.

III. Discussion

The eight examples I have given above represent a variety of languages— Spanish, German, French and Chinese. Spanish is the most common, playing a crucial role in five of the eight shows cited above. This is not surprising given the prevalence of Spanish speakers, Latinx culture and Spanish language in the U.S., especially in big cities such as New York and L.A. where all but two of the cited examples take place.[2] Making Spanish a major player in these dramas reflects a current reality in an ever-evolving demographic landscape where Latinos are the largest ethnic minority in the U.S., a percentage that

---

[1] Not speaking Chinese myself, I cannot specify Mandarin or Cantonese, both of which are present in New York City's Chinatown.

[2] *Monk* takes place in San Francisco and *Bones*, normally in Washington, D.C., was on location in New Mexico. *The Closer* takes place in Los Angeles. All *Law & Order* episodes take place in New York City as do *Castle* and *White Collar*.

continues to grow. Next year when the new census data is collected (provided that questions of citizenship are not included), it will be fascinating to see how this population has continued to grow.

Moreover, the use of Spanish serves to create a more realistic ambiance, to make the New York City on TV match the New York City in real life, which imbues the TV shows with more authenticity (Lopez & Bucholtz, 2017). But is the use of Spanish mere linguistic exhibitionism (Pandey, 2016)? Again, the answer to this question is mixed. On the one hand, the Spanish language is used by the English-speaking characters in *Law & Order, Law & Order: SVU*, and *Bones*. The audience hears non-native speakers using Spanish in real interactions, short though they may be. In *Castle* and *The Closer*, the Latino characters interpret Spanish into English (although Detective Sanchez on *The Closer* does use Spanish in other episodes). Taken together, there does seem to be something cross-cultural occurring that might transcend mere linguistic exhibitionism. The dialogue serves an ideological purpose (Bednarek's (2018) thematic/ideological function), conveying messages about the importance of Spanish, at least in certain professions or locations.

As I said at the outset of this chapter, if we consider the detective or mystery-solving genre more globally, including L2 use is not necessarily new. What is new, perhaps reflective of the realities of instant access in our world today, is the immediate and communicative nature of the decoding that occurs. Often in the past such decoding involved reading or deciphering ancient texts or symbols, such as in novels like *The DaVinci Code* or in films such as the *Indiana Jones* franchise. This type of knowledge is still shown to be useful, such as in the episode of *Law & Order: Criminal Intent* in which reading knowledge of German is crucial. But, more generally, the L2 use that occurs today in television often involves understanding spoken language in a real communicative context where messages are being delivered either to the detectives themselves or to a third party. This may also reflect trends in the way languages have been taught in schools for the last thirty years, using the Communicative Approach (cf. Krashen, 1982). Language is no longer seen as a stale object to be studied or read in books, but rather a living, vital instrument for expressing meaning and ideas.

In several of the interactions detailed above we see translanguaging (Otheguy et al., 2015) occur. For instance, detectives and witnesses in the *Law & Order, Law & Order: SVU*, and *Castle* employ both Spanish and English. The detectives in these shows have an instrumental interest in using Spanish—it is the means to the end of solving the crime. They use the linguistic resources that they have available to them (Spanish and English) to achieve the result of obtaining crucial information. In the examples, it is the speaking of the L2 that is most important, focusing us again on the communicative aspect of language use.

Another trend that comes forth in these examples is a focus on linguistic information. In the examples from *Bones* and *Law & Order: Criminal Intent* explicit metalinguistic analysis occurs. Cam talks about the American accent associated with the difference in pronunciation of /p/ and /t/ in Spanish versus English. Detective Nichols cites the conflation of present perfect and simple past in languages like German, French, and Italian. Although no full representation of linguistics as a field occurs, this contrastive analysis of language, comparing English with other tongues, is unusual and may represent a move toward greater inclusion of linguistics as a tool in the toolbox of investigators in this genre, much as medical analysis, forensic anthropology, psychological profiling, and techniques of DNA analysis are now ubiquitous on television. This may portend a popularization of the field—the next big TV show could popularize linguistics in the American imagination, much as the film *Arrival* (2016) did.[3]

Another issue of interest, which I touch on in other chapters, is the use or non-use of subtitles and the effect this has on the audience. Analysis of these examples through that lens would certainly yield additional conclusions, but it is beyond the scope of the current chapter. It is my hope that others will systematically engage this area of research in the future.

IV. Conclusion

To close, I want to return to an idea I brought forth at the end of Chapter 1. That is, the power that depicting different languages and, by extension, different peoples and different cultures can have on the viewing public. This representational phenomenon does more than simply highlight globalization, it tells us something about America itself. It not only recalls the immigrant history that many of us share, but it invites us to welcome others, who may not be as far removed from those ancestors who first came to make their lives in the U.S. or who may, indeed, be those first immigrant pioneers themselves. Strangers in a strange land—a land rendered, perhaps, a bit more transparent because of American music, films, and, ironically, television that is exported to the farthest concerns of the globe. Television presents an opportunity to experience diversity in a non-threatening way that may make us more open-minded and willing to accept those who are different from ourselves with less

---

[3] In fact, within a year or two of the episodes cited in this chapter, several television shows in this genre did use the linguistic idea of idiolect in English, i.e., the personalized dialect that one speaks or writes, as germane to solving the crime. Examples include: *Bones*, "The Future in the Past" (Hanson et al., 2012); *The Mentalist*, "Red in Tooth and Claw" (Harper & Zisk, 2013); and *Elementary*, "Possibility Two" (Goffman & Mann, 2013).

trepidation and more hope. With the Trump Administration's harsh stance on illegal immigration, including child detainees on our Southern border (Sacchetti, 2019), immigration policy is on the minds of many Americans. The coming 2020 presidential election in the U.S. will only serve to increase focus on this volatile and important issue. If the detectives on TV can decode the other, maybe the regular American can as well.

Part II:
Language Learning

Chapter 4

Xiaolin Monks Master Metaphor: Acquisition of Second Language Idioms in Children's Television

I. Introduction

Second language (L2) acquisition of idioms and metaphorical language is a daunting process. The learner, influenced by first-language assumptions of world framing and interpretation, must determine how such issues transfer into idiomatic L2 usage. Beyond rudimentary communication, incorporating metaphorical language into one's repertoire in an L2 indicates greater sophistication and in-group membership. It requires not only linguistic knowledge, but understanding of L2 culture and ideology. All of these elements are important for assimilation into an L2-speaking culture. Equally important, however, is tolerance on the part of L2 speakers for difference, linguistic and otherwise.

With this in mind, in this chapter, we examine the use (and misuse) of idioms and metaphors in the children's animated series *Xiaolin Showdown*, created and produced by Christy Hui for Warner Bros.' Kids WB, which ran for fifty-two episodes from 2003 to 2006 (Motz et al., 2003). This cartoon series follows the adventures of four *Xiaolin dragons*, pre-teen heroes from different parts of the globe, who search for ancient artifacts called Shen Gong Wu in order to save the world from domination by an evil witch and her boy-genius sidekick. We will look at language use by the non-native speaking monk-in-training, Omi and his compatriots in an effort to better understand how ideas such as linguistic and cultural difference are being represented to children in popular television. In addition, the ways in which metaphorical language is dealt with can convey messages about tolerance of difference, an important idea in an increasingly multicultural country like the United States. Although the protagonists are not real people, the behavior demonstrated in these small-screen episodes do characterize ways in which real children (and adults) behave toward one another and do provide a snapshot of our own culture and its reaction to the use and misuse of metaphorical language by native and non-native speakers alike.

II. Background Research

Previous L2 studies have addressed such issues as transfer in idiomatic L2 use (Kellerman, 1979; Irujo, 1986), idiom processing by non-native speakers of English (Cooper, 1999), metaphor comprehension by L2 speakers (De Cunha, 1991), and the role of chunking and phonological memory in idiom acquisition (Ellis, 1996). De Cunha's (1991) work is of particular interest because of her focus on education and learning as they relate to metaphor comprehension:

> Given the prevalence of metaphor in language and given that language is a main medium of learning, it follows that knowing how metaphors are processed and what constraints exist on their comprehension is bound to contribute to understanding the learning process. (1991, p. 2)

In addition, Li (2003) proposed a conceptual metaphor and image-based pedagogy to teach English metaphors, idioms, and proverbs to L1 Chinese first- and second-year university students. He tested this approach in a series of experiments, finding some support for the idea that the learning of metaphorical language could be facilitated using his techniques, which involved explanation of the concepts behind metaphorical language in English, as well as the imagining of mental images related to metaphorical language.

Imagine the number of young children who watched *Xioalin Showdown* when it aired in the early 2000s. As we will see below, children are given a roadmap to understand that language is not always literal through the misunderstandings and explanations given to Omi and his friends about metaphor use in English. Although this does not relate to how children process metaphors in real-time interactions, it does provide one possible way that they receive explicit instruction about what metaphors are and how they function in language. This explicit knowledge about how to interpret metaphors could lead to more successful understanding.

In first language, Nerlich, Clarke, and Todd (1999) find that: "Understanding the use and comprehension of metaphor and metonymy in language acquisition has important implications for language teaching, especially for reading and comprehension and later on for writing and composition" (p. 379). From this work, we can see why an early understanding of metaphor can have lasting impacts as students advance through their education. *Xioalin Showdown* potentially made invaluable contributions to young L1 English speakers' knowledge of their language, making it a model for other children's programming. This is especially true, when we consider research by Siqueira and Settineri (2003) that provides evidence that children as young as three-years-old are already able to understand some figurative uses in their L1 (p. 203). The additional explicit information on metaphor provided in *Xiaolin*

Showdown can perhaps increase this understanding for children who have some natural affinity for metaphor comprehension, or it can lay the groundwork for such understanding in those children without it, for both L1 and L2 learners.

Danesi (1992) argues that metaphorical competence should be taught explicitly in the L2 classroom. He conducted two experiments in this area that revealed that even advanced students had little knowledge of the conceptual system of the L2. However, both experiments had very low participant numbers making it impossible to hew to any strong generalizations. He also alluded to the importance of the conceptual system of a language to indicate differences in culture. Teaching these systems could increase overall cultural understanding.

All told, previous research on the topic of L1 and L2 metaphor acquisition indicates the importance of several useful ideas. First, explicit instruction in metaphor comprehension seems to be of worth for both first- and second-language learners (Nerlich et al., 1999; Siqueira & Settineri, 2003). Language learners' better understanding of metaphors could lead to increased language gains in their own written expression and reading comprehension (Nerlich et al., 1999). Second, understanding how learners process metaphors in order to comprehend them could lead to increased insight into the process of language acquisition more generally (De Cunha, 1991). Finally, when L2 students learn about how native speakers encode metaphors in the target language, there may be gains in awareness of cultural differences leading to a greater apprehension of the target culture (Danesi, 1992).

III. Data Analysis

In this chapter, I examine the use of metaphor in the children's animated television series *Xiaolin Showdown*. You may recall from above that this program features four pre-teen heroes, known as *Xiaolin* dragons, each from a different country, searching for ancient artifacts to stop an evil witch and her sidekick from taking over the world. Table 1 (following page) displays a brief sketch of each main character, including first language (L1) and country of origin.

I looked at all 13 *Xiaolin Showdown* episodes in Season 1 for occasions in which metaphorical language was used. I found a total of 54 "Metaphor Episodes" (ME), sometimes produced by one character alone, sometimes produced in an interactional context. Then, based on the content of each episode, I categorized the MEs into 10 distinct types. Some MEs fell into more than one category type. Table 2 (following page) summarizes the distinct episode types and the number of tokens of each type. Only the first ME type, Incorrect Production, is further subdivided into those MEs with correction and those without, as can be seen in the table.

Table 4.1: Summary of *Xiaolin Showdown* Characters.

Character Name	Description**	L1	Country of origin
Omi*	*Xiaolin* monk-in-training	Chinese	China
Clay*	Old-style cowboy	English	Texas, USA
Raimundo (Rai)*	Street-smart	Portuguese	Rio de Janeiro, Brazil
Kimiko (Kim)*	Hip-hop tech whiz	Japanese	Tokyo, Japan
Dojo	Dragon sidekick to the *Xiaolin* dragons	Chinese	China
Master Fung	Trains the *Xiaolin* dragons at the *Xiaolin* temple	Chinese	China
Jack	Evil boy genius	English	USA
Wuya	Hailin witch	Chinese	China

* Xiaolin dragons.
**Most descriptions taken from DVD packaging.

Table 4.2: Metaphor Episode Types and Tokens.

Metaphor Episode Type	Number of examples
Incorrect production With correction Without correction	26 (15) (11)
Failure to understand/interpret	10
Colorful metaphors	9
Metaphor/Idiom with translation/interpretation	8
Current Slang	16
Unexpected Correct Usage	10
Metalanguage	2
Fun with language	1
Literal Interpretations	2
Double Meaning	1

Below we will explore each ME type, analyzing specific examples of each one. Following this section, I will engage in a broader discussion of the significance of these MEs in the series.

A) Incorrect production

There was a total of 26 examples of this type in which the metaphor is produced incorrectly in some way. Of these examples, fifteen included an explicit correction of the incorrectly produced metaphor, while eleven did not. The vast majority of these tokens (25/26) are produced by Omi, a non-native speaker of English.

Below, in examples 4.1-4.3, there are several examples of this type of ME. In each case, as noted above, it is Omi who produces the problematic metaphor. In example 4.1, after a training exercise, Omi is trying to say that he did not do his best. Instead of the idiomatic "I stink" that he is trying to use, Omi comes up with the more literal "I smell bad." Raimundo corrects Omi's idiomatic usage by providing the correct expression (I stink) and then teases Omi by reusing his initial attempt at the phrase (I smell bad) to insult him ("and you smell bad, too"). This last bit, although insulting, provides further information to Omi with regard to the difference between the phrases that could be key in helping Omi to understand how "I stink" is used metaphorically, but how "I smell bad" only has a literal meaning.

> (4.1)
> Omi: I foolishly and shamefully lost a quarter second on the
>   sandbags. As you might say, **I smell bad**.
> Rai: I stink, not I smell bad.
> Omi: I stink?
> Rai: Yeah, and you smell bad, too.
> (Motz et al., 2003)

In example 4.2, Omi has bested Raimundo at some aspect of their training and attempts to trash talk him. Here again, Omi deploys incorrect metaphors with the respect to parts of the body, first saying "in your head" and then "talk to my fingers." In the first case, Raimundo helpfully provides a correction, "in your face," but no correction is given for "talk to my fingers" in the second instance. Of course, Omi means "talk to the hand," a common expression in the early 2000s that the creators assume watchers will be able to furnish on their own. Thus, in example 4.2, we have two separate instances of this ME type, one with correction and one without.

(4.2)

Omi: Yes. **In your head**, Raimundo.

Rai: In your face.

Omi: **Talk to my fingers**.

(Motz et al., 2003)

A couple of final exemplars of this ME type come at the end of 4.3 below. Here we again find two metaphors used by Omi, one that elicits explicit correction and one that does not. In the first bolded example, Omi uses "pushing your arm" in lieu of "pulling your leg," which Clay provides. At the end of the exchange, Omi says, "my badness" instead of *my bad*. This is not corrected for similar reasons to those discussed above: as a common phrase of the day, creators likely expected that viewers could easily access the correct phrase in their everyday lexicon.

(4.3)

Fung: In today's training we will divide the *Shen Gong Wu* among
              you. The exercise is called–Omi?

Omi: *Xiaolin* Surprise.

Clay: Sounds like an appetizer.

Fung: This is an advanced training technique that relies on a
              powerful inner force we call–

Omi: Oh, oh! The instincts of the tiger.

Fung: Which is? Omi?

Omi: The ability to predict your opponent's next move.

Rai: Yeah, like you can really read minds or something?

Omi: I knew you'd say that.

Rai: You, you did?

Omi: No, I am only, as you say, **pushing your arm**.

Clay: Pulling his leg?

Omi: Oh, **my badness**.

(Motz et al., 2003)

B) Failure to Understand/Interpret

The second type of ME involves failure to understand or interpret a metaphor. Ten total tokens of this type were found. Many of these interactions involve Omi or Raimundo in some way, including all of the examples below. Although Rai corrects Omi in examples 4.1 and 4.2 above, he has difficulty understanding some of the more colorful, less current metaphors used by some of his friends (interactions 4.4, 4.5, and 4.6 below). But, there is evolution in understanding as evidenced in interaction 4.7, from a later episode in the series.

In examples 4.4 and 4.5 below Rai expresses frustration at his inability to interpret the metaphors used by Clay and Omi respectively. In both cases, the metaphors are somewhat elaborate and relate to a cultural context that is outside of Rai's experience. In both cases, he asks, "What?" indicating that he has not understood and needs further clarification. In example 4.6, although Rai asks "What?" again, Clay cannot be bothered to explain the metaphor. The writers may have believed this metaphor was more easily understood and thus chose not to provide an explicit interpretation. Finally, in example 4.7, Rai seems to have learned something from interacting with his friends when they use metaphors. When Master Fung opines, "life is a river, it has ebbs and flows," Rai is willing to venture his own interpretation, "You mean, you win some, you lose some?" (Motz et al., 2003). This example shows Rai's growth with respect to his own understanding of metaphor and may reflect the evolution of some viewers' understanding of how metaphors work or it might inspire those who are still learning to make guesses about how to interpret metaphorical language.

(4.4)

Clay:	**Just get us on the range Dojo and we'll do the cow roping**
Rai:	What?
Kim:	I think he means, get us close and we'll find it
Rai:	So why didn't he just say it?

(Motz et al., 2003)

(4.5)

Dojo:	You're on your own.
Omi:	**A net cast wide catches more fish.**
Rai:	What?
Kim:	I think he's saying we should split up.
Rai:	Would it kill you guys to just say what you mean?

(Motz et al., 2003)

(4.6)

| Clay: | Raimundo, partner, it's pretty late. Maybe you oughta give that stuff a rest? |
| Rai: | No way, I am going to learn everything I can about the shen gong wu. |

Clay: **Doesn't do any good to close the barn door after the horses get out**.
Rai: What?!
Clay: Never mind.
(Motz et al., 2003)

(4.7)
Fung: I sense disappointment.
Omi: Shame forbids me from speaking of my wacky failure.
Clay: Omi lost a Xiaolin Showdown.
Fung: Young monk, you must learn that **life is a river, it has ebbs and flows**.
Rai: You mean, you win some, you lose some?
Fung: Precisely Raimundo.
(Motz et al., 2003)

Omi, too, has difficulty understanding some metaphors (oftentimes because he lacks specific cultural knowledge), similar to his metaphor production issues in the first type of ME. However, as we see above in 4.5 and below in 4.10, Omi is also capable of producing complex metaphorical language. Yet he can't understand the language in interactions 4.8 and 4.9 below. In both of these interactions, Omi insists on a literal interpretation of what is said. But in 4.10, he produces an elaborate metaphor that his companions cannot interpret. Omi may represent the contradictions that one finds in children, who can be quite perceptive on the one hand, while lacking some forms of specific knowledge or experience on the other. Or, he could represent the L2 learner/speaker for very similar reasons: L2 speakers may have a complex understanding of the world and expressive abilities in their L1, yet may lack specific, crucial cultural knowledge in their L2.

(4.8)
Omi: These are lion claws. Very similar…
Rai: But **no dice**.
Omi: Ooo, dice. Are we looking for dice, too?
Rai: (Shakes head)
(Motz et al., 2003)

(4.9)
Rai: Prepare to **cough up candy**!

Omi: Are you suggesting that I have stored candy inside my mouth. That would be most unsanitary.

Rai: Pick a cup! (Omi picks correct cup) Enjoy the tooth decay.

(Motz et al., 2003)

(4.10)

Dojo: It's the Star Hanabi.

Kim: I'm guessing that's a Shen Gong Wu.

Dojo: Yeah, it must be inactive. That's why I didn't notice before.

Omi: But if it activates, Jack and Wuya will be all over it like **kiju flies on a sunberry blossom**. (Blank stares)

Omi: I miss Clay and his colorful metaphors.

(Motz et al., 2003)

C) Colorful Metaphors

There are nine examples of colorful, over-the-top metaphors in the data sample. These elaborate, homespun metaphors are mostly Clay's domain, as he produces five of the nine examples. Examples 4.4 and 4.6 above as well as 4.11 below illustrate the point:

(4.11)

Clay: Dojo, why are you acting jumpier than **a long-tailed cat in a room full of rocking chairs**.

(Motz et al., 2003)

That Clay should produce the majority of this ME type is not surprising. He represents a speaker from the Southern U.S., specifically Texas. Southern speakers are often stereotyped for using this sort of colorful language, including vivid metaphorical language (cf. Mitchell, 2015; Queen, 2015, for greater discussion of this phenomenon).

D) Metaphor/Idiom with translation/interpretation

We have already seen several examples above of this type of ME, in which one character produces idiomatic or metaphorical language that is then interpreted by another. A total of eight examples were culled from the data. We see examples of this ME type in interactions 4.4, 4.5, and 4.7 above. Interaction 4.12 provides an additional example. Here Rai uses metaphorical slang ("rank") to describe a volcano's odor and Omi interprets it for those in the viewing audience who may not be aware of this usage.

(4.12)
Rai: Oh, that's **rank** yo!
Omi: **The volcano's odor is most stinky**. Are you sure you smell a
          shen gong wu?
Dojo: Does Clay wear his boots to bed?
(Motz et al., 2003)

E) Current Slang

The fifth ME type, uses of current slang, takes place almost exclusively in
Episode 9, "My Honey Omi," which takes place in New York City. Fourteen of
the sixteen total examples of this type come from this episode. In the episode,
Omi befriends Jermaine, an African-American boy from New York City, who
eventually helps him win a *Xiaolin* Showdown.

What's interesting about this episode is Omi's interaction with this new dialect
from both the standpoint of interpretation and production. In interactions 4.13
through 4.15 below, we see Omi have flashes of understanding of the unfamiliar
idioms of this dialect. In examples 4.16 through 4.21, Omi even manages to use
a few expressions correctly (cf. 4.16-4.18).

In 4.13, Omi defaults to a literal interpretation of the term "grill," while
managing to correctly interpret the meaning of "smack you down" as a
challenge. Interaction 4.14 demonstrates the uncertainty that Omi feels about
this new, more slang-filled dialect. He cannot reliably interpret Jermaine's use
of "off the hook" or "layin' it down hardcore." Nor does Omi understand the
usage of "tight" in example 4.15.

(4.13)
Bballer1:   You jackin' my game, punk? I oughta **bust your grill**.
Omi: But, I have no grill. I am vegetarian, a most healthy lifestyle.
Bballer2:   Don't go playin' baldy, or we'll **smack you down**.
Omi: I am not certain, but I think you may be challenging me.
Bballer2:   Got that.
(Motz et al., 2003)

(4.14)
Jermaine: That was **off the hook**, man!
Omi: It was? Uh…is that a good thing?
Jermaine: No doubt, no doubt! You was **layin' it down hardcore**.
Omi: This was my intention, I think.
(Motz et al., 2003)

(4.15)

Jermaine: Omi, dawg, your size is too **tight**!

Omi: Should I loosen it?

Jermaine: Most definitely not, my friend, most definitely not.

(Motz et al., 2003)

After he has some exposure to the new dialect, however, Omi is ready to try it out for himself. In examples 4.16 to 4.21, Omi acquits himself fairly well, using terms like "representing" (4.16), "up in my business" (4.17), "all that and a bag of chips" (4.18), and the victorious taunt "say my name" (4.20) correctly. He still makes some minor errors though, such as: "obtained game" (4.19), "angry skills" (4.20), and "peace on" (4.21) (Motz et al., 2003).

(4.16)

Jermaine: Now that's what I'm talking about! Omi, playa, playa! I knew you had it in you!

Omi: Am I, as you say, **bling-blinging**?

Jermaine: Definitely.

Omi: Jermaine, while I enjoy **representing**, I must not let it divert me from my quest.

(Motz et al., 2003)

(4.17)

Jack: Omi, I challenge you to a Xiaolin Showdown.

Omi: Jack Spicer, why are you always **up in my bus-i-ness**?

(Motz et al., 2003)

(4.18)

Jack: But, don't worry, I got the answer. Meet my first-round draft pick.

Omi: I am not feeling like **all that and a bag of chips** anymore.

Jermaine: For real.

(Motz et al., 2003)

(4.19)

Omi: Jermaine, we are doing well. Perhaps I have **obtained game**.

Jermaine: It's got game, Omi. And, yeah you definitely—

Jack: Got no chance!

(Motz et al., 2003)

(4.20)
Omi: Oh yeah! We win! **Say my name**, Jack Spicer! Oo, I have
                angry skills.
Jermaine: Mad skills.
Omi: Correct!
(Motz et al., 2003)

(4.21)
Jermaine: Hey, Omi, here's a souvenir!
Omi: Thanks! **Peace on**!
Rai: Uh, peace out.
Omi: That too!
(Motz et al., 2003)

These attempts by Omi to use an unfamiliar dialect are interesting. What could be the significance of such attempts? I believe that they convey an important message to viewers, especially those learning a new language: It is crucial to try new language. Mastery does not come without practice. In an unfamiliar linguistic situation, Omi is willing to take chances in order to learn.

F) Unexpected Correct Usage

This category, unexpected correct usage, is again of particular interest with respect to Omi, our L2 English speaker. He produces six of the ten examples. Most of them we have just seen in the previous category. Another, the term "small boned," follows in 4.22, from Episode 4, providing evidence that Omi does have some engagement with current terms used in pop culture. Once again, we see Omi taking linguistic risks, trying and sometimes succeeding with terms that are not part of his standard way of speaking.

(4.22)
Clay: Hold your horses, partner.
Kim: It's Omi's turn.
Clay: Give the little fella a chance.
Omi: While I appreciate your help, I must point out that I am not
                little. I am **small-boned.**
Clay: Um, my mistake, little…partner.
Omi: Ah, at last, the golden tiger claws are mine to wield. Golden
                Tiger Claw—
Dojo: Stop everything! We got a hot one!
Fung: A new Shen Gong Wu has revealed itself.

Omi:	Talk about **rotted timing**.
Kim:	Rotten timing.
Omi:	That too.

(Motz et al., 2003)

G) Metalanguage (2)

Occasionally, characters make conscious reference to language use and interpretation, using metalanguage. There are two such instances of metalanguage use in the data. They can be seen in 4.10, reproduced here for convenience, and 4.23. The metaphor is bolded, while the metalinguistic reaction is underlined. In both cases, explicit reference is made to the preceding metaphor. It's clear from these examples that viewers' attention is drawn to language use.

(4.10)

Dojo:	It's the Star Hanabi.
Kim:	I'm guessing that's a Shen Gong Wu.
Dojo:	Yeah, it must be inactive. That's why I didn't notice before.
Omi:	But if it activates, Jack and Wuya will be all over it like **kiju flies on a sunberry blossom**. (Blank stares)
Omi:	I miss Clay and his colorful metaphors.

(Motz et al., 2003)

(4.23)

| Omi: | You are supposed to **hand-scrub the floors**, Raimundo. |
| Rai: | You are being too literal. |

(Motz et al., 2003)

H) Fun with Language

Not only do all the very colorful metaphors and, in some sense, all examples indicate a certain pleasure that the characters take in using metaphorical language, but there is at least one example where Omi makes overt reference to the fun they are having with language (see underline below):

(4.24)

| Wuya: | Yes, yes, a thousand times yes. |
| Rai: | Okay, okay, just **jerking your chain**. |

Clay: That's funny. **A jerk jerking a chain.**
Omi: A **jerk jerking a chain**. <u>Most amusing, Clay</u>.
(Motz et al., 2003)

Here Omi repeats Clay's joke, which might be indication enough of the fun being had with language. But Omi goes further by offering an explicit appreciation of Clay's language use. Although I have not chosen to include this exchange as an example of metalanguage in the previous section, potentially it could be counted there as well. It is a clear indication that having fun with language is a part of the ethos of the show.

I) Literal Interpretations (2)

In at least two cases there are literal interpretations of what is being said. The first is from 4.23 above (reproduced below for convenience), where Rai tells Omi he is being too literal. In this case, Rai is assigned to hand-scrub the floors, but is using a mop instead. Rai's comment "You're being too literal" communicates to Omi that using the mop is in keeping with the idea of hand-scrubbing the floors, since he is operating the mop with his own hands. In 4.25, Dojo saves the pre-teen warriors by breathing fire, then makes reference to his small size after Clay uses the metaphor that Dojo had "a real fire brewing in him." The metaphor, meant to indicate Dojo's determination to save them, is contrasted with the literal idea of Dojo's 16-ounce size. In both cases, an explicit distinction is being made between the literal and the figurative meanings of what is being said. This distinction could be useful to viewers trying to parse the difference between meaning in the material world and metaphorical meaning.

(4.23)
Omi: You are supposed to **hand-scrub the floors**, Raimundo.
Rai: <u>You are being too literal</u>.
(Motz et al., 2003)

25)
Omi: I believe we owe our salvation to Dojo.
Clay: I always knew **he had a real fire brewing in him**.
Dojo: <u>'Bout 16 ounces to be exact</u>.
(Motz et al., 2003)

J) Double Meaning

The final category of ME has to do with double meaning. In 4.24 above, the double meaning of "jerk/jerking" is evident: "jerk" as in a mean person, and "jerking" as in pulling. In 4.26 below, we see a different approach to double meaning. In this case, the interpretation is deliberately unspecified or ambiguous to make either or both interpretations possible. Here Kimiko is fighting her robotic doppelganger made of metal. Thus, the phrase "test her *mettle*" could equally be interpreted as "test her *metal*." This situation also gives the phrase "a little harder-edged" an ambiguous meaning—is the robot literally harder-edged because it is made of metal or is it simply more ruthless? This wordplay could also be interpreted as having fun with language, however because it is not as explicit as the other example in that category, I have not included it there.

(4.26)

Kimbot:	Hi there.
Kim:	What is that?
Jack:	Kimiko, meet Kimiko. Or, should I say, meet your match. She's you.
Kimbot:	Hi there.
Jack:	Only, a little perkier. (Kimiko kicks Kimbot) And, a **little harder-edged**. Go on, **test her metal/mettle**.

(Motz et al., 2003)

IV. Discussion

There are several questions that we can pose based on the data we've looked at. These are:

- What does the problematization of idiomatic language usage indicate?

- What are the implications for native and non-native youngsters acquiring language?

- What does this anecdotal representation tell us about L2 idiom acquisition?

- What broader implications does this multiethnic, multilingual cartoon have for society in the U.S.?

In order to answer these questions, which I will return to shortly, it's most useful to consider the lessons that can be gleaned from the interactions around the production of metaphors and idiomatic language.

For example, L1 and L2 English-speaking children can gather rather sophisticated lessons from the production and interpretation difficulties of metaphorical language that are laid bare in the metalanguage and corrections we've seen in the language episodes above. First, both sets of children, L1 and L2 English speakers, can begin to understand that learning this idiomatic, metaphorical aspect of language is hard. Moreover, they see the characters on the show make errors and may realize that it's okay to make mistakes themselves when deploying this language. As a corollary to this idea, they may also realize that it's okay to be corrected as it forms a necessary part of the learning process, especially for these more difficult aspects of language production and interpretation. Finally, based on Omi and Rai's abilities to eventually interpret metaphorical language correctly (cf. B above for difficulties understanding), children watching will realize that, in time, they, too, will develop a framework by which to correctly understand and interpret this type of language.

There are other lessons that children learn about language as well. From Clay's colorful metaphors and other such examples, children begin to understand that language can be fun, imaginative and, even beautiful. From metaphors that are interpreted and/or explained and from the literal interpretations of metaphors, children learn two important ideas: 1) sometimes people don't always say what they mean, and 2) sometimes language has a meaning beyond the most literal or direct interpretation.

The use of slang provides children with lessons about dialect difference. They are provided with evidence that different dialects exist, and that these dialects are influenced by the experience of different peoples, places, and cultures. More indirectly, usage and explicit recognition of slang and other dialectal features invite children to be unafraid to try on different linguistic hats. If we see language as a proxy for culture, this lesson could also be interpreted to mean that they should not be afraid of difference, rather they should embrace it.

In terms of the examples above with metalanguage and double meanings, children will develop a sense that language is complex, but accessible if you learn the right tools. We can view this lesson as an invitation to explore language further. Perhaps young viewers are being invited to think critically about what we say and how we use language.

In terms of broader implications beyond language, it is clear that this series invites children into a world where difference is embraced. This embrace of difference is evident in the different skills and talents, linguistic and otherwise, of the main characters. In terms of language, it creates a safe environment to explore and to experiment. Moreover, there are implications for education: language comprehension, leading to eventual production as well, can open doors. Learning to decode metaphorical language can lead to better educational outcomes, resulting in access to knowledge that might be otherwise inaccessible (cf. De Cunha, 1991; Nerlich et al., 1999). Also, learning about the conceptual system of another language provides potentially invaluable clues about the culture that uses that language (cf. Danesi, 1992).

V. Conclusion

To conclude, I'd like to return to the questions I posed earlier.

- What does the problematization of idiomatic language usage indicate?

Children learn that language is not always denotative or literal. Language is a creative tool that they have at their disposal.

- What are the implications for native and non-native youngsters acquiring language?

The way idiomatic language is used in this series creates an opportunity for youngsters to grow and develop their linguistic skills (cf. Nerlich et al., 1999). Moreover, as Danesi (1992) indicates, teaching about metaphor, which I would argue that *Xiaolin Showdown* is doing implicitly, can increase cultural, and perhaps cross-cultural, understanding.

- What does this anecdotal representation tell us about L2 idiom acquisition?

It would seem that idioms in the second language require some explicit instruction as Danesi (1992) suggests. L2 learners may be able to decipher some metaphorical/idiomatic uses through transfer (cf. Kellerman, 1979; Irujo, 1986) or more general processing strategies (Cooper, 1999; De Cunha, 1991), but others will require native speakers to provide explanations of meaning. This could contribute to greater cultural understanding per Danesi (1992), but at the very least such exchanges will increase negotiation of meaning (Long, 1981, 1983a, 1983b), a key feature of L2 acquisition. As an avenue for future research, for any scholars with knowledge of Portuguese and/or Mandarin and English, it would be interesting to review the misuse of idiomatic language by Raimundo and Omi to determine if idioms in the characters' L1s or if aspects of their native cultures are being incorrectly transferred to the L2 context. Unfortunately, such an analysis is beyond my own abilities to complete. However, it could shed an interesting light on cultural differences that might influence language use.

- What broader implications does this multiethnic, multilingual cartoon have for society in the U.S.?

As stated above, the multiethnic, multilingual nature of this cartoon indicates an embrace of difference, linguistic and otherwise. In many places, the U.S. itself is very diverse. Even in places in the U.S. without great diversity, this cartoon may open viewers' minds to those who are unlike themselves and incite curiosity about others. It is a reflection of the U.S. itself in the diversity of its characters.

To get another perspective on the way language is used in *Xiaolin Showdown*, I reached out to series creator Christy Hui. I asked her the following questions:

1) As series' creator, what role did you foresee/intend that language would play in the series?

2) If you did have specific goals for the way language was used in the series, what informed the choices that you made?

I will conclude this chapter with her insightful remarks:

"Language is the DNA of a TV show. It gives the show an overall tone... It is also an essential tool to give a character a unique 'voice', as you see in the case of Omi, Clay, Rai and Kimiko. Each of them has a unique speech pattern.

Language helps tell a story and create great dialogue. That's what makes a show worth watching... I want to create a sense of "East meets West" exotic-ness, with proper English pronunciation. And yet avoiding stereotypical minority accent heard in many kids' TV series with Eastern elements. As such, I request that our central character, Omi, speaks with no Chinese accent and thankfully, the network and studio bought it. Having said that, I do like to have fun with Omi's dialogue; his unique speech pattern offers the show a great deal of comic relief. We also love writing dialogue for minor characters, like

Tubbimura—oversized ninja—who speaks in traditional Japanese samurai voice.

Giving the series a fresh, exotic feel language-wise is another objective. We created terms and jargons that are both familiar, yet exotic-sounding simultaneously. It took time to develop these terms and some of the Shen Gong Wu names. For me, one of the most rewarding things is to hear kids on the street repeating Xiaolin jargons, such as "Gong Yi Tan Pai!" Ironically, adults have a much tougher time remembering these terms than kids do. I think this is a result of so much foreign content made available to kids in America nowadays. Reality is that our world has become increasingly smaller. We are indeed living in a global village, think how popular Japanese games / anime have become over the years."

--Christy Hui, Creator and Producer of *Xiaolin Showdown*
(personal communication, July 1. 2019)

Chapter 5

Ugly French:

Learning a Second Language as an Adult

I. Introduction

Learning another language can be a difficult process at any age, but especially hard for adult learners. On the popular *telenovela*-based series *Ugly Betty*, principal character Daniel Meade begins season three learning French to reconnect with the French-born "son" he never knew he had. Meanwhile, his son D.J. is simultaneously learning English. Daniel does poorly; his son does better. This mirrors predictions in second language acquisition based on age. But, why expose American primetime watchers to this process? Why choose French as the language being learned when *Ugly Betty* is based on a Colombian *telenovela*? These are the questions I will tackle in this chapter after further exploration of the language learning process by Daniel, an adult learner, and his son, a child acquiring a second language.

II. Data

As I mentioned, Daniel is learning French in an attempt to make a connection with D.J. He has a strong emotional motivation for learning French, to show his son just how much he cares, and wants to be able to communicate with him in his native language. Despite this strong incentive, Daniel still proves to be a poor language learner. He is barely able to string together a coherent sentence, makes little attempt to mimic a native-sounding accent, and stammers in his efforts to speak French. Nevertheless, like many adult learners, Daniel is able to cobble together a complex construction or two, even using the subjunctive correctly at one point, demonstrating the power of fully-developed cognition in the language-learning process.

D.J., Daniel's son, does better learning English. Initially, he speaks only in French, although he is clearly able to understand everything that is going on around him right from the beginning. Despite his slower start, soon he is able to speak in full sentences that are quite long, including the coordinating conjunction 'and'. He maintains a strong French accent in his English, which would not necessarily be expected. Given his young age and his access to native-English speakers, one would expect his phonological development to be further along. Nonetheless, D.J. does demonstrate some knowledge of native English fillers (e.g., um, uh) in spite of his strong accent. He even makes an effort to use English slang.

Let's look at the data more closely. These data come from episodes one and two of the third season of *Ugly Betty*, entitled "The Manhattan Project" (Horta & Nelli, 2008) and "Filing with the Enemy" (Fields & Spiller, 2008) respectively. In "The Manhattan Project," there are two scenes in which L2 acquisition and use can be observed. In "Filing with the Enemy" there are three such moments.

In the first episode, we observe the Meade family sitting down for dinner. Present are Alexis (Daniel's post-operative transsexual sister, and D.J.'s true father), Claire (Daniel and Alexis' mother, D.J.'s grandmother), Daniel, and D.J. During the meal, Daniel asks D.J. to finish his dinner before moving on to dessert, some chocolate cake. This results in a conflict in which D.J. refuses to eat more dinner and is sent to his room accordingly. We see in this scene that D.J. does not use English, although he clearly understands what is being said to him in English. Both turns he has in this scene are in French. To express his desire for cake over dinner, *Je veux ma gâteau*, ('I want my cake') and to say he will not eat anything further, *J'ai pas faim* ('I'm not hungry') (Horta & Nelli, 2008). Ironically, in this first of these utterances, there is a gender error for the word *gâteau*, which would seem to indicate that the actor playing D.J. is a learner of French himself. Daniel uses one French word, *déjeuner* ('lunch'), to indicate the meal as opposed to the dessert to follow: "Hey, *déjeuner* first, then dessert, right?" (Horta & Nelli, 2008). In other words, it seems Daniel can use only an isolated word in French at this stage and that D.J. is not yet ready to speak in English.

Later that evening, in the second scene of the episode featuring French, Daniel and D.J. make amends for their earlier dispute. D.J.'s initial apology is in French, *Je suis désolé* ('I'm sorry') (Horta & Nelli, 2008), still not trying out his English. Daniel attempts to explain how, as father and son, he and D.J. are bound to have disagreements but that he loves his son regardless. In the course of this explanation, Daniel loosely translates a couple of words and phrases: "[Things] are not always going to be so great. *Pas si bon*," and "We're in this together, *ensemble*." He ends with a rather straightforward formulaic utterance: "*Je t'aime beaucoup*" ('I love you very much'). In response, D.J. uses his first and only English phrase in this entire episode of *Ugly Betty*: "I love you, too" (Horta & Nelli, 2008). It is also highly formulaic, and more or less a direct translation of what Daniel said to him. Thus far, we have Daniel making short French utterances of one to three words or using highly formulaic speech. D.J. also uses highly formulaic speech to this point.

In the second episode of season three, "Filing for the Enemy" (Fields & Spiller, 2008), D.J. and Daniel have the first of their three conversations at the southern tip of Manhattan, after taking a break from playing catch. Daniel must speak with D.J. because the youngster's French grandparents are interested in obtaining custody of him and returning him to France. This exchange, nine turns total, is the longest of the language episodes found in this data.

(5.1)

Daniel: God, you're gettin' good at this, aren't you? Are you having fun?

DJ: Oui. Good time.

Daniel: Well, I figured since you had to start school tomorrow, we might get in one more day of hooky.

DJ: Uh, hooky? Like, uh, prostitute?

Daniel: No, no. No prostitutes. Only when you're older. I mean (clears throat) not at all, son. No, I just thought we'd talk, you know, about important stuff. So (clears throat) you, uh, you have grandparents back in France. Do you--do you miss them?

DJ: Oui. I love them very much. Maybe, uh, we can visit?

Daniel: Yeah. Yep. Sure.

DJ: You, uh, don't want to talk more?

Daniel: Nah. You know what? I think that's enough talking. Come on.

(Fields & Spiller, 2008)

Daniel makes absolutely no attempt whatever to use French. D.J., on the other hand, aside from two *oui*'s, speaks entirely in English. His first utterance is a bit stilted in English, "*Oui*, good time" in response to Daniel's question whether or not he is having fun. But, in the rest of the exchange, we see productive use of non-formulaic English that, aside from the accent and the French filler *euh*, is akin to anything a native speaker might produce. In fact, when he does not understand what hooky is, he asks for clarification, proposing a definition for a similar-sounding English word he knows: "Euh, hooky? Like a prostitute." This question about language demonstrates a characteristic of a good language learner. Asking a question when you don't understand produces more language and keeps the interaction going, which results in more language data for the developing second-language system, a process called negotiation of meaning (Long, 1981, 1983a, 1983b). Daniel answers D.J.'s inquiry as his father, an adult caretaker trying to educate his non-native speaking offspring, an expected response (Scarcella and Higa, 1981; Cathcart, 1986). A final linguistic feature to note in D.J.'s speech is the use of English "uh" as opposed to French "euh" as the filler in his final utterance, "You, uh, don't want to talk more?" Learning the fillers in a second language is a process that escapes many language learners, a slight tell that they are not native speakers even if they do not have an accent. Here, D.J. has already begun acquiring this most subtle of native-speaker features.

In the second exchange between Daniel and D.J. in "Filing with the Enemy," Daniel again fails to distinguish himself as a French speaker.

(5.2)
Daniel: Like I said, uh, remember not to get too hung up on any one girl. You're--you're young. You gotta play the field.
DJ: Quoi?
Daniel: And listen in class, okay? That's what I told you. Um, écouter le teacher.
DJ: Oui. Papa, uh, your French is, uh, how you say—suck-ky.
Daniel: Just have a good day.
(Fields & Spiller, 2008)

Upon seeing D.J. off at his first day of school (at a French-speaking school) Daniel relies on his earlier strategy and goes back to single word translations of things he has already said in English: "*écoutez*" for 'listen'. He tells D.J. to "listen in class...*écoutez le* teacher." In this utterance, we also see Daniel's failure to acquire even simple vocabulary in French, like "teacher", although he does manage to translate the definite article, "le" for 'the'. Whereas D.J.'s first utterance is an unremarkable "*Quoi?*" his second, "Papa, euh, you're French is, how you say--suck-ky" is worth taking note of. Here he is trying to use a native English slang expression, "sucky". Already, his language knowledge starts to show sophistication as he attempts to be *au courant* ('up-to-date') with peers his own age.

Finally, the last language episode produces interesting data for both of our learners.

(5.3)
DJ: Yes! Papa. Look I made it to the next level.
Daniel: Hey, uh, would you come here for a second? Uh, there there's something I want to ask you. It's important. Um, okay, so your grandparents want you to come live with them in France. Comprends?
DJ: Oui, oui.

Daniel:	Um, mais, uh, je veux que tu, uh, habites avec moi. I-I-I want you to live here with me. Look, I guess I guess what's m-most important here is what do you want?
DJ:	You are my father. And I want to stay with my father.
Daniel:	Okay. Great. Uh good. So we'll stay together, and, um, and we're gonna fight for that. Come on. Let's see how good you are.

(Fields & Spiller, 2008)

Daniel ultimately tells D.J. that his grandparents wish to take him back to France with them and asks what he wants. Again D.J.'s utterances are completely in English, with the exception of an understandable "*oui*" in response to Daniel's question, "*Comprends*?" 'understand' in French. His accent in this scene is particularly strong, yet his two sentences in English are well constructed and free of pauses, hesitations, or fillers. He even manages to use "and" to put two ideas together with no difficulty, "You are my father and I want to stay with my father." Daniel's language use is also interesting in this scene. He asks D.J. if he understands using French, "*Comprends*?" but this lacks the obligatory subject pronoun "*tu*" which could have been placed before or after the verb to ask the question correctly, "*Tu comprends*?" or "*Comprends-tu*?" Without the subject pronoun, this question looks like an adaptation of Spanish "*entiendes*" or Italian "*capisci*". So, once more Daniel is in error. However, his next utterance in French, "Uh, *mais* uh *je veux que tu* uh *habites avec moi*," aside from a few minor hesitations, is a flawless deployment of the French subjunctive, one of the most difficult things for learners to acquire. So, how does Daniel manage this feat? Generally, adult learners, having already fully acquired a first language, have the cognitive capacity to learn more complex structures. That being said, most English learners of French have the tendency to use a personal infinitive construction in this instance, something along the lines of "*Je veux que tu rester avec moi*," failing to conjugate the second verb, using the infinitival form instead of the requisite subjunctive. Thus, either Daniel asked someone to translate his wishes into French and memorized the correct form or has much greater abilities in French then he has demonstrated to this point. The former seems the more likely scenario.

III. Discussion

The fact that D.J., a child, has an easier time learning English than Daniel does as an adult learning French is in keeping with what research in the field of second language acquisition would predict. D.J. undergoes a silent period, a period in which he does not use English, while he is presumably puzzling out how the English system works. Not all learners pass through a silent period, although it is particularly common in child second-language learners (Hakuta, 1976; Itoh & Hatch, 1978; Saville-Troike, 1988). D.J. then progresses to the next stage of his productive second-language abilities: formulaic speech, in which he produces English expressions as unanalyzed wholes or chunks. This also fits in with the developmental stages one might expect for a child learning a second language (Ervin-Tripp, 1974; Hakuta, 1976; Itoh & Hatch, 1978). We have one such example: "I love you, too." Between the use of formulas and fully productive speech in the second language, there is a stage of structural and/or semantic simplification (Ellis, 1984). In the case of D.J. we see a semantic simplification in the utterance, "*Oui*, good time." Ellis (1982) characterizes semantic simplification as an omission of content words such as nouns and verbs that we would expect in native-speaker speech. Thus, the verb we might expect, as in "I'm having a good time" or "This is a good time," is not present leaving us with only "good time." In this same exchange, D.J. demonstrates several characteristics of a good language learner. He asks for the definition of the word "hooky" which results in the negotiation of meaning and further opportunities for language use and acquisition. Additionally, he uses the English-language filler or hesitation, "uh" instead of French, "euh". Finally, in this and future exchanges, he uses English almost exclusively and that English is well constructed and fluent with no grammatical errors. He even uses slang, "suck-ky" and links two ideas using "and". In short, in the few language events in these episodes of *Ugly Betty* we observe the evolution of D.J. from monolingual French-speaker to competent French-English bilingual, who uses translanguaging strategies (Otheguy et al., 2015), employing French and English together to communicate. This is typical of what one might predict for a child learning a second language, especially in an environment where he is surrounded by the second language.

    The same cannot be said for his father, Daniel. Daniel has no evolution across the episodes in which we observe his use of French. In the first two scenes involving French from the first episode, he begins with only isolated words, "*déjeuner*", "*pas si bon*", and "*ensemble*", simple translations of ideas he is trying to convey in English. He does use one formula, "*je t'aime beaucoup*," but as with child learners, the use of formulaic speech is not unusual for adults. In fact, this particular formula could merely be an extension of Daniel's translation strategy. Given his fully developed cognitive system, translating a simple phrase of three to four words would not pose significant difficulties. In the first scene we considered from the second episode, Daniel does not even use French at all, followed by the next scene in which he employs the translation strategy once again, producing merely "*écoutez le...*" before petering out, unable to translate the word "teacher". Finally, in the last scene between Daniel and his son, we do arrive at the beginnings of potential evolution of Daniel's knowledge. He manages to produce "*Comprends?*" which I discussed earlier as being an ungrammatical utterance in French, but perhaps this could be seen as a semantic simplification. And, of course, Daniel's crowning achievement, his fully grammatical use of the subjunctive in the sentence, "*Je veux que tu habites avec moi.*" This could be seen as further use of a formulaic expression or, as I suggested earlier, an application of his translation strategy employing his fully developed cognitive capacity to make certain that the phrase is completely correct. He has the emotional motivation to do so, as with this utterance he wishes to convey how much he wants his son to stay with him. In any event, Daniel's language-learning trajectory does not even approach the success his son achieves. This is typical of an adult learning a second language, especially while not immersed in the L2 environment. He has limited success, gives up at moments and, from time to time, is capable of surprising feats of expression.

IV. Conclusion

But these two relatively accurate portrayals of language learning by both child and adult raise the question, why expose American primetime watchers to this process? Why faithfully represent the difficulties expected for adult learners acquiring a second language and the relative ease experienced by child learners? Perhaps this could be seen as a cautionary tale. For viewers watching Daniel struggle with French as his son easily outpaces him in English it might be a convincing message for the importance of learning a language early in life. This can be interpreted in such a framework as positive publicity for language education. Moreover, the message of intercultural understanding always subtly at play in a program such as *Ugly Betty*, which often straddles two languages, two cultures, two identities, is bolstered by the inclusion of yet another language and culture. The attempts made to bridge the language gap between Daniel and D.J. recapitulate the ways in which the program itself is constantly bridging the different cultures and identities represented by its characters. Betty is herself a Latina with two languages, two cultures and a hybrid identity. By advocating for early learning of different languages and cultures, this storyline is in keeping with the underlying message of *Ugly Betty*: celebration of cultural and linguistic diversity and the synergistic effects of such diversity on our society. In essence, D.J.'s learning of English and adaptation to American cultural norms can be seen as representing the openness of American society to outsiders. Daniel's putative attempts at learning French can be taken as a sign of the readiness of our own society to meet others with a willingness to accept their differences and make some concessions or adaptations of our own. In short, this interlude of father and son learning each other's languages is a positive model for more global acceptance of difference in our increasingly diverse American society, where different languages and cultures are in continual encounter.

But, why choose French as the language being learned when *Ugly Betty* is based on a Colombian *telenovela*? One might have expected Daniel's son to be from a Spanish- or Portuguese-speaking country given the Latin American genesis of the original *Betty la Fea* from Colombia. In fact, it begs the question, are there issues of class or prestige at play? Perhaps it is the best answer to this question in my view. With a number of Latinx characters already, the choice of French may have been made to distinguish this storyline from others in the drama. Another plausible explanation is the importance of Paris and France in the fashion world. Using French makes sense if the writers/producers wanted a language linked with high fashion, as the program centers on a fashion magazine. Of course, with that in mind, one might have imagined Italian as another possible mother language for Daniel's son.

Even with these ideas, it's hard to get away from the strange, snooty prestige that French offers as a linguistic pedigree. Similarly, in Chapter 1, I noted that French has been used in other programs to represent sophistication or cachet.[1] The French are often seen as snubbing Americans or too good for us in the popular imagination, however untrue these perceptions may be. To insist on French calls to mind those negative stereotypes. At the same time, France holds an allure in the American psyche, as beautiful images of grand public monuments and art-filled museums possessed of rare masterworks and castles in picturesque countryside coexist with these negative tropes of the French. French still trades on its reputation as the language of kings and diplomacy. Linking French with the son of a rich magazine publisher can be viewed as bringing issues of class to the fore. Of course, this could also be evidence of the commodification of languages as they vie for value, as Pandey (2016, 2019) suggests in her study of prize-winning literature. Recall, also in Chapter 1, we saw another example of French being elevated in the American consciousness as a *sexy* language. Although we will never know if this choice was simply made without thinking or after great reflection, the possible valence of the viewer's reaction may be shaped to some extent by this linguistic selection.

In closing, I must note how fascinating it is to have seen a primetime television series in the U.S. represent language learning. There is so much that this process opens our eyes to, and it so rare for adults to have the chance to

---

[1] The episodes I cited were *Trophy Wife*, "Back to School" (Seidell & Sohn, 2014) and *Partners*, "The Key" (Kohan et al., 2012). Certainly, these are not the only shows on American television that have used French to symbolize sophistication or cachet.

consider all the difficulties and pleasures that this particular broadening of one's horizon can encompass. One can only hope that this representation will lead those who may have viewed it when it aired or who may yet view it on Netflix or Amazon to consider the possibilities that linguistic and cultural diversity can offer to the individual and to the society as a whole.

Chapter 6

Let's Learn A New Language, America!
Fact and Fiction in Representations
of Language Learning on TV

I. Introduction

To learn a new language presents many challenges as we saw for Daniel in the previous chapter. One must adapt to new grammatical structures; one must produce new shapes of the mouth to pronounce strange new sounds; one must be unafraid to make mistakes in the name of communication. However, television represents learning, and, on occasion, losing another language as a simple process of mind over matter, a switch to be turned on and off at will. Television portrayals of language learning often oversimplify not only the process of learning a language, but also the content of what one learns. Television mythologizes language acquisition (and, to a much lesser extent, language loss), transmitting these fables to a mass audience. In addition, television provides us with interesting information about how language learning is perceived in the U.S.

The mythologization of which I speak has been seen in television programming ranging from prime-time sitcoms and soaps to tween-targeted high school sitcoms and cartoons. The data analyzed in this chapter come from episodes of *American Housewife*, *Brooklyn Nine-Nine*, *The Middle*, *Modern Family*, *Schooled*, *Speechless*, *One Tree Hill*, *Pretty Little Liars*, *The Simpsons*, *10 Things I Hate About You*, and *Ben 10: Ultimate Alien*. Each program depicts either incidents of language study/acquisition and/or the voicing of attitudes toward language study. In addition, I will consider an episode of *Lost* that fittingly portrays language loss, as well as an episode of *Modern Family* that depicts a different cause of language loss. I will explore these TV representations of language learning and loss, seeking to understand the effects of these portrayals on popular attitudes toward these phenomena.

II. Data and Discussion

In the teen sitcom *10 Things I Hate About You* (Covington et al., 2009c), to impress a girl, one character "learns" French from scratch, on his own, in the space between two episodes, so that he can then tutor his love interest. In the pilot episode (Covington & Junger, 2009a) of this Shakespeare play (*The Taming of the Shrew*, 1590-1592) turned movie starring Julia Stiles and Heath Ledger (*10 Things I Hate About You*, 1999) turned eponymous sitcom, two teenage sisters move from Ohio to California with their gynecologist father. Similar to the movie, the older of the two sisters, Kat, is serious, focused on doing well in school and on causes such as environmental awareness, while her boy-crazy younger sister, Bianca, dreams of nothing but being popular and dating boys. In the first episode, Bianca, after realizing in part her dream of being on the cheerleading squad (she is made mascot because the captain of the squad is jealous of her beauty and likability), says to her friend Cameron, "Now I can focus on passing French," lamenting further, "it's way beyond what I had in Ohio." Cameron, in love with Bianca despite the fact that she believes him to be gay (as we find out in a subsequent episode), offers, "Uh…uh…I could tutor you, I mean, if you want." He follows up this offer with a sentence of complete gibberish and several fronted high back vowels, as in *tu* and *bu*, to which Bianca responds, "See, I didn't get any of that. You're a lifesaver." This scene ends when Bianca walks away and Cameron admits, "I gotta learn French" (Covington & Junger, 2009a).

And learn French he does, or so we are led to believe in the next episode, "I Want You to Want Me" (Covington & Junger, 2009b). Early in this episode, Cameron tutors Bianca in French. He has her repeat a series of romantic come-ons in French (*"Tu es très gentille,"* 'You are very nice;' *"Je te trouve très belle,"* 'I find you very beautiful') leading to an invitation to go out with him, also in French (*"Est-ce que tu veux sortir avec moi?"* 'Do you want to go out with me?') (Covington & Junger, 2009b). Upon uttering this last phrase, he offers her a bunch of red carnations—needless to say he doesn't get the date, but not because of his flower choice. Immediately after she repeats his last utterance, albeit somewhat incorrectly (*"Est-ce que tu sortir avec moi?"*), he asks if she understood what he had said. Her answer, "See that's the problem, great with the repeating, not so great with the understanding. But, I'm guessing it was about flowers" (Covington & Junger, 2009b). Poor Cameron, his French is good enough to pass in this three-sentence lesson, although he does mispronounce *gentille*, but ultimately he doesn't have enough game to get Bianca to view him as a serious romantic interest. Plus, she thinks he's not interested in girls.

Moving beyond the interplay between the sexes, let us consider what these examples indicate about second language use. As I mentioned above, the French lesson we see is all of three sentences long. In it, also already noted, Cameron, the "tutor", mispronounces one word—not bad for having learned an entire language in mere days. But, the question of how much he actually learned is an open one. As anyone who speaks a second language knows, especially those who've learned from books at school or on their own, he certainly didn't learn enough to say he had "learned French" as had been his stated goal in the pilot episode. The Foreign Service Institute of the United States Department of State suggests that 600-750 hours of in-class language instruction are necessary to learn French well enough for "Professional Working Proficiency" in the language, or a score of "Speaking-3/Reading-3" on the Interagency Language Roundtable scale (U.S. Department of State, n.d.). Did he learn just enough to impress the girl then? Perhaps. With only three sentences uttered in French, anything is possible. It must be noted that, aside from his slight mispronunciation of *gentille*, his pronunciation did correlate well with native-like pronunciation. Suffice it to say, however, that the expectation that the average high-schooler is going to be able to learn another language quickly enough, on his own, to impress a girl is ridiculous at best.

There is another interesting aspect to this example, though: Bianca's ability to repeat without truly knowing what she is saying. The trope represented here, that of the unsophisticated high school learner just repeating rote phrases with no understanding of what she is saying, unfortunately, presents a compelling and realistic picture of many high school and college language learners (although Duff (2000) does make a case for the value of repetition in the language classroom). The fact that she fails to repeat the third phrase correctly, leaving out the modal verb (*veux* 'want') indicates her lack of understanding quite convincingly. She is merely doing her best to repeat, not to understand. She admits as much as the scene ends, "[G]reat with the repeating, not so great with the understanding," and she runs off to plan a carnation sale to raise money for the cheer squad, inspired by the flowers Cameron offers. As she leaves, Cameron utters in melancholy exasperation, "*Sacré bleu!*" (Covington & Junger, 2009b). Again, however, his pronunciation could be better.

The *Pretty Little Liars* explore second language learning at the high school level in their aptly titled episode "Je Suis Une Amie" (Holdman & Grismer, 2011) or 'I am a friend.' In the episode, the boy accused of killing the four main female protagonists' girlfriend is under house arrest awaiting trial. However, the girls are no longer convinced that he is the culprit; on the contrary, they believe he may have valuable information about the crime that could lead to the real killer. So, one of them agrees to tutor him in French, of course.

In their first tutoring session, Spencer, the young girl, and Toby, the accused teenage murderer, sit on his front stoop where she hands him a copy of *L'attrape-cœurs*, "The Heart-Catcher," Toby translates after reading the title aloud. "It's '*Catcher in the Rye*,' I guess there's no literal translation. But it helps to read a book you already know in English," Spencer responds before telling him their teacher would like him to review the "conditional tense" (Holdman & Grismer, 2011).

This scene strains credulity in several ways. First, if Toby were reviewing the conditional *mood*, it's highly unlikely that he would be reading an entire book in French, especially one as sophisticated as Salinger's 1951 classic *The Catcher in the Rye*. Second, even if he were reading an entire text in French, it is difficult to imagine that any language educator worth his or her salt would assign a novel written by an American when there is a long list of French masterpieces more culturally appropriate and suited to the task. The idea that one merely reads a work that one has read in English and then compares that to the French translation seems, in some ways, an exercise designed for a much more advanced student of the language interested in issues of translation theory. Moreover, it harkens back to an earlier era of grammar-translation pedagogy abandoned over fifty years ago. Richards and Rodgers (2001)[1] explain grammar-translation pedagogy thus:

> As "modern" languages began to enter the curriculum of European schools in the eighteenth century, they were taught using the same basic procedures that were used for teaching Latin. Textbooks consisted of statements of abstract grammar rules, lists of vocabulary, and sentences for translation. Speaking the foreign language was not the goal, and oral practice was limited to students reading aloud the sentences they had translated. (p. 4)

In short, it's simply not believable.

Later, in talking to her friend Emily about her interaction with Toby, Spencer questions Toby's guilt. She expresses her doubts and indicates that she is trying to investigate his involvement by helping him with his French in the hopes of getting to know him better and uncovering some other connection to their murdered friend. Emily retorts, "Spence, you can't figure all that out sitting on his porch conjugating verbs." Spencer counters, "Well, you don't know what those verbs are" (Holdman & Grismer, 2011).

What's interesting in this scene is the way in which Emily denigrates Spencer's activities as a French tutor. From the earlier extreme of one learning French by reading whole novels in French, now we have a perspective at the other end of the spectrum: learning French is merely about conjugating verbs.

---

[1] Richards and Rodgers (2001) provides a comprehensive history of language teaching methods through the turn of the 21st century.

This perspective is unfortunately more in keeping with what many high schoolers come to see as learning a second language. In a strange wardrobe choice, in later scenes that take place the following day, Spencer is adorned with a beret. She really must know French since she wears culturally appropriate outfits, albeit a bit *vieux-jeu,* 'old fashioned.'

At the end of this particular episode, just before the credits, we see a scene of an old record player, on which someone, presumably the real killer, begins to play a record while arranging tools that s/he will use to mislead the protagonists in future episodes. The record plays, "Learning French can be a fun activity for families, friends, civic groups or clubs. By listening to these long-playing, high fidelity records you can speak French fluently in as little as six weeks. We're going to start with the French verb *être,* which means 'to be.' Ready? Let's begin. *Prêt? Commençons. Je suis.* 'I am.' *Je suis.* 'I am.' *Je suis.* 'I am'..." (Holdman & Grismer, 2011). If it seems hard to believe that after only six weeks, one could speak fluently, it is. The record's promises do not equate to real-world results. Again, think of the 600-750 hours the Foreign Service Institute suggests is necessary (U.S. Department of State, n.d.). There are 1008 hours in six weeks. If we reserve eight hours for sleep per day, that leaves us with 672 hours remaining. Essentially, to complete the required 600-750 hours suggested, the learner would need to do almost nothing else but study French or the learner would have to sleep significantly fewer than eight hours per night. Either way, again, it seems that we have a misrepresentation of how easy it is to learn another language.

In the "Lists, Plans" (Richardson & Davola, 2010) episode of the CW soap *One Tree Hill,* it's character Brooke Davis who begins to learn French in the wake of losing her clothing company "Clothes Over Bros." Lacking inspiration after her loss and in the midst of re-imagining her dream wedding because she no longer possesses the funds to realize it, her fiancé Julian finds an old list of goals that she had once planned to accomplish. Among these goals is to learn French. In the type of grand romantic gesture that abounds on the small screen, Julian endeavors to inspire Brooke by helping her to accomplish the aspirations she listed long ago.

Brooke starts her car one morning to find that instead of the radio, her speakers emit, *"Bonjour! Je suis Paul. Au revoir. C'est la vie. Merci beaucoup.* These may be French phrases you're familiar with by now. But soon you can live in Paris and never have to speak English again. How does that sound?" (Richardson & Davola, 2010). In all honesty, it sounds like this language learning program is overpromising, just like the record at the end of *Pretty Little Liars.* To make this more credible, the CD case she finds is for a three-disc set at least.

When she returns home from her errand later in the day, she finds a box with a note on it, "*Mettez cela sur (Put this on.)*" (Richardson & Davola, 2010). It's a good thing there's a translation because I think a native speaker of French, especially one who had never studied English, would have trouble deciphering the meaning of this particular gesture. A friend and native speaker of French suggested that "Mets ça" or "Mettez ça" would have been the appropriate translation. In the box is an Oktoberfest dress; Julian's attempt to help Brooke realize another of her listed goals, attend Oktoberfest.

No one expects Julian's French to be more than remedial at best, although one does expect online translators, even in 2010 to be good enough not to produce such a butchered phrase as "*Mettez cela sur*" to translate "Put this on." In fact, around the time when I first saw this episode in 2010, to test this notion, I plugged the phrase "Put it on" into several translators and was surprised by the results: *Mettez ceci dessus* (Yahoo Babelfish), *Mettre cette question à* (Google translate), *Mis cela* (Free translation online), *Mettre ceci* (Bing translator). The Bing translation came closest, although the verb remains inconveniently in the infinitive. It must be said that when I added the word dress to the phrase, "Put this dress on," Google translate came up with a better translation: "Mettre cette robe," but again, the verb remains unconjugated. However, when I moved the particle "on", the translation got awkward again, "Put on this dress" became "Mis sur cette robe," another poor translation. I tried this experiment again with Google Translate in 2019 and it appears that the correct translation is now given. How far we've come! Nonetheless, despite the evolution of Google Translate over the years, poor translations still occur on a regular basis. On that count, this TV show accurately represents the continued inefficiencies of online translators: part of the phrase is translated well, the rest *laisse à désirer*, leaves something to be desired.[2]

In the last scene in the episode using French, Brooke and Julian share another romantic moment where Julian confesses that he cannot wait to have a family with his future wife. She in turn responds, "*J'adore.*" He

---

[2] In the 2019 series finale episode of *Life in Pieces* called, "Reverse, Burden, District, Germany" (Adler & Reid), problems with online translators are highlighted when Matt gets an e-mail offering him a job in Germany. In the fourth story of the episode "Mattoberfest," he puts the e-mail through an online translator only to get a stilted English translation: "You are being the job. Please take with us breakfast on the Tuesday subsequent to next. Cannot translate" (Adler & Reid, 2019). Note the inclusion of the portion of the e-mail that the computer simply "cannot translate." Although a fictional representation, it does indicate that online translators are still not perfect.

retorts, "Wow, one day and you're already speaking French" (Richardson & Davola, 2010). While in the scene, it's clear that he's not being serious, it may give false hope to those interested in learning a language among the audience members, that integrating your new linguistic knowledge into conversation will be so simple. Not to mention, the phrase Brooke utters is the name of a popular women's perfume, meaning that she may not have really learned anything at all; she may simply be recycling a phrase she already knew.

In "It's Not Easy Being Gwen," an episode of the cartoon series *Ben 10: Ultimate Alien* (Wayne & Youngberg, 2011), the teenage character Gwen is studying for a French exam in the midst of the other activities of her hectic life (addressing family reunion invitations for her mom, teaching an algebra class, battling giant toads with her cousin and boyfriend). In the beginning of the episode, while running, she studies by listening to her mp3 player and repeating the phrases given. This study method smacks of an earlier time, one focused on audiolingual pedagogies rather than on the more communication-focused methods of today's language classroom. The audiolingual method was based on a behaviorist stimulus-response-reinforcement model, in which learners memorized and performed dialogues and repeated pattern drills. It was a "speech based instruction with the primary objective of oral proficiency, and dismissed the study of grammar or literature as the goal of foreign language teaching" (Richards & Rodgers, 2001, p. 58). We saw a similar audiolingual focus in both *Pretty Little Liars* and *One Tree Hill*. In fact, other shows depict learning another language using tapes or CDs: Phil and Claire Dunphey learn Italian on *Modern Family* using language tapes (in "Blasts From the Past," Chandrasekaran et al., 2019) and Katie Otto learns French in *American Housewife* ("The Otto Motto," Donovan et al., 2017). Returning to Gwen's learning, the sentences she repeats are direct translations of English sentences, also not in keeping with more modern pedagogical practices. As an example, the mp3 player says, "Listen and repeat. Would you like some grapefruit? *Voudriez-vous du pamplemousse?*" (Wayne & Youngberg, 2011). The first three phrases Gwen practices are all related to grapefruit. The fourth phrase, "I would like a waffle iron. *Je voudrais un gauffrier,*" (Wayne & Youngberg, 2011) is equally obscure. In a subsequent scene before her exam, Gwen walks down the school corridor practicing the forms of the past subjunctive, "*que j'aie rempli, que tu aies rempli, qu'il ait rempli, que nous ayons rempli ...*" (Wayne & Youngberg, 2011). Not only is the verb *remplir* 'to fill' in keeping with the obscure nature of the vocabulary Gwen is learning, the past subjunctive is among the last learned and most obscure of tenses used in conversational French.

Does this choice of vocabulary and grammar truly represent what is happening in high school French classrooms across the country today? Not by a long shot. That students would be studying a chapter focused on breakfast foods and implements while at the same time combining that with the past subjunctive seems far-fetched at best, especially considering the primacy of communication in today's second language classroom. Practicing obscure vocabulary and grammar, although possible at the high school level, would not be the most effective use of class time. Moreover, beyond knowing the words for grapefruit and waffle iron, having them included over and over again in sample sentences, when they are such low-frequency lexical items, would overestimate their importance in the language.

While Gwen's study techniques and the material she is studying seem out of sync with current practice, it is curious that the writers of this episode or the producers of the show chose to represent these choices. This misrepresentation of what it means to study French could indeed have real-world consequences. When one considers that children younger than the age when second languages are started in schools likely watch this program, they may have a false sense of what it means to learn French. They may view it as lacking value, given the obscurity of the vocabulary and grammar studied. Additionally, for any kids studying French in school already and struggling, this could add to their sense that French is useless and that the things they are learning, probably much more practical than grapefruits and waffle irons, are as well.

Above, I mentioned Katie Otto's journey learning French from CDs on *American Housewife.* I'd like to discuss this episode, "The Otto Motto" (Donovan et al., 2017), in greater depth. Main character, Katie Otto, quits everything, including learning conversational French from CDs (the audiolingual method, once more), which she was doing for a planned trip to Paris with her husband that never happened due to the birth of their three children. In the episode, when her husband Greg points out that Katie has trouble sticking with projects by calling her a quitter, she accuses him of not having listened to the CDs either. He replies, "*Bien sûr que je l'ai fait,*" 'Of course I did' (Donovan et al., 2017). Greg suggests that Katie take a French immersion course at the Education Institute, a local venue for adult education where Greg, a professor, happens to be offering a history class. To motivate Katie he tells her that if she can say, "I am not a quitter in French" he will stop calling her a quitter in English (Donovan et al., 2017).

As the first day of class arrives, she is "kind of excited" for French class (Donovan et al., 2017). In the classroom, we see the chalk board with the following phrases and verbs conjugations:

Beginning French
Bonjour classe

Verbe: AVOIR	Verbe: ALLER
Meaning: TO HAVE	Meaning: TO GO

J'ai = I have	Je vais = I am going
Tu as = You have	Tu vas = You go
Il a = He has	Il va = He is going
Elle a = She has	Elle va = She is going
Nous avons = We have	Nous allons = We go
Vous avez = You have	Vous allez = You go
Ils ont = They have	Ils vont = They go
Elles ont = They have	Elles vont = They go

(Donovan et al., 2017)

The professor is dressed like a 1950s schoolmarm, although her sweater is red as is her lipstick—just enough sex appeal to fit American notions of the French *femme*. She holds a folder in her crossed arms and begins, "Veuillez retirer votre guide d'étude," 'Please take out your study guide' (Donovan et al., 2017). In the dialogue that follows, we see things start to go downhill for Katie very quickly.

(6.1)

Katie:	I'm sorry I did not get one of these handouts.
Prof:	En français, s'il vous plaît.
Katie:	Was I supposed to print one out at home because my husband has not set up the printer, so...
Prof:	[Emphasizing each syllable] En français
Katie:	OK, I don't speak fran-çais. That's why I'm here.
Prof:	[Each word very distinct, like speaking to a child] Dans cette classe, nous parlons seulement français.
Katie:	Are you pretending you don't speak English right now? Because I am not pretending that I don't speak French.
Prof:	Classe?
Class:	En français.
Katie:	Bunch of kiss asses.

(Donovan et al., 2017)

Here we see some positive language teaching techniques. Insistence by the professor on the use of the target language, French, in class, for instance. Using the board to write down important information, such as the verb conjugations, is also good, although I'm not sure many would see the need to include English translations in modern foreign language pedagogy. The hope would be to create a context to understand the meanings of the verbs. It must also be noted that the translations associated with the conjugations for the verb *aller* use two different verb tenses in English: the simple present (you go, they go) and the present progressive (I am going, he is going, she is going). Although the present tense in French can be translated with either, in addition to the present with do-support, i.e., "I do go," mixing these tenses without further clarification or explanation could be very confusing to students. Nonetheless there are some positives present. On the other hand, the intransigence of the professor and her unwillingness to engage Katie in English for even a moment, creates anxiety and negativity not only for Katie but for viewers who may have had their own "en français" moment in their language learning past. Many have studied language learning anxiety and Ellis (2006, pp. 691-97) provides a good summary of viewpoints in the field of second language acquisition. It should be noted that, although the jury is still out on the exact effects of anxiety on language learning (positive, negative, or a symptom of more generalized difficulties in learning a foreign language), many believe it to be a significant impediment for some if not many L2 learners.

Later in the episode, Katie gives voice to her negative experience in the classroom while meeting up with friends at a café. Katie laments, "I don't understand a word. I wish the teacher would teach me phrases that I really need to know, like, 'Please open this window, I would like to jump out'" (Donovan et al., 2017). Her friends suggest that she quit or ditch class, but she can't quit because of the bargain she made with her husband (i.e., he'll call her a quitter), and she can't ditch because her husband teaches his class right down the hall. Her friends suggest that she kiss her husband at the door to his classroom then sneak outside where they will pick her up to hang out. Before class is over, they will return her to the Education Institute.

Just before the next class, Greg and Katie are at home getting ready to leave. Greg tries to integrate French into their conversation, to no avail.

(6.2)
Katie:	You ready for class?
Greg:	Oui.
Katie:	We what?
Greg:	Non. Oui.

Katie: We what?
(Donovan et al., 2017)

At this point, it's clear that she has learned very little in class—she confuses French *oui* 'yes' for the personal pronoun *we* in English, leading to a humorous interaction. Following this exchange, they go to the Education Institute together where they part ways to go to their respective classes, the French class Katie is taking and the history class Greg is teaching. But, of course, Katie does not go to class, immediately leaving the building once Greg can no longer see her. As she opens the door to leave the building, she hits her French teacher with the door by accident. The French professor exclaims, "Ou eee" /u i:/, to which Katie, fed up, replies, "You're in America. Say ouch" (Donovan et al., 2017). Her negativity toward French is on full display. In fact, in a later scene after Greg discovers that Katie has not been attending her French class they have the following exchange:

(6.3)
Katie: Look, I tried it, I didn't like it, so I stopped doing it. Why
             shouldn't I quit something that's making me *misérable*?"
Katie: And besides, face the facts, I do not need to learn French!"
Greg: So, no Paris?
Katie: We have three kids' college tuitions to pay for. We were
             never going to go…to Paris.
Greg: Hey, we may never get to France. But you sure have a
             negative French attitude, lady.
(Donovan et al., 2017)

Here, not only is Greg attacking Katie for giving up on French and their dreams of visiting Paris together, but he is also attacking the French, implying that they are negative people.

So what turns Katie around? Why does she eventually try to learn French? In a word, guilt. It turns out that she comes face to face with her own lack of grit when she tries to read a bedtime story to her youngest daughter, Anna-Kat. Greg bought her *Madeline* in French (entitled *Madeleine* in French), which Katie tells her daughter she can't read. She goes on to say that she doesn't think that she will ever be able to, but Anna-Kat tells her that she can do anything if she keeps up with her class (Donovan et al., 2017).

At the end of the episode, Katie has a surprise for Greg. She makes the house look like a small French café and presses her children into service as the wait staff. Her oldest daughter Taylor brings out wine and welcomes Katie and Greg to her humble Parisian café with more of a German than French accent. Their son brings menus and recommends the *boeuf bourguignon* in English with a passable French accent. He then rips the menus out of their hands after Greg orders. Greg comments, "very authentic," another negative commentary on the French. Finally, Anna-Kat brings *Madeleine* to the table for the entertainment. Katie reads a few lines in French. Her accent is not fantastic but it is understandable (Donovan et al., 2017).

> (6.4)
>
> Katie: [Reading from Madeline][3] À Paris, dans un vieille maison
>   aux murs recouverts de vigne...[4]
> Greg: Listen to you, reading French.
> Katie: Je ne suis pas un crétin.
> Greg: And speaking it—where did this come from?
> Katie: As Anna-Kat says, I can do anything
> [Montage of Katie learning French]
> Greg: Thank you for seeing this through.
> Taylor: Oh great, so now that you stuck with French, I have to
>   stick with drama?
> Greg: Oui
> Taylor: We what?
> [Parents share a look]
> (Donovan et al., 2017)

In the brief montage of Katie learning French via the audiolingual method we see her listening to CDs and repeating. First, as she's driving she hears, "*Je vais à la plage,*" ('I'm going to the beach') after which she rolls eyes, but repeats nonetheless. Then, as she's doing laundry, she hears and repeats "*Comment allez-vous?*" ('How are you?') with more focus and interest. Finally, she is reading part of *Madeleine* to Anna-Kat in French, "*Elle n'avait pas peur des souris*"

---

[3] Oddly, the version she is handed is the English version.
[4] Although what Katie reads is the first page of a recent French translation *Madeleine* (Bemelmens, 1985) of the original English text *Madeline* (Bemelmens, 1939), it is not the full first line. The full first sentence is written over two pages: "À Paris, dans une vieille maison aux murs recouverts de vigne" (p. 5) "vivaient douze petites filles" (p. 6). Original English text: "In an old house in Paris that was covered with vines
Lived twelve little girls [in two straight lines]" (bracketed text appers on p. 7 of the French version) (pp. 1-2). In this scene, Katie mispronounces *aux* (no direct translation in this context) to sound like *un* 'one' and *vigne* 'vines' to sound like *vie* 'life'.

(Donovan et al., 2017). The pronunciation is not perfect, but looking at the original French version of the book, it is clear what line she is reading. [5]

Katie's language learning does seem plausible in some ways. First, she is motivated. Motivation has been shown to be a key factor in language learning (Gardner, 1985). Second, she does appear to put in time listening to her CDs while doing various activities in the montage. However, the phrases taught in the montage are rather disconnected from the type of language that she eventually produces in the last scene. Much like Gwen's *pamplemousse* sentences, what she hears on the tapes, while more useful, is still unlikely to get her to where she ends up.

We also need to consider how this episode presents negative views on language learning, especially in a classroom setting. Consider the depiction of the French teacher as unyielding and pretentious. Katie would rather jump out of a window than sit through French class. Of course, we saw negative portrayals of language learning in the *Pretty Little Liars* episode as well. In that episode, learning French is reduced to just conjugating verbs. These shows are not the only ones to present a negative perspective on language learning.

In *The Middle*'s "Roadkill" episode (Brown & Chemel, 2016), Sue needs to declare a major at college. She is considering German, Theater, and two other majors. Her German professor encourages Sue by telling her that she has a real ear for German. Sue's mother, Frankie, tells Sue's father, "German? Theater? Where's the future in that…We can't let her choose from four insane majors" (Brown & Chemel, 2016). Later in the episode, Frankie tells Sue that she's "all over the place" with respect to choosing a major (Brown & Chemel, 2016). Sue responds by telling her mother that her assessment is not true, in German. Clearly, Sue is shown to be very interested in German, but is discouraged from pursuing it because Frankie believes it will not lead to a successful future. In the end, Sue majors in hospitality and hotel management because she can use her German if she works abroad. A happy resolution, but the denigration of foreign language study is difficult to ignore and likely represents the view of a significant portion of the viewing public.

A similar negative view of language learning is expressed in the ABC show *Schooled*, set in the 1990s. In the episode that I discussed in Chapter 1, "CB Likes Lainey" (Howard et al., 2019), long-simmering tensions between

---

[5] The end of this line "peur des souris" is quite clearly rendered in French by Katie. The first part of the line, "Elle n'avait pas" is more difficult to understand. By looking through the French version of Madeleine I was able to discern the full line: "Elle n'avait pas peur des souris" (Bemelmens, 1985, p. 17).

Spanish teacher Ms. Taraborelli and gym teacher Coach Mellor come to a boil over the school's new website. Principal Glascott forces the two to design the school's website together in order for them to bond and bury the hatchet. It appears to be working as Ms. Taraborelli teaches Coach Mellor about the web and piques his interest, until they begin to fight again. At one point, Ms. Taraborelli tells the principal, "I will never find common ground with Gym Teacher Rick." To which, Coach (Rick) Mellor responds, "And I will never learn Spanish because of her! And also because it's hard" (Howard et al., 2019). Here Coach Mellor explicitly expresses the idea that learning Spanish is hard.

In a similar vein to this episode of *Schooled* and the *American Housewife* episode, the second season *Speechless* episode "D-I—DIMEO A-C—ACADEMY" (Chun et al., 2018), also discussed in Chapter 1, attacks language teachers. In the episode differently-abled JJ's mainstream school will not let him graduate because he has not met the requirements to do so. His mother Maya goes to the school to confront the principal, Dr. Miller, who has brought with her all of JJ's teachers to back up her position. Maya negotiates with each teacher and comes to an agreement with each one. In the end, Dr. Miller stands firm and Maya accepts her position because the principal says it's best for JJ because he is not yet ready to graduate. I would draw your attention to the brief interaction that Maya has with JJ's French teacher:

(6.5)
French teacher: JJ will not pass French.
Maya: JJ will pass French, 'cause you don't actually care
                    and you hate your job.
French teacher: Au revoir.
(Chun et al., 2018)

Here, the language teaching professional is accused of both hating her job and not caring about her students. This accusation is simply insulting to those of us who teach a foreign language, at whatever level. Often language teachers get to know their students quite well because the interactive nature of the language classroom, which leads students to reveal a great deal about who they are and their interests. Taken together, these episodes (from *American Housewife, Pretty Little Liars, The Middle, Schooled,* and *Speechless*) convey some rather disturbing messages about learning a foreign language—it's boring and difficult; the teacher won't care about teaching you; learning another language won't lead to a career success—that are just not true. Moreover, as we saw in the *American Housewife* episode, there are also some negative stereotypes associated with the speakers of languages other than English. In particular, the French are assumed to be rude, inflexible, and mean.

Returning to the idea of language learning, in contrast to the implausible language learning depicted in *10 Things I Hate About You*, *Pretty Little Liars*, *One Tree Hill*, and *Ben 10: Ultimate Alien*, the classic *Simpsons* episode, "The Crepes of Wrath" (Meyer et al., 1990), follows Bart as he becomes an exchange student in France. In fact, however, instead of living with a pleasant host family and amusing himself with French siblings and parents, he essentially becomes slave labor for two deceitful brothers who own a vineyard and put antifreeze in their wine! *Oh, mon Dieu!* But after two months when his captors send Bart to fetch more antifreeze in the pouring rain, he attempts to speak to a police officer. Unfortunately, the policeman replies, "Excusez-moi, je ne parle pas anglais," 'I do not speak English' (Meyer et al., 1990). He continues to try to explain his situation, but after the policeman offers him a piece of candy and apologizes again for not understanding, Bart walks away disheartened. Alone in the pouring rain, he laments, "I'm so stupid. Anybody could have learned this dumb language by now. Here I've listened to nothing but French for the past *deux mois. Et je ne sais pas un mot. Eh, mais je parle français maintenant. Incroyable!*" (Meyer et al., 1990).[6] He flags down the policeman once more and explains to him what his "host parents" have done to him in detailed, error-free, and relatively well-pronounced French.

Bart, after a two-month-long almost total immersion experience in France, learns to speak French. Given his age, 10 years old, it's certainly possible that he could have made such progress in that time. Putting aside the fact that his pronunciation probably would be better than it is and the fact that his vocabulary is quite advanced for a 10-year-old—he knows the word for rescuer, *sauveteur*, translated 'savior'[7]—it's still the most realistic depiction of a language-learning experience of the ones that we've considered so far. Here more realistic consideration is given to time of exposure to the language and to the learning context. And, despite the devious "host parents" Bart gets stuck with, it's also a rousing endorsement of study abroad for language learning. Bart's experience is reminiscent of Daniel's son D.J. in *Ugly Betty* from the previous chapter.

In a similar, more realistic depiction of language learning, Adrian decides to learn Spanish for his wife, Rosa on *Brooklyn Nine-Nine*. The episode, "Kicks" (Guest & Appel, 2017) finds Rosa thinking that Adrian is cheating on her because there was a credit card charge for a restaurant called La Palapa—two entrees and one flan. Being a detective, she deduces that they shared the flan.

---

[6] '…two months. And I don't know a word. Hey, but I speak French now. Incredible!'

[7] Unfortunately this is generally someone who saves a boat.

In truth, when Rosa confronts Adrian about having a mistress it is revealed that Adrian has been studying Spanish to impress Rosa's father.

(6.6)

Rosa:	I know about your mistress. I know about La Palapa. I know about the flan.
Adrian:	Babe, wait.
Rosa:	Oh, I've been waiting. I waited all night to do this. We're done. It's over.
Adrian:	What? No. [Groans] [Sighs] I don't have a mistress. That woman's name is Señora Reyes. She's my Spanish teacher.
Rosa:	Oh, please.
Adrian:	No, I'm serious. The only reason we were even at La Palapa was so I can practice ordering in Spanish. Ah by the way, [speaking Spanish subtitled in English] The restaurant told us to share the flan.[8]
Rosa:	It did?
Adrian:	[Speaking Spanish subtitled in English] I'm learning Spanish to impress your father.[9]
Rosa:	Oh, my God. Oh, my God. Adrian, I'm so sorry. You must be so mad at me.
Adrian:	What? No, of course I'm not mad at you. Are you kidding? Jealousy's, like, the hottest emotion.

(Guest & Appel, 2017)

From this scene, we can discern that Señora Reyes knows what she is doing as a language teacher. Bringing Adrian to La Palapa to have an authentic experience ordering in Spanish is the type of highly contextualized learning environment, interacting with native speakers, that is likely to produce comprehensible input (Krashen, 1982) and negotiation of meaning (Long, 1981; 1983a, 1983b), two pillars of second language learning. Similar to Bart's experience in France, this experience will help develop Adrian's Spanish language knowledge and skills.

As a final, short example of more realistic portrayals of language learning on TV, we can look to the "All Things Being Equal" episode (Straton et al., 2017) of the sitcom *Modern Family*. In this episode, which I discussed in Chapter 1,

---

[8] El restaurante nos dijos [sic] que compartir el flan.
[9] Estoy aprendiendo español para impresionar a tu padre.

patriarch Jay and son-in-law Phil enter into a business partnership owning a car lot, where people pay for parking near the downtown. They need to hire an attendant to manage the lot. They interview two candidates, Joan and Tibor. Tibor is a non-native speaker of English who is depicted with very limited English language proficiency. While being interviewed for the job, Tibor is only able to answer "Tibor" and "Is good" (Straton et al., 2017). Jay believes that his limited ability to interact with customers will be an asset, but Phil gets his way based on the flip of a coin and Joan is hired. Jay eventually fires Joan because she is too personable and engages customers in long conversations when entering the lot, causing a line of cars to form waiting to get into the parking lot. Jay justifies his decision: "We're gonna hire that Tibor guy. He barely speaks English, but there'll be no chattiness although I did try that with Gloria, and eventually they watch so much TV they figure it out" (Straton et al., 2017). Jay admits that while Tibor is a good choice from his perspective now, eventually he will learn to speak English, like Jay's wife Gloria did, by watching TV. The idea that TV can be a good way for naturalistic learners (i.e., those living in an English-speaking environment not formally studying the language) to acquire English is not so far-fetched. In fact, TV provides contextualized input, if not interaction, in the L2 that can be very beneficial to learners. Thus, this method of language learning could help Tibor (and others) learn English. Also, there is the meta joke of a character on a TV show suggesting this notion, as if non-native English speakers were watching at that moment, improving their English.

Bedarnek (2018) explores this very idea by collecting and analyzing data from 582 advanced L2 English German university students. She asked her participants about their TV watching habits, particularly as it concerns watching U.S. television series. She found that the vast majority of respondents watch English-language series (her examples are mostly from the U.S.) without subtitles (81.5%). "Students also indicated that they found such TV series useful for learning (better) English" (p. 223) at a rate of roughly 81%. Many of the students surveyed will become English teachers. Bedarnek asked them whether they would use English-language series in their own future classrooms to exploit them for their pedagogical value. A little more than half of those students who responded to this question said they would do so often or very often (p. 223).

Let's move on from these instances of language learning to a representation of language loss. In the *Lost* episode "The Package" (Zbyszewski et al., 2010), the Korean-speaking character Sun loses the ability to speak English after hitting her head during a chase. While trying to flee Locke, Sun looks to see if he is gaining from behind and turns forward to hit her head on a tree in her path. The resultant bump on the left side of her head impedes her ability to

Part III:
Subtitles & Stereotypes

Chapter 7

Tu Vuo' Fa' L'Americano:
Italian Use on Primetime TV in America

I. Introduction

As we've seen thus far, the use of languages other than English has become ubiquitous on American popular television in recent years. Foreign languages are used in a variety of ways: to access important clues in solving a crime (see Chapter 3), to explore myths about language learning (see Chapter 6), to create humor (see Chapter 1), and to problematize what it means to be a speaker of another language in a mostly monolingual American context (see Chapter 1), among others. Although used less frequently than other foreign languages on American TV (e.g., Spanish), Italian nonetheless has a place in this trend. Thus, in this chapter, I will discuss uses of Italian language and representations of Italian speakers, be they natives or non-natives, on American popular TV in an effort to understand the messages being conveyed to viewers about Italian, and Italians/Italian-Americans in particular, and foreign languages and speakers of languages other than English more generally. I will examine examples from episodes of *CSI*, *The Simpsons*, *Rules of Engagement*, *30 Rock*, *How I Met Your Mother*, *Happy Endings*, and *Modern Family*. Scenes from these sources raise questions about such issues as computer translation and subtitle use, employing another language to conceal the truth (cf. Chapter 1), and stereotypes of Italian speakers, Italians, and Italian-Americans, as well as why foreign language use may be funny to American audiences (as we also explored in Chapter 1).

II. Data

I'd like to begin with this last idea, why using Italian, or foreign languages more generally, is funny to American audiences. Let's consider an example from *30 Rock*. In the episode "Alexis Goodlooking and the Case of the Missing Whiskey" (Riggi & Slovis, 2012), Liz Lemon, played by Tina Fey, is coerced into pretending to be the girlfriend of her coworker Frank. Frank has lied to his Italian mother, Silvia, played by Patti Lupone, about having a relationship with Liz to cover up an affair with one of his middle school teachers. Liz resists his coercion by refusing to come to dinner at Frank's mother's home, so he tells his mother that Liz is sick. Concerned for Liz, Silvia somehow gets into Liz's locked apartment (with Frank) and cooks a meal to help Liz recover. Silvia explains, "Frank said you couldn't come to dinner because you weren't feeling well. But I know the best thing for a fever is food, wine, and cheek pinching! So I packed everything up, prayed to the patron saint of locked apartments, and here we are" (Riggi & Slovis, 2012). Liz tries to resist again, but Silvia is firm, "You don't have a say in this! Now, lie down [pushes Liz onto sofa]. While I'm here, you do nothing. As we say in Italy, [speaking Italian subtitled in English] all you have to worry about is farting.[1] [Speaking English, she places a huge plate of food on Liz's lap and shoves food in Liz's mouth] Eat an arancine." Liz ceases resisting, "I love our little family" (Riggi & Slovis, 2012).[2]

As I have discussed before on several occasions, this is yet another example of ethnic humor (Mintz, 1996). In this example, the laugh line is delivered in Italian with English subtitles. Although this example does not so much play on the linguistic elements of ethnic humor (despite the character having a slight accent and the use of an aphorism with the word "farting" in it), the caricature of Silvia as an overbearing, overly caring Italian mother is clear—she breaks into Liz's house and cooks a huge meal merely because Frank tells her Liz is sick.

In two separate studies reported in Madon et al. (2001) looking at stereotypes associated with various ethnic groups according to U.S. undergraduate students, Italians were perceived as "loyal to family ties" (p. 998). Since, as Frank's "girlfriend" Silvia considers Liz family, Silvia's actions only reinforce this stereotype. Indeed, in a third study, Madon et al. examined if stereotypes of different ethnic groups became more or less favorable over time. Undergraduate students considered stereotypes associated with various groups including Italians from the 1930s, 1950s, 1960s, and 1990s. The researchers found that stereotypes associated with Italians in the 1990s were more favorable than those of earlier eras. Because of this increase in favorability, they posited an unexpected effect: "modern members of stereotyped groups may confront stereotypes more frequently than did previous members of stereotyped groups" (p. 996). In other words, the stereotypes may be more pervasive given their favorability. Because of the trajectory of favorability in the late 1990s, it is possible that these stereotypes

---

[1] "Tutto quello che dovete preoccupare è scoreggiare." Here, the pronunciation of *scoreggiare* 'to fart' sounds more like scoggiare (missing the second syllable), which is, unfortunately, not an Italian word. The subtitled translation, if the word had been correct, is reasonable.

[2] For languages other than English, the English subtitles have been added when provided onscreen. When no English subtitles were present, speech in a language other than English that is not subtitled has been added by the author whenever possible.

have only increased in their association with Italians. Perhaps today Italians and family ties are even more strongly linked. We see this stereotype with Silvia above and we will see it again in other examples below.

The overbearing, overconcerned mother trope becomes even more obvious in a later scene in Liz's office. In an elaborate scheme to fix Frank's life by getting his mother to accept his much older girlfriend, Liz lies to Silvia on the phone, telling her Frank is sick. Silvia shows up to the office with a live chicken: "Frankie! Are you okay? *La donna di scoregge*[3] called and said you were sick, so I came by to make you chicken soup. [Holds out chicken] Where can I kill this?" (Riggi & Slovis, 2012). The idea that Silvia plans to kill the live chicken that she is holding to make chicken soup for her son demonstrates a farmer's sensibility that recalls an Italy that hardly exists today, as that kind of "homemade" cuisine has been replaced by supermarkets and restaurants in much of the country, especially the cities. However, this kind of stereotype, more of Italian-Americans than of today's Italians, still works as ethnic humor. Especially juxtaposing the character's country ideas with New York City. Language does play a role in the scene, lending authenticity (Lopez & Bucholtz, 2017) to Lupone's character, Silvia—she uses the short phrase "*la donna di scoregge*" in Italian giving her the air of an actual Italian, while adding to the humor of the scene. Of course, the audience would have to recall the mispronounced word from earlier in the episode and make the connection between *scoreggiare* 'to fart' and *scoregge* 'farts' to get this joke. From this *30 Rock* episode, it's clear that one of the functions of Italian use and Italian characters on American TV is to create humor by playing off of the associated stereotypes.

As a final example from this episode, as Liz enacts her plan of bringing together Frank, Silvia, and Frank's girlfriend Lynn, she appeals to Silvia in terms that Liz thinks Silvia will understand. Silvia rejects Frank and his girlfriend's relationship because they met when Frank was her student in middle school and because of their age difference, calling it "weird" and indicating that they shouldn't be together. Liz has the perfect reply: "[Y]ou know what else shouldn't go together? Veal, fennel, lemon, cheese, and pork. That's right. Your meatballs. Lynn and Frank are just as good as your meatballs" (Riggi & Slovis, 2012). The metaphor is apt because it builds on the ethnic humor of food-focused stereotypes associated with the Italians and Italian-Americans in the episode.

---

[3] 'The lady of farts.' The audience would have to recall the mispronounced word from earlier to get this joke.

Let's come back to the idea of authenticity that I mentioned earlier. In the short-lived situation comedy *Go On*, about a recently widowed sports radio commentator, Ryan King, working through his grief in a support group, Italian is used to add authenticity to a storyline in the episode "Gooooaaaallll Doll!" (Webster & Holland, 2013). In this episode, King, played by Matthew Perry, decides that he must go on his first real date since losing his wife. He does go on a date, meeting a woman whose company he finds very enjoyable. The woman, however, is being considered for a job in Milan. At the end of the episode, she propositions King and tells him that this will be their only opportunity to be together as she has been offered the position in Italy and will be leaving the very next day: "I got that job. I leave for Milan in the morning, so I have just a few hours, and I'd like to spend them in your bedroom....*Voglio passare la notte con te, carino*" (Webster & Holland, 2013). Here again, the use of Italian by the female character is meant to lend credence to the idea that she will be taking a job in Milan, leaving for Italy in the morning. Moreover, what she says in Italian, "*Voglio passare la notte con te, carino*," ('I want to spend the night with you, dear') is seductive and sexy. However, if you don't speak Italian, you can only infer what she wants from what is happening on screen while she is saying this foreign phrase—it is not subtitled. I'll come back to this issue a little later in this chapter. In short, the use of Italian appears to be two-fold in this scene: to create authenticity and to imbue the moment with an alluring foreignness. If you remember from Chapter 1, speaking a foreign language can be viewed as sexy.

Another scene that uses Italian to imply passion, both anger and love, comes from the *CSI: Crime Scene Investigation* episode "Double Fault" (Byer et al., 2013). In this episode, lab tech David Hodges has been keeping his engagement to an Italian woman a secret from his coworkers. When she finds out, she is not pleased.

(7.1)

Elisabetta: Non riesco a capire come mai non hai mai detto a nessuno niente di me.[4]

David: I-I [Attempts to speak]

Elisabetta: What is the problem, baby? Are you ashamed with me?

David: Elisabetta, mio amore, please calm down. Calmati.

---

[4] I can't understand why you haven't told anyone anything about me.

Elisabetta:	Calmati. No. Potresti avere all spoiled. L'avvocato mi ha detto che non sarei in grado prendere una carta verde.[5] Do you understand me?
David:	Sì. Sì. Sì.

[Scene shifts to co-workers looking on from a distance]

Female coworker:	Who is that?
Male coworker:	Hodges' fiancée.
Female coworder:	Fiancée?!
Male coworker:	Yeah. Shh. I'm trying to figure out what she's saying. If my translate app is correct, it's something about a green card.
David:	Don't worry. Everything will be okay.
Elisabetta:	Okay?
David:	Sì. Bene.
Elisabetta:	Non è okay. Hai capito. Mi stai trattando come se io non esistessi.[6] Like I'm invisible, or what? Mm-mm.
David:	Ti amo. No, it's-- I didn't want to tell anybody about you yet. Non-non sono pronto.
Elisabetta:	David, perché sempre piedi freddi?[7] Cold toes?
Male coworker:	Oh, she means cold feet.
Female coworker:	Hey, shh.

[David turns, glares at coworkers, then turns back to Elisabetta]

David:	No. No cold feet.
Elisabetta:	Allora, cosa c'è? Dimmi! Ti sei innamorato di qualche altra donna? There is another woman in your life? Qualche bionda bimbo americana?[8]
David:	No, wait
Male coworker:	Oh, she thinks there's another woman.
Female coworker:	Yeah, I got that.

---

[5] David: Calm down.
Elisabetta: Calm down. No. You would have [all spoiled]. The lawyer told me that I wouldn't be able to get a green card.
[6] It's not okay. Do you understand? You are treating me as if I don't exist.
[7] David: I'm not ready
Elisabetta: David, why? Still have cold feet?
[8] So, what's wrong? Tell me! Are you in love with some other woman?... Some blonde American bimbo?

David:	Elisabetta there is only you. Sei l'unica donna che io amo.
Elisabetta:	Tu mi fai impazzire.[9] You drive me crazy, David, you know that? I love you. [Kisses David passionately]
Male coworker:	I have never been jealous of Hodges until this moment.
Female coworker:	Mm-hmm, yeah.
Elisabetta:	Now everybody knows who I am.
(Byer et al., 2013)	

This scene is rather complicated with several aspects to discuss. First, there is the issue of subtitles—there are none at all, although a good portion of the scene is in Italian. Previous moments in the story make it easy to understand the reason for Elisabetta's anger. Additionally, a male and a female colleague watch the fight from the background of the scene. The male colleague's "translate app" provides other useful information: the fight is about their impending marriage and Elisabetta's green card aspirations. Hodges understands his fiancée without difficulty and even uses a few Italian phrases of his own: "*amore mio...calmati,*" "*ti amo,*" "*non sono pronto,*" "*sei l'unica donna che io amo.*" Also fortunate for the audience, Elisabetta translates herself, repeating more or less verbatim in English several of things she says in Italian. Finally, it is worth noting that there is a moment of ethnic humor in the scene. Elisabetta mistranslates the Italian "piedi freddi" into "cold toes," although the original Italian phrase means 'cold feet.' She is promptly corrected by Hodges' colleague, in an attempt by the writers to add humor it would seem and to ratchet down the anger in the transition to the passionate kiss at the end.

The stereotyping of Italian language and culture in the form of Hodges' fiancée's passionate argument with him about their nuptials is clearly reductionist. Italian, and all the stereotypical qualities associated therewith, is used to create a foil for the Hodges character's cold rationality—a bright spark in the otherwise frigid lab drama. Americans often think Italian speakers are arguing because discussions seem loud and heated—that stereotypical Italian passion that the writers are playing off of. In my own life, I have experienced this phenomenon. Once, for example, I was on the phone speaking in Italian with an Italian friend and, after the phone call ended, my American colleague asked me

---

[9] David: You're the only woman that I love.
Elisabetta: You make me crazy.

if we were fighting about something. My colleague seemed genuinely surprised when I told her that we were just making plans for later that evening.

The role of translation and lack of subtitles in this scene are quite interesting. The Italian character seems like a very competent English speaker, translating her own words with little hesitation or difficulty. She could probably very easily express her anger in English, but her passion might be constrained in a second language. Additionally, the Hodges character seems to understand quite readily, but he also uses Italian to appeal to his fiancée and their love for one another. Again, Italian is associated with love and passion. Both of these characters make strong cases for learning another language—meet the man/woman of your dreams if you can speak another tongue. This passion only seems to reinforce the persistent stereotype that Italians are associated with family ties (Madon et al., 2001), as David and Elisabetta will be married.

Finally, the "translate app" is a crucial plot device for explaining critical aspects of the conversation for the non-Italian-speaking public. It is not clear how the app functions—is the colleague typing in text or merely using some sort of speech recognition? Also, not clear is how useful such an app could be from across the room if speech recognition were being used. If not, then the colleague using the app must have some knowledge of how to spell in Italian or a very good ear. Perhaps not to translate "*carta verde*," but other aspects of the discussion would not be so easy to figure out. I am not sure how effective translator apps are, but earlier I expressed my continued skepticism of such tools as online translators. They are improving with time, but there is still quite a ways to go for the technology to be very effective at understanding context to provide high-quality translations. In other words, I find this aspect of the scene somewhat difficult to believe.

Returning to the idea of humor, *The Simpsons* use Italian to hide the truth with amusing results in the episode, "The Real Housewives of Fat Tony" (Biasucci & Kramer, 2011). Before discussing the episode, let's consider the continued prevalence of the mob boss stereotype. Schaefer (2011) holds that:

> While as a group Italian Americans are firmly part of middle America, they frequently continue to be associated with crime. In 2009, three New Jersey mayors were indicted for corruption and while not all of them were Italian and at the core of the scandal were five Syrian American rabbis, newspapers quickly dubbed it "New Jersey's Italian Problem." (p. 175)

Marge's sister Selma marries Fat Tony, a stereotypical mob boss with a heart of gold, who uses Italian only incidentally. Before proposing to Selma on his boat, he says, "In this *matto, svitato*[10] world, you've got to hold on to the good things" (Biasucci & Kramer, 2011), as his men hold a captive's head under the water in the background. He then sings the famous operatic aria *Con Te Partirò*[11] after she says yes. This type of language use merely links him to his Italian heritage adding the veneer of authenticity, but is not used consistently by Fat Tony throughout the episode. To my mind, this usage serves as an example of Pandey's (2016) linguistic exhibitionism, mere ornamentation without any deep discoursal roots.

In the course of the episode, we discover that Selma is not Tony's true wife, but a "goomar" (*comare*), literally 'godmother', but meant here as mistress. The Italian used during Tony and Selma's wedding ceremony was employed to hide this fact:

(7.2)

Homer:	Tony, we have to leave. For the record, I want to emphasize we're not leaving because today is "cleanup."
Tony:	Leave? Why?
Selma:	Because you have a girlfriend!
Tony:	Oh. It is true, but it is not what you think.
Tony's wife:	[Drives through the backyard fence in her car] Where is she? Where is this other woman?
Selma:	You're the goomar?
Tony's wife:	I'm Fat Tony's wife. You're the goomar.
Selma:	You're nuts. And I've got the ring to prove it.
Tony's wife:	[Scoffs] That's a goomar ring. This is a wife ring.
Homer:	That's a wife ring? Marge, don't look.
Marge:	This doesn't make any sense. There was a wedding. You exchanged vows.
Tony:	I can explain. **If you spoke Italian, which I knew you did not, you would have known that those were goomar-goombah vows.**
[Flashback to wedding]	
Priest:	[Speaking Italian subtitled in English] Do you, Selma, agree to be Fat Tony's goomar for the rest of your life?
Selma:	[Speaking Italian subtitled in English] Yes.

---

[10] 'crazy, screwed up'

[11] "I will go with you"

Priest:	[Speaking Italian subtitled in English] And do you, Fat Tony, agree to take Selma as your goomar until she busts your chops in front of your business associates?
Tony:	[Speaking Italian subtitled in English] Yes.[12]
...	
Tony's wife:	You missed my first open house as a licensed real estate broker for this *brutta puttana*?[13]
Selma:	I've hit on enough pizza boys to know what that means.[14]

(Biasucci & Kramer, 2011)

In this scene, Tony knows that the vows at his wedding to Selma are false. The fact that Selma cannot speak Italian, nor can anyone in her family makes this subterfuge possible. We also observe that Fat Tony's real wife uses a phrase in Italian, "*brutta putana*," to lend authenticity to the character in another show of linguistic exhibitionism.

Additionally, we see stereotypes of Italian-Americans throughout this episode. For instance, when Marge and Homer come to Tony and Selma's home, he introduces them to his overly muscled nephews, S-Money, Jell-O Shot and the Occurrence as well as his tanned-to-a-crisp niece, Tushy, who studies Italian-American design at Sandy Hook Vocational Institute (in New Jersey, one presumes). These characters are an obvious reference to the *Jersey Shore* (Salsano et al., 2009) cast, with the Occurrence and Tushy quite obviously Mike "The Situation" Sorrentino and Nicole "Snooki" Polizzi. Moreover, both Fat Tony's wife and Selma are caricatures of Italian-American women we might see on television, with big hair, tight clothes, and flashy jewelry—a mix of *Jersey Shore* and *The Real Housewives of New Jersey* (Diefenbach et al., 2009). Moreover, Tony's mother is portrayed making her own pool noodles, a play on the word "noodles" as she makes different varieties. Tony, floating on an inner tube in the pool, shows Homer "pool fusilli" and "pool ziti" and suggests that his mother can "make him one special" (Biasucci & Kramer, 2011) with what looks like an exaggerated pasta

---

[12] Priest: Vuoi tu, Selma, essere la goomar di Tony Il Grasso per il resto della tua vita?
Selma: Sì.
Priest: E tu, Tony Il Grasso, prende Selma come la tua goomar finché non ti rompe i coglioni in presenze ai tuoi compari?
Tony: Sì.
[13] 'ugly whore'
[14] The Italian used in this scene is mostly correct in terms of grammar and pronunciation.

maker. His mother looks like the stereotypical Italian widow, in a dark gray frock with a black shawl covering her head and shoulders. Upon seeing Homer, she exclaims in Italian-accented English, "Mother Mary herself couldn't make a noodle big enough to float this one" Then, in a further nod to stereotyping, she blesses herself," In nomine patris et filli" (Biasucci & Kramer, 2011).

Also in this episode, there is a subplot that revolves around Bart's ability to sniff out truffles in the forest. Bart and Lisa, playing in the forest, realize that he has this ability when they run into Luigi, the owner of the Italian restaurant in Springfield. He is there trying to find truffles himself using his pig, Numbnose, that he flew in from Italy. This character, widely acknowledged to represent a stereotype, speaks English with an Italian accent. The idea of the Italian/Italian-American character searching for ingredients in the forest recalls the Silvia character from *30 Rock*. These rustic depictions of Italians are part and parcel of the older stereotypes associated with them in the U.S.

In Chapter 1, I discussed a scene from the "Anniversary Chicken" episode of the sitcom *Rules of Engagement* (Haukom & Mancuso, 2011), in which Italian is also used to hide crucial information in relation to a beautiful Italian woman. During the episode, the character Russell takes an Italian-speaking woman, Sophia, out on a date, but because he does not know Italian he forces his assistant Timmy to translate for him. Timmy is compelled to translate vulgar messages for Russell throughout the date, which continues throughout the night as Russell and Sophia sleep together. At the end of the episode, Russell enlists Timmy to translate his desire for Sophia to leave.

It is at this point, if you remember, that Timmy makes Russell pay for his actions. Russell wants Sophia to leave, but instead, Timmy tells Sophia that Russell would be willing to marry her so that she could get a green card. Similar to *The Simpsons* episode discussed above, Timmy uses his knowledge of Italian to put one over on Russell, demonstrating how knowledge of a second language can be used to conceal information from those who are ignorant of that language. The point is humor, and subtitles are used to make the joke clear to viewers. But, as I noted in Chapter 1, representing the idea that speaking another language can result in negative consequences for those who do not speak that language is a dangerous game. Some monolingual English speakers could be insulted by the implications of this idea, or worse, they may feel threatened by those who speak languages other than, or in addition to, English (Queen, 2015, p. 203 makes a similar point). In the current political climate nationally, immigrants or those perceived to be the other for any reason, are often targeted. Sewing the fear of those who speak languages other than English, even in a humorous way, could be misinterpreted as something very negative.

We should note that once again, the representation of an Italian woman in the scene from *Rules of Engagement* exudes sex, sensuality, and passion. We can see a trend toward a definite trope for younger Italian women: beautiful, sexy, passionate, energetic. The "Romeward Bound" episode of *How I Met Your Mother* (Tatham & Fryman, 2013) features a scene with another beautiful Italian woman. In this episode, Lily is contemplating a job offer in Rome but she would have to move there with her husband, Marshall, and their baby. Lily has fears and concerns about the move, about her ability to do the job, and about what Marshall's life will be like when he gives up practicing law to be a stay-at-home dad. She worries that his life will become, "an angsty, existential black-and-white Italian movie" (Tatham & Fryman, 2013). Cut to a scene in which we see a well-dressed Marshall at an outdoor café table sipping espresso. He makes eye contact with a beautiful, Italian woman at a neighboring table. She strikes up a conversation:

(7.3)

Italian woman:	[Speaking Italian, subtitled in English] What do you do for a living?[15]
Marshall:	I used to be a lawyer.
Italian woman:	[Speaking Italian, subtitled in English] And what are you now?[16]
Marshall:	I don't know anymore.
Italian woman:	[Speaking Italian, subtitled in English] Why don't you and I move to Minnesota where I will learn your mother's recipe for ham casserole.[17]

(Tatham & Fryman, 2013)

Although the words coming out of the Italian woman's mouth are comical (and subtitled to convey the humor of the scene), she fits several aspects of the trope outlined above. She is very beautiful; she is meant to exude sex and passion, although more smoldering this time. This contrasts the Italian mother trope portrayed by Patti Lupone in *30 Rock* as well as Fat Tony's mother in *The Simpsons*.

---

[15] *Che lavoro fai?*

[16] *Cosa fai adesso?*

[17] *Perché non andiamo a vivere in Minnesota vicino a tua madre dove imparerò la [sua] ricetta per lo [stufato] al prosciutto.* Words in brackets are guesses at what was meant; what is actually said is either incorrect or pronounced incorrectly.

In a later scene, Lily herself experiences an existential crisis related to her job. She worries that if she takes the job in Italy, she will end up losing it because it will not go well. This time, it is Lily who is pictured in the black-and-white café scene. The same Italian woman strikes up a conversation with the same opening line, "*Che lavoro fai?*" 'What do you do for a living?' In this case, Lily tells the woman that she "used to be an art consultant." The woman responds, again in Italian with English subtitles, "My husband used to be married to an art consultant. Here he is now!"[18] (Tatham & Fryman, 2013). Marshall shows up on a *vespa* with baby Marvin strapped to his chest.

This *How I Met Your Mother* episode includes other stereotypical visions of Marshall: wearing a white sleeveless undershirt feeding his baby and making pasta by hand. These images seem more in keeping with a view of Italy as the Old Country instead of a modern European nation. This is similar to Tony's mother in *The Simpsons*; it seems that in America today being Italian-American (or just Italian) is a mash-up of *Jersey Shore* (Salsano et al., 2009) and *The Sopranos* (Chase et al., 1999). In fact, later in "Romeward Bound," after Lily has decided to take the job in Rome, we see Marshall dressed in his best white mafia don outfit (cf. Schaefer, 2011 above) from an earlier era strolling through little Italy. He exclaims the word "Madonna" (in the Italian-American dialect) when he finds out via text that Lily has changed her mind about the job again (Tatham & Fryman, 2013). In some ways, Italian or Italian dialect, more precisely, has become a marker of a particular ethnic subculture, much as Yiddish marks the New York Jewish community in the popular American imagination. It has become a shorthand to tell you about the character, to indicate a particular type.

Modern Family's "Blasts From the Past" (Chandrasekaran et al., 2019) episode also explores Italian stereotypes. In the episode, first discussed in Chapter 1, Phil and Claire learn Italian to prepare for a cycling trip in Italian. At first, we have the trope of Americans speaking another language poorly:

(7.4)
Phil: [speaking Italian, English subtitles] Italy is truly the most
            beautiful country, no?
Claire: [speaking Italian, English subtitles] Yes. The food is
            delicious and the people are nice.
Phil: [speaking Italian, English subtitles] Let's stop. And kill that
            old man for directions.

---

18 'Mio marito era sposato con una consulente di arte. Eccolo adesso!'

Claire: [speaking Italian, English subtitles] Our Italian has gotten
               very big. [19]
Phil: We're taking a four-week bicycle trip through the vineyards
               of Italy!
(Chandrasekaran et al., 2019)

In this case, it's mostly small lexical errors that result in humor (e.g., "kill that old man for directions;" "our Italian has gotten very big"). But what Phil and Claire say represents clear stereotypes of Italy: it's a beautiful country with delicious food and nice people. But the stereotyping in this episode takes a darker, more negative turn (especially in the #MeToo era):

(7.5)
Phil: So we've been hitting the language tapes, the, uh the
               stationary bikes, and a couple of times a day, I wolfishly
               whistle at Claire to prepare her for that timeless Roman
               charm.
Claire: I can't believe after all those nights at Fratelli's talking
               about going to Italy, it's actually happening.
Phil: [Italian accent] Ohh, American lady! Why do you do this to
               me?
Claire: Don't make me practice my slap on you again. Mm.
(Chandrasekaran et al., 2019)

Here, by the use of Phil's fake Italian accent, Italian men are stereotyped as sexually aggressive, with the word "wolfishly" heightening the danger present in the stereotype. Claire must threaten to slap him to keep his urges under control.

In all of the examples we've looked at thus far, Italian language and stereotypes about Italians and/or Italian-American culture seem inextricably linked. In addition to the stereotypes connected to strong family ties and those associated with younger and older women and the mafia, we have the

---

[19] Phil: *L'Italia è davvero il paese più bello del mondo, no?*
Claire: *Sì.. Il cibo è delizioso e le persone simpatiche.*
Phil: *Ah, fermiamoci. Uccidiamo quel vecchio per le direzioni.*
Claire: *Nostro italiano migliorato molto.*
Phil's pronunciation of "fermiamoci" sounds more like "fermioci". Claire's use of *migliorare* in the last line is the correct verb for "to improve"; the incorrect translation of "*migliorare*" as 'to get big' in the subtitle seems a deliberate attempt at humor.

Jersey Shore and *Real Housewives* stereotypes also linked with Italian-Americans. In fact, some of the stereotypes represent earlier beliefs about Italians and Italian-Americans that seem more connected with an era much earlier than with today. For instance, the idea of Italians killing their own animals, or searching the forest for their own food, or the Italian widow draped in black from head to toe—these seem more likely to represent Italians/Italian-Americans among earlier generations in the U.S.

John Markert's (2004-2007) research on Hispanic stereotypes in *The George Lopez Show*,[20] demonstrated that Hispanic and non-Hispanic viewers tended to identify with George López as just the guy next door with the same difficult in-laws and problems with his kids that everyone has without focusing on language use per se. Hispanic viewers expected the show to be in English while non-Hispanic viewers didn't realize the characters were all proficient in English until questioned about this fact. I mention this study because, in contrast to Latinos in the current American imagination, Italians are well integrated in America and American culture, most having immigrated to the US over a century ago. The Italian language used by Italian Americans, as represented by Fat Tony, for instance, is only vestigial, easily replicated by non-Italian-Americans like Marshall. In much of the U.S., Italian-Americans are so mainstream that using Italian language serves to create just that bit of distance necessary to satirize Italian-Americans without offending, with the idea that the audience is in on the joke. Even if the portrayals are potentially negative, the distance created by the over-the-top stereotype inoculates the writers/producers and allows the audience to laugh without derision. With respect to "true" Italians, they are mostly depicted by beautiful women and imbued with sex appeal and passion, positive qualities, if at times overblown in the portrayals.

Let's come back to the idea of subtitles for just a moment. In this *Modern Family* scene as well as in the scenes from *30 Rock, The Simpsons,* and *Rules of Engagement,* subtitles were used so that the joke would not be lost. In contrast, in the *CSI* episode subtitles are not used. There, a different strategy of having the characters translate the scene at various points and in various ways as it progresses is employed. Perhaps this makes the second-language use seem more authentic in the dramatic genre as opposed to the comedies, where the L2 use is played for laughs. The joke would not be as funny if it had to be translated by the characters on screen; the subtitles are a necessary part of the humor. In some sense, the stakes are lower in the drama and the

---

[20] Also known as *George Lopez.*

immediacy of understanding everything that is being said is reduced to knowing only key moments or ideas.

In terms of learning or speaking a second language, a number of myths are perpetuated on American television (we've considered some of them in Chapters 5 and 6). In a scene from the *Happy Endings* episode, "Like Father, Like Gun" (Libman et al., 2011), the old wives' tale about being able to speak a second language only when drunk is highlighted. Two friends, Alex and Penny, are seen hungover at brunch discussing what they did the night before. Alex marvels at the fact that Penny was able to speak fluent Italian the night before. Cut to a scene of Penny rattling off in Italian (subtitled in English) to two men, "So I said to him, 'You want me to get in a Jacuzzi with prostitutes? Who am I? Silvio Berlusconi?'"[21] (Libman et al., 2011). I mentioned the use of subtitles earlier—I remind the reader that this is a common use of subtitles in the sitcom genre so that the viewers can easily understand the joke. In fact, one of the men leaves Penny a voicemail in Italian, but she can't understand it, despite having studied in Florence for a semester in college.

Both women wonder why Penny was able to speak Italian the night before, but can no longer. They realize that Penny was drunk the night before. There is a drinking montage as the women seek to test that theory. Surrounded by a number of empty mimosa glasses on the table, Penny listens to the message again. She easily translates what is said: the Italians want to meet up with the two women again that night. This scene relates to research done by Guiora et al. (1972) decades ago that showed that "ingestion of small amounts of alcohol, under certain circumstances, does lead to an increased ability to authentically pronounce a second language" (p. 426). The study also showed that consuming excessive amounts of alcohol had a negative effect on L2 pronunciation. So the representation of this myth does not stand up to scrutiny.

In this episode, we also see a negative portrayal of the ugly American. Penny's friend Alex does not understand Italian and thus feels left out. Because of this, she acts out in an insulting manner when she and Penny meet up with the Italians again. In the scene in question, Penny is once more engaging both men in conversation in Italian on one side of the table. Alex, on her own on the other side of the table unable to understand what is being said, takes some of her hair in her hand and uses it to form a mustache over her lips as she exclaims in a fake Italian accent, "Hey, I'm Mario. I'm gonna win-a" (Libman et al., 2011). The negative perspective on second language use that I discussed in reference to the

---

[21] *"Io gli ho detto, 'Vuoi che io mi butti in Jacuzzi insieme alle prostitute? Ma chi sono? Silvio Berlusconi?'"*

Rules of Engagement scene, where Russell cannot understand that his assistant
is offering him up as a husband, is turned on its head in this scene. Alex comes
across as petty and childish because instead of asking her friend and the Italian
speakers to speak English, she acts out a stereotype from Mario Brothers.
Moreover, she concludes, "Why would I even want to be there if I can't
understand anything?" (Libman et al., 2011). This portrayal represents an
interesting stereotype of Americans as incurious about other peoples and
cultures. Taken in the context of the episode, it seems like a challenge to look
beyond our own language and culture.

In the inevitable conclusion to Penny's storyline with the Italians, she takes
one of them, Mossimo, home with her. The morning after they consummate
their interest in each other, Penny wakes up sober to find her Italian love
interest making coffee. He begins to tell her a story about the dream he had that
night. Mossimo speaks Italian, but is subtitled in English. He starts, "This
morning I woke up from a dream..."[22] (Libman et al., 2011), as Penny quickly
realizes that she can't understand him because she is not drunk. She begins
searching the kitchen for alcohol, but all the bottles she finds are empty. The
Italian continues, "...only to find myself in a sweeter dream. You are a bright
spot in a dark and desolate world marred by personal tragedy. My father was a
cruel drunk who used to beat me with a belt" (Libman et al., 2011).[23]
Throughout what Mossimo says, Penny nods, says "Mmm-hmm", and starts
laughing at points as she cannot find any alcohol. Unfortunately, her poor
Italian lover reaches the sad climax of his tale as she finds some vodka in her
freezer and takes a swig. Mossimo continues, "Finally, one day his belt
broke...but the next day he came home with a new belt...a championship belt
from an amateur boxing competition. There was nothing amateur about the
beating I took that night"[24] (Libman et al., 2011), while Penny, still not
understanding, smiles from across the kitchen, gives him two thumbs up, and
laughs again. Not comprehending her reaction, Mossimo asks, "Penny, why
must you laugh at my sadness?"[25] (Libman et al., 2011). He excuses himself and
leaves. Despite the humor in this scene caused by Penny's inability to
understand and, thus, her inappropriate reaction to Mossimo's story, we cannot
get away from negative stereotypes: the tough Italian father beating his son.

---

[22] *"Stamattina, mi sono svegliato da un sogno."*
[23] *"...per poi trovarmi in un sogno più dolce. Penny, tu sei luce in un mondo desolato di
tragedia. Mio padre mi picchiava tutte le sere con un [sic] cintura."*
[24] *"Fino a che un giorno si è rotta. Il giorno dopo, lui è tornato a casa con una cintura
nuova...una cintura che aveva vinto in un gara amatoriale di pugilato. Non c'era niente
di amatoriale nella botta che io ho preso quella sera."*
[25] *"Penny, perché ridi della mia tristezza?"*

Why must the story that Mossimo tells involve being beaten by his father? Would it not have been possible to tell an equally sad tale that did not play into negative stereotypes about Italians (and by extension Italian-Americans)?

Turning back to the "Romeward Bound" episode of *How I Met Your Mother* (Tatham & Fryman, 2013), we see another storyline related to language learning. The character of Marshall supposedly took a week of Italian in college, but still remembers one phrase according to his friend Ted. The phrase, "Andiamo fratello, non mastroianni tutti i Funyuns" 'Come on, bro, don't bogart all the Funyuns' (Tatham & Fryman, 2013) seems a highly unlikely one to learn in the first week of Elementary Italian. You'll notice that the writers chose an interesting way to translate Marshall's one Italian sentence, substituting the last name of a similarly well-known Italian actor, Marcello Mastroianni, for the verb bogart, from Humphrey Bogart of course.[26] However, it does represent the fun aspect of learning another language—the beauty and power of trying to find a way to translate ideas from your first language into another one—as we see at the end of the episode when we finally hear this phrase used. After his wife Lily has turned down her dream job in Italy, she and Marshall sit on the steps of their building. She expresses her fears to Marshall, who tries to encourage her. Eventually, this encouragement takes the form of Marshall repeating his one Italian phrase ten times with different inflections. The first two times he uses the phrase, the subtitles reflect the meaning as rendered above, but as he continues, the subtitles change to reflect different meanings.

(7.6)

Lily:	I'm a hick from Brooklyn who's terrified of living more than ten subway stops from where I was born.
Marshall:	Okay, Lily, if I can move from St. Cloud, Minnesota, to New York City, then you can move to Rome.
Lily:	We know nothing about Italy. We have no friends there. We don't speak the language.
Marshall:	[Speaking Italian, subtitled in English] Come on, bro, don't bogart all the Funions.[27, 28]
Lily:	Okay, so you know that one sentence. Can you say anything else?

---

[26] Urbandictionary.com defines bogart as "To keep something all for oneself, thus depriving anyone else of having any."

[27] *"Andiamo fratello, non mastroianni tutti i Funyuns."*

[28] This spelling of Funyuns used in the subtitles is not the official spelling by Frito Lay.

Marshall:	[Speaking Italian, subtitled in English] Come on, bro, don't Bogart all the Funions.
Lily:	That-that was the same sentence. You just changed the inflection.
Marshall:	[Speaking the same Italian sentence eight times, subtitled in English] Okay! Fine! Maybe the only sentence I know is 'Come on, bro. Don't Bogart all the Funions.' But I know, in my heart…that you understand me anyway…because no one else has ever understood anyone…better than you and I understand each other. Is this trip going to be scary? Yes. Do I like the idea of not knowing the language? Of course not! But I believe we can do this. I love you, Lily. I love you.
Lily:	I love you, too. All right. We're going to Italy.
Marshall:	*Sì!*

(Tatham & Fryman, 2013)

The different use of subtitles here, to explain in English what Marshall is saying to his wife by repeating his inscrutable Italian catchphrase with varying inflections, is a somewhat novel use. This use of subtitles is meant to represent the idea that even if Marshall and Lily are not speaking the same language, they still understand one another. This proves to be the case, as Lily responds to Marshall's "I love you," said with the words, "*I Funyuns*, Lily. *I Funyuns*," by saying, "I love you, too."

IV. Conclusion

Suffice it to say that Italian has an interesting place among second/foreign languages used on American television. We've seen how it can be used in creating ethnic humor or comic situations through the concealment of information, how it is used to add authenticity to certain characterizations, and how it is used to perpetuate language-learning myths. The most striking aspect of what we've seen seems to be the inextricable link between language and culture in the case of Italian. I believe this results from the Italian language having a fixed locus of national origin and the long history of Italian-American stereotypes in the U.S. Language plays a role in amplifying those stereotypes for the purposes of comedy. As Giacomo Leopardi, famous Italian poet, philologist and philsopher said, *"Chi ha il coraggio di ridere è padrone del mondo."*[29]

---

[29] Whoever has the courage to laugh is master of the world.

Chapter 8

How I Met Your Foreign Boyfriend: What Primetime TV Tells Us About Popular Attitudes Toward L2 English Speakers[1]

I. Introduction

Popular media have long shaped societal views in America on a variety of issues. They have been responsible for both perpetuating stereotypes on the one hand, and presenting evidence to contradict, and sometimes even tear them down, on the other. Television has, perhaps, the most pervasive power in this domain, given its ubiquity in American society. A negative portrayal of a given racial, ethnic, or minority group can do great damage to that group's image in the collective American psyche. Whereas, a positive storyline revolving around a minority character can help mainstream that minority group by erasing racial, ethnic, and cultural differences, essentially presenting the message, "Hey, they're just like us." Of course, the questions surrounding who the *they* and the *us* might be are ever-evolving depending upon the expected target audience of a given program. Nevertheless, the power of television to impact American attitudes toward a given group or culture is undeniable.

In this particular work, I am concerned with how television portrayals of second-language speakers can be interpreted to determine the possible effects these portrayals have on popular attitudes toward speakers who have English as a second language. Specifically, my analysis will focus on a scene from the CBS sitcom *How I Met Your Mother* in the context of the episode in which it appears. This analysis will be considered with reference to other television portrayals in which second-language (L2) speakers, particularly those who may speak Spanish as a first language (L1) or may be bilingual, are highlighted. Before taking on that task, however, let us first consider some current research studies on language attitudes towards L2 English speakers.

---

[1] This paper was first published in Patricia Donher (Ed.). (2010). *Barbarians at the Gate: Studies in Language Attitudes*. Newcastle upon Tyne: Cambridge Scholars Publishing.

II. Background Research

Lindemann's (2005) study explored linguistic prejudice against L2 English speakers from a number of foreign backgrounds by college undergraduates. She used two tasks to assess these attitudes, a map-labeling task in which 79 undergraduates labeled world maps with descriptions of the English of international students from those regions and a country-rating task in which 208 undergraduates were given a list of 58 countries and asked to rate the "correctness, pleasantness, and friendliness" of the English spoken by natives of those countries (p. 191). In the country-rating task, Mexican English, although rated as the most familiar of non-native varieties, was not rated very highly for pleasantness or correctness (p. 193). In a cluster analysis of all three scores (*friendliness, pleasantness, correctness*) only three Latin American varieties (from Costa Rica, Colombia, and Brazil) were in the second tier of nations rated positively (first-tier being most countries where English is the native variety; most Western European nations were also in the second tier, including Spain). In the third tier were the other Latin American nations (including Mexico and Argentina) (p. 194). As for the map-labeling task, Mexico becomes a proxy for all of Latin America and receives relatively negative evaluations. Some descriptors include, "sloppy," "lazy sounding," and not "respectable" (p. 203). In the introduction to her research, considering previous studies, Lindemann says, "The relationship between speakers' perceived origin and reactions to their speech is . . . relevant to fair treatment of (perceived) non-native speakers" (p. 188). She cites job discrimination as a possible consequence. From this research, it is evident that Latin American varieties of L2 English are generally perceived with prejudicial attitudes. This is of particular importance given the focus the current research has on L2 English speakers from L1 Spanish backgrounds.

Durkin and Judge (2001) studied children's reactions to pro- and anti-social behaviors by foreign and native speakers of English in television (p. 597). The researchers had 144 English-speaking children of 6-, 8- and 10-years-old view short programs in which the same group of actors portrayed positive and negative social behaviors in the context of either an English-speaking family or a family speaking an artificial language created for the study to avoid pre-existing biases (p. 601). It was expected that the children would have negative reactions to the "foreign" language and to the antisocial behaviors and that this effect would be additive (p. 600). In fact, the researchers did find that all groups preferred the prosocial to the antisocial condition, regardless of language. Additive effects for language were seen in the 6- and 8-year-olds, but by age 10, social behavior rather than language was the most significant factor in determining positive or negative attitudes (p. 608). The authors conclude their study:

The mass media, especially television, are pervasive sources of information and ideas about foreign people, and are sometimes negative in the ways in which minorities are represented. The present findings indicate that the valence of the social portrayal may interact with developmental changes in prejudice and either heighten or ameliorate a tendency toward unfavorable judgments of outsiders. (p. 610)

Clearly this conclusion is of great importance in that it indicates that not only language, but the social context in which that language is presented can affect children's perceptions of and attitudes toward a given group. Presumably, adults would also be vulnerable to the formation of prejudicial or negative attitudes based on whether characters demonstrate pro- or antisocial behaviors.

Dobrow and Gidney (1998) also find language to be an important factor in children's animated programming on television in the late 1990s.[2] Using trained coders, they analyzed a sample of 12 animated programs for kids, representative of the 76 such programs on various networks in the Boston area at the time, in terms of "a variety of personality and visual characteristics as well as for dialect and foreign accents" (p. 105). Citing previous studies that found negative portrayals of African-, Asian- and Latino-Americans could have negative consequences on the self-concept and self-esteem of young people of the given ethnicity, the authors state that "Language is a powerful means of signaling social and personal identity. In fact, it is one of the principal means by which we distinguish members of our own and other communities" (p. 107). Language is a way we assess and make judgments about others—their education, their intelligence, their social status, whether they are native or foreign. In this study, the data demonstrate that "villains consistently used non-American accents" (p. 105). That such a negative characteristic should be bound with foreign accent bespeaks a clear bias against foreigners or those who do not speak an unaccented American variety of English.

Considering other manifestations of racism in ambiguous contexts, Mastro et al. (2008), looked at the effect that exposure to television depictions of Latinos has on the judgments of Caucasian viewers. The results showed that racial identification and media ambiguity did have a subtle influence on viewers' evaluations of Latinos as well as an effect on the self-esteem of the

---

[2] Some of their sample programming, such as *Flintstones*, although still on broadcast television, was conceived and originally aired many years earlier.

Caucasian viewers (p. 5). Again, it is clear that media images do have the power to affect viewers' opinions of themselves and others.

III. Latino Television Characters

Latino characters have been and are present in several primetime television series in recent years. There is Betty Suarez, heroine of the sitcom *Ugly Betty* (Hayek et al., 2006) on ABC. Comedian George López has an eponymous sitcom (*George Lopez*, Helford et al., 2002) on the same network, where one also finds Eva Longoria Parker playing Gabrielle Solis on *Desperate Housewives* (Cherry et al., 2004). The ABC network also ran the short-lived sitcom *Freddie* starring Freddie Prinze, Jr. (Prinze et al., 2005) in the 2005-2006 season. In addition to these characters, the character of Fez on *That '70s Show* (Mandabach et al., 1998), portrayed by the Venezuelan-raised Wilmer Valderrama, was also a fixture on the Fox network for eight seasons from 1998-2006. Certainly, there are other Latino/a characters of recent vintage to be considered; however, the aforementioned provide an interesting representative sample of how television deals with portrayals of minority roles.

I should first mention that, of these characters, none is exclusively Spanish-speaking. In fact, none use Spanish with any regularity beyond the occasional word or two, at all. All, however, could be perceived to be bilingual. Gabrielle Solis, although nominally Latina, does not communicate her Hispanic identity in any way. She is the stereotypical fashion-loving, over-spending suburban woman, with much more in common with the characters in *Sex and the City* (Darren Starr Productions, 1998) than with the other Latino/a characters mentioned above. However, the very fact that Eva Longoria Parker, a beautiful Latina actress, plays Gaby Solis has raised the profile of Latino/a performers in all media. In fact, Eric Deggans did a cover story for *Hispanic* magazine on Eva Longoria and other Latinos/as on television in 2005 (2005b).

In this same issue of *Hispanic* a cover story specifically about Freddie Prinze, Jr. and his new show, *Freddie*, also appears (Deggans, 2005a). The show is based on Prinze, Jr.'s life growing up with all women after the untimely death of his father when he was young. Again, Freddie, the character, seems more like your average everyday all-American late twentysomething; he is assimilated and homogenized. He, like Gaby Solis, does not speak Spanish, although he does understand it as evidenced by the interesting twist to this particular show: the presence of his grandmother, *who does not speak English*. Her lines are subtitled in English but she speaks exclusively in Spanish. The impact of this character is evident when one considers she is the first character to speak only in Spanish on an American TV show (Wilson, 2006, p. A10). The Spanish-speaking character is positively assessed in *People* as "a

Puerto Rican grandmother who shares her sarcastic pearls of wisdom in Spanish" ("Freddie," 2005, p. 44).

Another show that revolves around a family with a non-native family head, this time a patriarch, is *Ugly Betty*. Betty's father, Ignacio, played by Tony Plana, is originally from Mexico, having crossed the border with the woman he loved to save her from an abusive husband. Although he does speak with a barely noticeable accent, his English is flawless. He watches Mexican *telenovelas*, and clearly understands Spanish, but apart from *mija, empanada, tortilla* and the like, he does not speak Spanish on the show. Nor, for that matter, does Betty or any member of her immediate family. For a series of episodes at the end of the first season, beginning of the second, the family members found themselves in Mexico, where Spanish was spoken, however not by them. *Ugly Betty* has been touted as "one of television's best series—a celebration of both the candy-colored diversion of fashion and the values of home and family" (Gliatto, 2008, p. 43). These last words of praise are interesting since the ideals of home and family are presented and held aloft in Betty's Latino household, with an immigrant father (who came to the U.S. illegally). This acceptance of the Suarez household as mainstream with typical American values represents another major shift in cultural perceptions in the U.S.

The George Lopez Show (TGLS), starring George López, much like *Ugly Betty*, is another show in which work life and the family play central roles. John Markert's (2004-2007) extensive study of *TGLS* analyzes the content of episodes from three of the four first seasons for stereotypes about Hispanics, a total of 49 out of 80 episodes—the first three episodes of the first season and 46 of the 52 episodes in seasons three and four (p. 150). He also includes focus group reaction from Hispanic and non-Hispanic participants (p. 151). Linguistically speaking, *TGLS* is another show where English is used almost exclusively in lieu of any Spanish. Only one character, George's Cuban-born father-in-law, has any discernable accent (p. 155). In his focus groups, however, no participant mentioned the use, or lack of use, of Spanish. Once prompted, Hispanics took it for granted that the show would be in English. Non-Hispanics, on the other hand, were not aware that all the cast members were proficient in English until asked about the character with the accent; according to Markert, "this challenged their belief that most Hispanics do not know English" (p. 155). Markert concludes the following from this reaction on the part of his non-Hispanic participants:

> It may be, then, that constant exposure to the English-proficient López family by viewers, though it is unlikely to abolish a widely held assumption, could reduce the underlying belief by non-Hispanics that Latinos do not speak English. This could, however, have some negative

results insofar as this assumption could make those who do speak Spanish all the more salient to viewers of *TGLS* and thus increase (rather than decrease) their negative reaction to Spanish-speaking Latinos. Support for this conjecture comes from the widely documented finding that television reality has more substance to viewers than material people in the real world. (pp. 155-56)

A final portrayal to consider is Wilmer Valderrama's character Fez on *That '70s Show*. The actor, a native speaker of Spanish who learned English upon coming to Los Angeles as a teenager,[3] played Fez—an acronym for Foreign Exchange Student, the spelling of which is modified to represent how it sounds ("Fez (That '70s Show)," Origins, ¶ 1)—with a non-distinct yet foreign accent that he developed. The origins of the character himself are never made clear, although many teasers were provided over the course of the eight-season run of the show. Of interest here is Fez' accented, non-native English. Of course, he is often harangued for his imperfect-sounding dialect, yet he is also an accepted member of the group of teenagers that make up the core of the show, which takes place in Wisconsin.

The characters presented above demonstrate a clear mainstreaming of Latino/foreign culture in the American television milieu. Gabrielle Solis as a new version of the American high-fashion beauty that every man covets, Betty's family as a typical all-American household, George López as just the guy next door with the same difficult in-laws and problems with his kids that everyone has (Markert, 2004-2007), Fez as part of the gang in the late '70s Midwest, even Freddie's Spanish-only grandmother recalling the immigrant roots of other cultural groups in the U.S., they all serve to undermine the distance that difference in language and culture can create. They *are* just like us. All of these portrayals contribute to more positive attitudes toward foreigners in the U.S., specifically Latinos and Hispanic culture.

---

[3] Valderrama was born in Miami but moved to Venezuela when he was three, only returning to the U.S. about ten years later. He claims, "'I didn't even know how to say 'Hi.' When people would ask me something, I had no idea what they were saying, and they would laugh at me. At lunch I'd hide from everybody"' (Jordan, 1999, ¶ 1).

IV. *How I Met Your Mother*

With this in mind, let us now consider the particulars of the speech event I will analyze below. In the second episode of the third season of the CBS primetime hit, *How I Met Your Mother*, called "We're Not From Here" (Harris & Fryman, 2007), principal character Robin returns to New York City with an Argentine boyfriend, Gael. Although Gael speaks accented English (like Fez and George López's father-in-law), it is clearly fluent and free of grammatical errors. In a discourse event between Robin and her native English-speaking friends regarding her relationship with Gael, Barney asserts that her relationship with Gael is temporary and cannot last. Upon Gael's arrival at the bar where this conversation is taking place, everyone assumes Gael will not understand if "big words" are used despite Gael's already demonstrated strong L2 abilities. Aspects of the conversation occurring before Gael's arrival are recapitulated using "big words" to conceal Robin's friends' negative commentary about the relationship between Gael and Robin. This portrayal raises questions about how popular culture represents L2 speakers, their legitimacy and capacities, not only as L2 speakers, but as thoughtful individuals who happen to speak another language before English. By analyzing the discourse event in the context of this particular episode, I will show how it is meant to be satirical. On the other hand, looking at this speech event in terms of the previous discussion of language attitudes research and other television portrayals of L2 English speakers, I will also demonstrate how it can easily be misinterpreted to cast a negative light on L2 speakers, specifically those of Latino origin. Let us begin by analyzing the speech event itself. (A full transcript of the speech event can be found in the Appendix.)

The moments leading up to Lily's suggestion that the group use "big words" to prevent Gael from understanding can be characterized by Barney trying to convince Robin that her relationship with Gael is doomed. He believes that, although she may assert otherwise, she has not changed and will revert to the "unevolved Robin" who will no longer have any need or desire for Gael. Barney says things like, "you haven't changed Scherebatsky" and calls Gael her "soon-to-be ex-boyfriend" saying she'll "dump his ass down the drain like sour milk" (Harris & Fryman, 2007). In this portion of the exchange, Robin defends her experience in Argentina and her relationship with Gael: "I feel like the Robin who left is not the same Robin who came back." She claims to have "evolved" and maintains that she is "enjoying living...life a bit closer to the way [she and Gael] did in Argentina." Barney asks for Ted's affirmation of his assertions—"Back me up here, Ted!"—but Ted, not wanting to get stuck in the middle, demurs repeatedly: "I'm just happy Robin's happy" (Harris & Fryman, 2007).

Even before Gael's appearance in the scene, Barney clearly expresses a negative opinion of him and, particularly, of the effect he has had on altering Robin's lifestyle and attitudes. Robin comes back from her time in Argentina claiming to be more relaxed and laid-back, less concerned with the aspects of her life in New York—which Barney enumerates as drinking scotch, eating red meat, smoking cigars, carrying a gun—that used to preoccupy her. In short, she has renounced those qualities that made her *New York Robin*. Barney goes on to list the new attributes she is presumed to have acquired from Gael while in Argentina: giving massages, wind-surfing, playing the bongos, not drinking, and adopting the positions of a vegan, peacenik hippie. This persona is highly antithetical to Barney who, even before seeing Gael, has already embraced a negative valence toward him. This negative valence prefigures the potential linguistic prejudice of the upcoming episode when Gael arrives at the bar. Barney's dialogue also insinuates a subtle judgment about Argentines, and perhaps by extension all Latinos, as only interested in pleasure, lacking ambition, and potentially not manly enough as evidenced by the comparison to a vegan, peacenik hippie. Thus, before ever appearing in the scene, Gael has already been reduced to a series of negative clichés and stereotypes, albeit in a comic manner.

It is at this point that Gael enters the bar. Lily, noticing his arrival, tells everyone to, "Switch to big words" (Harris & Fryman, 2007). Essentially, the dialogue that follows, which uses "big words," recapitulates the arguments and discussion of the earlier moments of the scene. Barney once more insists that Robin and Gael's break-up is imminent because they are such different people. He claims that Robin will "recognize [her] dearth of compatibility with [her] paramour, and conclude [their] association." Robin continues to defend her transformed self and her relationship with Gael. She calls her journey "transformative" and it "reassert[s] [her] commitment to both [her]...paramour and the philosophies he espouses." Barney calls on Ted to back up what he is saying—"Support my hypothesis, Ted"—but once more, Ted repeats his refrain, in somewhat more elaborate verbiage, "I'm just jubilant my former paramour is jubilant" (Harris & Fryman, 2007).

So, how about these "big words?" A closer reading of the dialogue calls into question the "big words" strategy. Most of the big words employed are Latinate in origin and have clear cognates in Spanish, a Romance language also derived from Latin. The vast majority of these cognates have meanings that correlate almost exactly with their equivalents in English. Table 8-1 below presents a number of equivalencies.

Table 8.1: Comparison of "big words" used in dialogue with Spanish equivalents.

English	Spanish	Meaning
Triad of solar periods	Tríada de períodos solares	Same
Compatibility	Compatibilidad	Same
Conclude	Concluir	Same
Association	Asociación	Same
Transformative	Transformativo	Same
Aforementioned	Ya mencionado	Already mentioned
Philosophies	Filosofías	Same
Espouses (v.)	Esposos/as (n.); esposar (v.)	Spouse (n.); to handcuff (v.)
Masticate	Masticar	Same
Gluteals [sic]	Glúteo	Gluteus (anatomical)
Support	Soportar	To support (different semantic range)
Hypothesis	Hipótesis	Same

As is evident from the table, a great deal of information about the conversation's content is still available to the Spanish-speaking Gael. Most of the "big words" used provide almost exact equivalents in Spanish: triad of solar periods, compatibility, conclude, association, transformative, philosophies, gluteals [*sic*], hypothesis. Others provide near-equivalents. "Aforementioned" clearly highlights the verb "to mention" as in the Spanish *ya mencionado*. "Espouses" has clearly phonological resonance with the Spanish nouns *esposos/esposas* (spouses) and the verb *esposar*, to handcuff, in Spanish. Both of these concepts, marrying a spouse or handcuffing oneself to something have the same metaphorical value as "espouses" does in the dialogue. Finally, for the equivalent of Barney's exhortation that Ted "support" him, there is the verb *soportar* in Spanish. It can have a different semantic value than "support" does in English, similar to that of the verb tolerate or *tolerar*, e.g., *no lo soporto*, 'I can't stand him.' That being said, the verb *soportar* does exist to provide some indication on how to interpret Barney's statement. Moreover, Barney's final statement in the exchange is relatively inconsequential as the truly damaging remarks regarding Robin and Gael's relationship precede it.

Aside from the directly comprehensible elements of the "big words" portion of the conversation, there are, in fact, two other "big words" that Gael could potentially decipher. The words "recognize" and "paramour" should not pose particular difficulties. "Recognize" is derived directly from Latin and although the Spanish version *reconocer* is quite different, if Gael has even rudimentary knowledge of Latin, he may interpret this correctly. "Paramour" on the other hand, should pose little problem as it is composed of elements that exist in Spanish: *para + amor*, for + love.

At this point, one might begin to wonder how effective these big, inscrutable, polysyllabic, Latinate words are at camouflaging the true meaning of the conversation, which I might add is being recapitulated, imprudently and unnecessarily, before the object of its scorn. The only words that are truly of an origin to which Gael would not necessarily have access or that have evolved in English and Spanish so differently as to be unrecognizable are perhaps: dearth, *penuria*; journey, *viaje*; reassert, *reafirmar*; and commitment, *comisión*. In this case, only the beginning of Robin's statement, "My journey was transformative, and I reassert my commitment to both the aforementioned paramour and the philosophies he espouses" (Harris & Fryman, 2007), remains mysterious or obfuscated. Thus, Barney's attacks, the principal material that one would hope to keep from Gael, remain accessible despite the change in register.

It bears mentioning that Gael's one contribution to the exchange is meant to convey his lack of understanding. He queries, "What are we talking of? Baseball?" (Harris & Fryman, 2007), I would like to draw particular attention to his use of the preposition "of" as a way to highlight his status as a non-native speaker. Although empirical, I would venture to bet that most native speakers of English would end this question with the preposition "about"—*What are we talking about?*—instead of "of". This rhetorical strategy employed by the writers serves to accent the already false nature of this exchange and Gael's supposed inability to understand or effectively participate.

Taking all of the above analysis into account, the encrypted conversation does not stand up to true scrutiny. Why, then, do the writers of *How I Met Your Mother* include this exchange? To answer this question, let us consider another major storyline that plays out in parallel to the eventual dissolution of Robin and Gael's relationship: Barney and Ted decide to pretend to be visitors to New York City in order to pick up "genuine" New York women. After noticing that all the women in the bar faun over Gael because of his "slightly mispronounced" words, they decide to adopt Midwestern accents, pretending not to be New Yorkers. Despite Barney's negative characterization of Gael's accent, this storyline could represent an overarching, more positive message: accents are sexy, thus too is foreignness. In this subplot, Barney and Ted do attract two women and follow them through a series of misadventures in New York City, including an uninspired meal at a chain restaurant and a mugging in an unsavory part of town. (Ted expresses concern about going there while in the cab, but Barney quiets him since they are not supposed to know the city at all). In the end, after being mugged, the possibility of imminent "thank God we're alive sex," as Barney puts it, is ruined when the women reveal they are not "genuine" New Yorkers at all, but from New Jersey. Ted refuses to go to New Jersey for sex, an inside joke for those familiar with the rivalries in that part of the country (Harris & Fryman, 2007).

The importance of this storyline lies in its satirizing of what it means to be native, an insider, versus foreign, an outsider. Both Ted and Barney are only pretending to be foreigners, yet despite their secret insider knowledge, they are unable to protect themselves from being mugged. In fact, in trying to play naïve and innocent sheep in wolves' clothing, they cannot admit the danger of venturing to the seamier side of Manhattan for fear of revealing their true identities and ruining their chances of bedding the "true" New Yorkers.

This game of double identities is key to understanding the satirical nature of the earlier conversation with the gang when Gael enters. For all the reasons I enumerated previously, it would seem that the writers of the scene are keenly aware of the false premise they propose at its outset: that Gael will not understand if "big words" are used. Gael, as representative of non-native speakers everywhere, is clearly competent in understanding and speaking English. And given the positive valence that Latinos have garnered lately in the characters of Betty Suarez, Gabrielle Solis, George López, Fez, and Freddie's grandmother, the writers are sending up the ignorance of those Americans who believe that having an accent in English equates to not being able to speak or understand English. Gael is foreign and clearly not a native-speaker of English and yet he can also be an insider in the same way Ted and Barney are insiders yet assume false, "foreign" identities as a ruse. Being from another country/culture or speaking another language does not intrinsically limit one's ability to assimilate a second language or, perhaps, more importantly, a second culture.

Is there not, then, a parallelism here? Having an accent, being a non-native speaker, does not in any way indicate a lack of intelligence or lack of understanding of the world around you. Does having an accent make you less of a person? Clearly not, which I believe is the whole point of this language episode, so overtly meant to problematize identity. Moreover, in light of issues such as the status of immigrants in the U.S., many legal and still others not, some who speak English fluently without accent and some who do not, this episode highlights identity in a complex way, much as the legal status of Ignacio Suarez, Betty's father, did before it was resolved. We are forced to ask, what does it mean to be a native-speaker, and by extension, a native?

The writers may have meant to satirize the unenlightened views of some of the viewing public, but the point of their exploration of language and accents could be easily misinterpreted. One need only consider journalistic and fan reaction to this episode to see some disturbing trends in the understanding of this language episode. Looking at blogged reviews and fan postings on TVGuide.com (Carlson, 2007), ign.com (Krause, 2007), tvoholic.com (Fred, 2007), channelguidemag.com (Mike, 2007), and tvsquad.com (Keller, 2007), all make mention of the scene in question in some way. All but the TVGuide.com blogger make explicit reference to Lily's suggestion that the group use "big words" to conceal their conversation from Gael, although all five sources do cite the scene itself. The ign.com recap says of the switch to big words, "When Gael shows up, Lily tells them to switch to big words. They do and Gael asks if they were talking about baseball. It was hilarious!" (Krause, ¶ 5). The channelguidemag.com review characterizes the "big words" as "outside of [Gael's] limited English vocabulary." According to the recap, "It works . . ." (Mike, ¶ 2). Only two of the blogged reviews question the idea of "big words." Tvoholic.com states, "Switch to big words! I don't know if it works that well in real life, but it was nicely done here" (Fred, ¶ 10). Keller's blogged recap on tvsquad.com poses a more direct question: "Does using big words around foreigners really fool them?" (More Fun, ¶ 1).

Although there is not a wholesale acceptance of this premise and the gesture at interrogation of this notion is present in the fan community, fan reaction, as evidenced by posted comments reacting to these blog reviews, is less nuanced. Several references to the scene in question, found in postings to TVGuide.com and tvsquad.com, merely sing the comic praises of the dialogue. However, on TVGuide.com lilyputty posted the following:

> When everyone started using 'big words' so that Gael wouldn't understand them. I about died. They did it so effortlessly, just as if that is the way they always talked. It was not only hilarious and well done but I liked that it showed that the writers aren't afraid to let the characters be smart. So often 'dumb' is funny, attractive or at least acceptable. I like that these guys are allowed to be smart characters. (Carlson, 2007, Comments Section)

Is there a subtle implication here that Gael, Enrique Iglesias' character, is "dumb" because he does not, cannot understand them? Froggirl on tvsquad.com invites a similar comparison: "The using big words was hilarious. My hubby and I do that in front of our kids sometimes" (Keller 2007, Comments Section). So, not only is Gael dumb, he is a kid. These types of comparisons, however unintended they may be, are troubling. Recall Markert's (2004-2007) words regarding viewers' expectations. First, since Gael is a Latin American who speaks English, Latinos in the U.S. who do not speak English might inspire a negative reaction as viewers will come to expect that

Latinos will speak English. Furthermore, the assumption that people with accents are unintelligent or childlike, intimated in the fan reaction cited above, could result from this scene, as people often take television reality as a proxy for the real world (pp. 155-56).

Further negative interpretations are possible based upon the way Robin and Gael's relationship progresses and eventually ends. Gael attempts to satisfy Robin by maintaining the positive aspects of their time in Argentina. His attitude is relaxed and friendly, as seen in the "big words" dialogue itself. His actions, on the other hand, are contrary to those we would expect from a good boyfriend. For example, he invites a band of Australian tourists to stay at Robin's apartment without her knowledge, in the throes of passion he throws Robin's laptop to the floor damaging it, and he gets food stains on her couch and clothes while trying to feed her—all this in trying to replicate the elements of their vacation romance. The storyline between Robin and Gael develops to show us how they are ultimately incompatible as she reverts to her "unevolved, scotch-swilling, cigar-smoking, red-meat-eating, gun-toting" self. This transformation, rather reformation, culminates in Robin chasing from her apartment the drum-playing, pot-smoking group of Australian tourists that Gael had invited to stay with them, wielding her own handgun. Of course, the effect is comic irony; however, it can be misread. Gael can be perceived as portraying antisocial behavior, albeit in a very nice, non-threatening way. Durkin and Judge (2001) indicate that negative, antisocial behaviors, such as taking advantage of someone's hospitality or damaging her property, can perpetuate negative stereotypes about and attitudes toward a given group. English produced by Argentines (as Gael is supposed to be) is already perceived quite poorly, in the third tier of Lindemann's (2005) study. Thus, this poor behavior on his part does little to redeem him or the group he could be said to represent.

V. Conclusion

All in all, given the writers' choices about the "big words" dialogue in concert with the totality of the episode, it is clear that satire is the desired effect. The satire seems to center more on the notion that vacation romances go awry when extended unduly or when one pretends to be something he or she is not. For example, Robin tries to assume the identity of the woman she was on vacation when she met Gael ("I feel like the Robin who left is not the same Robin who came back"). It is untenable and ultimately cannot be sustained. They are very different people and she cannot deny her true self simply to maintain their relationship. Ted and Barney try to assume the identity of the naïve newcomer to the big city, the stranger in a strange land. In due course, this too proves more trouble than it's worth, resulting in nothing but negative consequences. However, one cannot ignore the way in which this episode, aptly titled "We're Not From Here," calls into question not only identity, but language and accent as proxies for and extensions of that identity. In the context of the electoral season that is and has been upon us since before this episode was written and aired, with the prominence of immigration, especially by Latin Americans, as a hot-button issue, perhaps the writers could have crafted their story with greater care. Although they may not intend it, the reading of negative stereotypes in this linguistic episode and in Gael's later behavior could have the inadvertent effect of reinforcing negative attitudes toward Latinos in the U.S. and undoing some of the positive work characters like Betty, George, and Gaby have done in recent years.

Chapter 9

Subtitling Language Subordination:
Linguistic and Ethnic Stereotyping on TV

I. Introduction

If it's not clear by now, languages other than English abound on American television. The small screen is rife with English speakers using languages such as French, Spanish, and Mandarin, as well as with native speakers of those languages interacting in their native tongues. Sometimes, as we've seen, these foreign languages are subtitled for an American audience—this technique is used in particular to achieve a humorous effect. In other instances, viewers are left to guess at what is being said based on the contextual clues provided on screen. Many times, the use of a language other than English is related to a stereotyped view of a given ethnic or foreign group (cf., Chapter 7, for instance). These occasions are often intended as ethnic humor (Mintz, 1996) as we've already seen. The problem with ethnic humor is that the caricatures portrayed can easily cross the invisible line into racist parody.

In this chapter, I explore how recent uses of Chinese language as well as Asian characters speaking accented English in relatively popular TV shows, specifically *American Dad!* (Fox), *Intelligence* (CBS), and *The Millers* (CBS), serve to enact racist stereotypes.[1] Moreover, I investigate the specific role of language subordination, a process that devalues non-standard language while validating the norms and beliefs of the dominant group (Lippi-Green 2012), with particular attention to the role that subtitles play in this process. In addition, I will make a broader connection to real-world acts of discrimination and racism against Asians and Asian Americans based on language using excerpts from the Report To The National Football League Concerning Issues Of Workplace Conduct At The Miami Dolphins (Wells et al. 2014), which details the harassment of Jonathan Martin and others by players within the Miami Dolphins organization within the last decade.

---

[1] I do discuss other relevant portrayals from additional shows, but the arc of the argument that I am making is very clearly understood in analyzing these three shows.

II. Linguistic Stereotypes on TV

In the fifth episode of the ninth season of the show *American Dad!*, entitled "Kung Pao Turkey" (Richter & Clouden, 2013) the main character and family patriarch Stan is forced to welcome his wife Francine's parents into his home for Thanksgiving. In one of the show's many conceits, including a talking fish and an alien, Francine, a blonde, blue-eyed Anglo woman, was adopted as a child by a Chinese couple, known on the show as Mah Mah and Bah Bah Ling, who speak accented and sometimes broken English. These linguistic differences are on display from the moment of their arrival to celebrate the Thanksgiving holiday. In an early scene, Steve, Stan and Francine's teenage son, answers the door when Mah Mah and Ban Bah ring the bell:

> (9.1)
> [doorbell rings]
> Steve: I got it! [opens door]
> [hands together, bowing slightly, utters greeting in Chinese]
> Bah Bah: Ah, your Chinese gibberish very mediocre. Either really
>   learn language or go broader.[2]
> (Richter & Clouden, 2013)

To begin discussion of this example, I first want to address the character Steve's use of Chinese. I do not speak any variety of Chinese myself, thus I cannot evaluate how poorly or how well the language is used here. On the other hand, I don' t believe that a knowledge of Chinese is necessary to understand what is going on in this example. In fact, I submit that, in some ways, the Chinese is irrelevant to what this interaction conveys. We can see the copula and article deletions in the transcript that give the clear impression of non-native speech. "Your Chinese gibberish very mediocre. Either really learn language or go broader" (Richter & Clouden, 2013). We're missing the "is" in the first sentence and the "the" in the second. Moreover, you'll also notice that their grandson Steve speaks "Chinese gibberish." This can be interpreted in both positive and negative ways. Seth MacFarlane, the creator of *American Dad!* is a well-known satirist. The writer of this episode, in keeping with that ethos, can be viewed to be lampooning the use of fake accents in television. This would be a positive reading, in which MacFarlane is

---

[2] For languages other than English, the English subtitles have been added when provided onscreen. When no English subtitles were present, speech in a language other than English that is not subtitled has been added by the author whenever possible.

critiquing reductive, if not racist, portrayals of ethnic characters. On the other hand, the use of the word gibberish as equated with Chinese language leaves something to be desired. It smacks of linguicism, or linguistic discrimination. It is also reminiscent of Hill's (1998) "Mock Spanish," which conveys "negative and racializing messages" by which "the linguistic behavior of historically Spanish-speaking populations is highly visible and the object of constant monitoring" (p. 684). According to Hill, this places value on whiteness. There is too much room for some segments of the audience to miss the critique and only find humor in the surface correlation of Chinese as gibberish, further elevating whiteness at the expense of other cultures/ethnicities.[3]

In a subsequent scene, the character of Hayley, Stan and Francine's daughter, is lamenting the loss of her boyfriend when her grandmother enters:

(9.2)

Mah Mah:	Hello, Granddaughter. We share room tonight. Aw, you look sad. What's wrong? Greasy face got you down?
Hayley:	No, I-I'm sad because this is the first Thanksgiving I've spent without Jeff.
Mah Mah:	Let me tell you what my mom tell me when I was your age: "Man you love die in space so you marry Bah Bah now." We need find you new man.
Hayley:	Thanks, Mah Mah, but I'm just not over Jeff.
Mah Mah:	That's because you still surrounded by him. Reminders everywhere. You need to get rid of his stuff.
Hayley:	Hey, that was mine!

---

[3] In one of Seth MacFarlane's other TV shows *Family Guy*, the episode "Tiegs for Two" (Viener & Langford, 2011) depicts a "Chinese" dry cleaner named Mr. Washee Washee, who speaks in the same stereotypically "broken" L2 English accent as Mah Mah. In a scene in which he and main character Peter Griffin are arguing over a shirt, Peter adopts Mr. Washee Washee's L2 English, appropriating his speech in what Bourdieu (1991) has termed a "strategy of condescension." The goal of such an action is to mock and eventually silence the non-standard speaker, what Foucault (1984) calls "disciplining of discourse" (cf. Chapter 12 for more on these ideas). In a later scene in which Peter is forced by his wife Lois to invite Mr. Washee Washee to his house for dinner to apologize, Mr. Washee Washee gets upset and bans the Griffin family from his dry cleaning establishment. As he storms out the door, he says, "Bing bong," a reference to an ethnic slur that makes fun of the way Asian languages sound, "Ching chong bing bong." This is clearly racist. For more on this slur, please see Lippi-Green (2012), pp. 292-297.

Mah Mah: Sorry. Here. Use my pipe till I replace. It work good,
                  make you cough a lot.
(Richter & Clouden, 2013)

This scene emphasizes once more the English being portrayed by the characters of Mah Mah and Bah Bah. Again, we have verb-tense errors and missing articles in dialogue such as, "We share a room tonight," ("we share" instead of we**'re** sharing), "you still surrounded," (instead of you**'re** still surrounded), "It work," (instead of it work**s**), and "What my mom tell me," ("tell" instead of **told**), and finally, "We need find you new man" ("find" instead of **to** find; "new man" instead of **a** new man).

As the story evolves, Stan expresses a range of ethnic stereotypes about his in-laws and their culture. What is most disturbing about the next scenes that I'll discuss concerns Stan's mistaken conflation of Chinese and Japanese peoples and cultures into a sort of pan-Asian hodgepodge.[4] In the first scene, Stan enters the kitchen sporting what appear to be briefs-style underwear in the colors of the NFL team associated with Washington, D.C., where the show is set. After complaining about the food to his wife, she suggests that he put on pants. In response, he asserts that his in-laws' "people" (or "you people" as he says) wear karate outfits as their default garb.

(9.3)
Stan: Francine, what the hell's goin' on in here? It should
                  smell like turkey and stuffing, not a medley of
                  longevity-inducing vegetables.
Francine: Stan, this is my mom's famous stir-fry. I thought we
                  could have it instead of sweet potatoes.
Stan: But that's not Thanksgiving! I don't want to see this
                  tiny corn! I don't want to see your tiny corn!
Francine: Put on some pants!
Stan: I'm not changing the way I dress on this most American
                  of days. This is traditional American Thanksgiving garb.
                  You know how you guys always wear karate outfits?
                  Well, this is Uncle Sam's version of that.

---

[4] Similar pan-Asian tropes can be seen in the *Family Guy* episode, "Tiegs for Two" (Viener & Langford, 2011). Mr. Washee Washee and Peter have a video game fight à la *Mortal Kombat*, in which a rising sun motif, more closely associated with Japan than with Mr. Washee Washee's supposedly native China, is prominent in the background.

Francine: Stan, just go watch some football. I'll call you when
               dinner's ready.
(Richter & Clouden, 2013)

In a later scene, he again mixes up Japan and China, dressing as Godzilla to
scare his in-laws away.

(9.4)
Stan: Now, we got to get these stupid idiots out of our house!
Klaus: I see. And how do you plan to do that?
Stan: Why, exploit their fears, of course. And throughout
               time, what has consistently been the Chinese people's
               greatest enemy?
Stan: [Enters dining room where Mah Mah and Bah Bah are
               setting the table dressed as Godzilla] Roar! [Walks up
               on table; inadvertently sets costumer on fire]
Mah Mah: [Putting out fire with water from vase] Godzilla Japanese.
(Richter & Clouden, 2013)

I would submit that this scene is meant to satirize of a segment of the
population in the U.S. who view Asians and Asian-Americans as all the
same, a monolith, but the danger here lies in the interpretation of the
humor.[5] Some viewers may simply stop at a surface reading of Stan dressing
as Godzilla to scare his Asian in-laws and not pick up on the deeper critique
of ethnic stereotypes, much like the Chinese gibberish joke that occurs
earlier in the episode.

Perhaps the most disturbing of the stereotypes expressed in this episode is
that of the Yellow Peril or yellow devil. According to Lippi-Green (2012), "The
construction of Asians as the 'Yellow Peril' [is] an image which arose in the
mid- to late nineteenth-century xenophobia and racism, in response to
increasing numbers of Asian immigrants" (p. 289). The Yellow Peril/yellow
devil stereotype found reinforcement in the twentieth century with the
bombing of Pearl Harbor during World War II. Not only were Asians "invading"
American shores like in the nineteenth century, they were underhanded and
untrustworthy. Asians "have a tendency to use natural wiles and treachery to

---

[5] Returning to the "Tiegs for Two" (2011) episode of *Family Guy*, there is an odd moment
of reverse ethnic humor in which Mr. Washee Washee tells Peter that all Americans look
alike. Peter replies, "look who's talking" (2011).

achieve their own ends. [...] Thus a prominent Asian stereotype is of an intelligent, clever, but crafty and unreliable person" (Lippi-Green, 2012, p. 287). In a later scene in the episode, Mah Mah is determined to set Hayley up with a new boyfriend from the Internet, Big Wang Bai, but has second thoughts about her plan.

(9.5)

Mah Mah:	Wait. What am I thinking? Big Wang Bai too good for Hayley. But not too good for Mah Mah.
Hayley:	I guess it wouldn't hurt to contact him.
Mah Mah:	No, no, no. No, he no right for you.
Hayley:	But I thought
Mah Mah:	He taken!
Hayley:	But it says here he's single.
[Mah Mah pulls a gong from out of nowhere and strikes it]	
Hayley:	What was that for?
Mah Mah:	Haven't you ever seen The Gong Show? You lose! Get out!
Hayley:	But it's my room.

(Richter & Clouden, 2013)

Here we see this duplicitous stereotype enacted. Mah Mah decides that Big Wang Bai is "too good" for Hayley. Mah Mah must have him for herself, putting her interests ahead of those of even her own granddaughter. Adding to the stereotypical sensibility of the scene is the use of the gong to cut off Hayley's objections. Conveniently the 70s talent show *The Gong Show* is mentioned, but it seems unlikely that that television program is the inspiration for the inclusion of this instrument associated with Asian cultures.

Recall that Mintz (1996) defines ethnic humor as "the construction of caricatures based on familiar ethnic stereotypes and linguistic humor—puns, malapropisms, double entendres, and accent play, including broad exaggeration and misunderstandings, which result from faulty pronunciation" (p. 20). That is certainly part of what's being portrayed in this *American Dad* episode, particularly because there are subplots related to Thanksgiving and Native American/Anglo relations at the time of the first Thanksgiving. But, more is happening as well. The infusion of stereotypical symbols of Asian cultures, like the gong, karate, and Godzilla, while satirizing the conflation of all Asian cultures also does some work reinforcing the belief that all Asians are the same. At the outset of this chapter, I made the point that these caricatures become problematic when they cross the line into racist parody. That's exactly what happens, especially in the last scene in which Mah Mah enacts the treacherous stereotype of the untrustworthy "yellow devil," reminiscent of Hanoi Hannah, infamous for broadcasting anti-American war propaganda during the Vietnam War. This is no longer humor, but rather trades on a vicious and pervasive stereotype.

Moving on from this discussion of *American Dad!*, I'd like to discuss two contrasting examples in which subtitles play a role in reinforcing stereotypes about Asians and Asian Americans on television. The first example, aired in December 2013, comes from the first season of the CBS sitcom *The Millers*. In the episode, entitled "Carol's Parents Are Coming to Town" (Bowman & Burrows, 2013), the family in the show puts on a front for the matriarch's parents, pretending that they are the picture of family harmony and bliss. Essentially, they make pretend that no one has gotten divorced, when in reality two members of the family have done so, by inviting their exes to spend Christmas with them. This leads Nathan, the protagonist, to call his best friend Ray, who is spending Christmas gambling in Atlantic City, playing Pai Gow, a Chinese betting game using dominoes. Nathan reaches Ray at the Pai Gow table to express his concerns that he may be feeling "Christmas Horny."

(9.6)

Ray:	Ni hao, Nate! I'm up $38,000! Whoop, I'm even.
Nathan:	Look, Ray, I am in big trouble here, man. Janice is here, in the house. My mom invited her.
Ray:	Janice is spending Christmas with you? I'm gone 12 hours! How did this happen?
Nathan:	Look, long insane story short, my mom is making Janice and me pretend that we're still married in front of my grandparents. And she looks good, man. The only way to stop myself from getting aroused is to look at my grandma, and that's weird. I'm scared, Ray. I'm scared that I'm Christmas horny.
Ray:	Damn it, Nate! [Turning to other Pai Gow players at the table and speaking Chinese rendered in English subtitles:] Give me a minute. My friend is Christmas Horny.
Pai Gow Players:	[In Chinese, rendered in English subtitles:] Oh no. Christmas Horny. Most dangerous horny.
Nathan:	I know, I know, I know. Look, I need help, man. I am losing control! I mean, my mind is going places. I mean, maybe I'm more than Christmas horny.

(Bowman & Burrows, 2013)

As you notice, Nate's friend Ray turns to the other Pai Gow competitors to ask for a momentary break in the game, speaking Chinese. As I mentioned earlier, I don't speak Chinese myself so I cannot say whether this is Mandarin or Cantonese, but for the purposes of my analysis, this distinction is irrelevant. Also irrelevant is how well the character of Ray speaks Chinese, given that a large swath of the American audience watching the show will not understand any variety of Chinese. What is of interest, however, is the subtitling of this exchange. You'll notice that Ray's Chinese is subtitled in perfect English, full sentences, no grammatical errors. The reactions by his Chinese-speaking competitors are subtitled as brief exclamations, "Oh, no. Christmas horny. Most dangerous horny" (Bowman & Burrows, 2013). This type of subtitling makes it seem as if, although speaking their native language, these characters still speak a broken language, where verbs apparently don't exist. Especially egregious is the last phrase, "most dangerous horny," which renders these native speakers not only unable to form a sentence in their own language but unable to do so in English as well. It subtly does double duty, undercutting the language abilities of these characters in a way that I would submit is wholly racist.

Interestingly, non-Asian characters have been portrayed on other shows speaking Chinese and other Asian languages well. On *Brooklyn Nine-Nine's* "Kicks" episode (Guest & Appel, 2017), Sgt. Teri Jefferts, who is African American, shares the story of how his girlfriend cheated on him during his year abroad in Japan. He speaks Japanese in a scene early in the episode and at two more points as the episode unfolds. When he is subtitled, the subtitles are rendered in grammatical standard English. In the *A.P. Bio* episode, "Overachieving Virgins" (Blickstead et al., 2018), an African American student running for Student Council President speaks Chinese to make promises to Asian students in order to win their votes. The one sentence he utters is rendered in perfectly grammatical English subtitles. Similarly, in "Grandma Dearest" from the series *Champions* (Geary et al., 2018), the Anglo character Matthew speaks Chinese in two scenes with his mother's Asian-American companion. Once more, in both scenes, his Chinese is rendered in error-free standard English. On *The Big Bang Theory's* "The Matrimonial Metric" (Ferrari et al., 2018), Howard Wolowitz, while having take-out Chinese with friends, calls the restaurant to get fried rice when their order does not include it. His Chinese is again subtitled in perfect American English, leading the viewer to believe that he speaks Chinese flawlessly.

In contrast to the episode of *The Millers* above, let's consider at a brief scene from another CBS show, the drama *Intelligence*, from the January 2014 episode "Mei Chen Returns" (Shimosawa & Williams), only several weeks after the airing of this episode of *The Millers*. Here an Anglo female character, Kate

Anderson, is seen running up to the gates of the Chinese embassy in London, seeking asylum. She bangs on the gates and, after expressing her fear in English saying "Help me!" three times in desperate succession, she engages the guard in Chinese. I reproduce the brief subtitled conversation below:

(9.7)
Kate: Call the Ambassador.
Guard: It's two o'clock in the morning.
Kate: Tell him Kate Anderson is here. [In English:] Please.
             [Guard walks off and begins an unintelligible
             conversation on walkie talkie]
(Shimosawa & Williams, 2014)

Now, Kate Anderson does not say much, however, what she does say is rendered in the subtitles in perfect English, leading us to believe that she has perfect command of Chinese. Again, the true evaluation of her Chinese abilities is irrelevant to the argument I am making. The illusion of an Anglo woman who speaks and understands Chinese perfectly is what is of interest. This is similar to the illusion of Ray, an African-American man who can speak perfect Chinese in *The Millers*. Coupled together, aired mere weeks apart, these images contrast to the representation of the Chinese speakers at the Pai Gow table with Ray, whose own language comes out as verb-less and broken when subtitled in English. Clearly Asian characters are getting short shrift, when it comes to being treated as speakers of fully formed and fully grammatical languages. I will say, however, to the credit of *Intelligence*, the guard at the embassy gate is subtitled in English in a manner consistent with the way the Anglo woman is—his Chinese is not portrayed as broken.[6]

So, why the "broken" English in the subtitles for *The Millers*? I would venture to guess that this is an attempt at ethnic humor, a type of caricature. Similar to the way *American Dad!* tries to use caricature and stereotypes as a way to create humor, this broken English is meant to elicit a laugh. But, just as in

---

[6] In the pilot episode of the medical drama, "Monday Mornings" (Kelley & D'Elia, 2013), after performing a complex procedure, Korean doctor Sung Park is taken to task by the hospital's Chief of Staff for misusing an English metaphor, saying, "...between rock and eight ball," instead of the correct, "between a rock and a hard place." He also asks the Chief of Staff if he means to "insinuate" instead of "insult" him. Based on these relatively minor errors—it is clear from the rest of the episode that Dr. Park is able to communicate quite effectively in English—the Chief of Staff essentially tells Dr. Park to come to his office the next morning to discuss his "language skills."

American Dad!, the laugh comes at the expense of the Asian characters, with nothing redeeming the episode with respect to the Asian characters. At least with *American Dad!*, an argument could be made that MacFarlane and company are trying to satirize racist beliefs, but with *The Millers*, no such argument can be made.

We cannot discuss the issue of racism and potential satirizing of racist beliefs without discussing two additional examples. First, let us consider *The Mick* episode entitled "The Dump" (Chinn & Sohn, 2018). In this episode, Aunt Mickey and housekeeper Alba chaperone Mickey's newphew Ben's school field trip to a trash dump. They find an unknown boy on the school bus when they return from the field trip. Mickey doesn't want to tell the school because she doesn't want to get in trouble. She decides that she and Alba should just take the boy back to the dump themselves, but the police are at the dump as they arrive. They decide to drive past, again fearing they will get in trouble.

Instead, they bring the child, who Mickey wants to call "Dump", home with them while they figure out how to return him, unintentionally kidnapping the child. Eventually, they decide to call 911 from a payphone to reach the detectives looking for the boy at the dump. Mickey makes Alba make the first phone call. Alba, a character originally from Guatemala who speaks English with an L2 accent normally, disguises her voice by faking a different accent. In the scene, Alba says things like, "Yo, yo, you jive-ass turkey. What's the skinny on the po-po down at the dump?" and "Shut your mouth, bacon, before I fry your greasy ass" (Chinn & Sohn, 2018). Mickey finds the accent offensive:

> (9.8)
> Mickey: What are you doing?
> Alba: [NORMAL ACCENT] I disguise my voice to protect my
>   identity.
> Mickey: Yeah. Yeah, I got that part. Did you have to be so racist? Is
>   that how you think black people talk?
> Alba: [NORMAL ACCENT] No! Who said anything about
>   talking like a black person? That was a cool white lady.
>   Oh, no, you're a racist for thinking that was a black voice.
> (Chinn & Sohn, 2018)

Mickey believes Alba is being racist by adopting an African-American English accent. In reaction, Alba accuses Mickey of being racist, questioning Mickey's assumption that she is trying to represent a Black person. This interaction is important because it sets up a later phone call to the police that Mickey makes, in which she also disguises her voice using an accent.

Before that call, however, Mickey tries to talk to the child, not knowing that he is hearing impaired. Because of his hearing difficulties, he does not respond. It is at this point that Mickey calls from a new payphone, choosing to use an Asian accent. Here is a redacted excerpt of the scene:

(9.9)

Operator:	911 emergency.
Mickey:	[Fake accent] Uh, yah, I kidnap-a from a sanitation center. I demand speak with most honorable policeman. [Alba tries to get Mickey's attention] [To Alba] Shh.
Hurley:	This is Detective Hurley. Who am I talking to?
Mickey:	[Fake accent] Oh, you talk to yourself, you don't shut your mouth. You listen to me. I have boy you seek.
Hurley:	Is the child unharmed?
Mickey:	[Fake accent] Yes, child fine!
Hurley:	Look, the boy is hearing-impaired, and his parents are very worried.

[Later in the conversation]

Mickey:	[Fake accent] Oh, sorry, no, no, no. I-- I have demand. Big demand. I-I ask one million American dollar. Uh, Greenwich Park one hour. *Arigato.* [Hangs up]
Alba:	Wha-- Ah, Mickey, that was very offensive.
Mickey:	Wh-What are you talking about? That's what you did. I picked an accent and disguised my voice.
Alba:	An Asian accent?
Mickey:	Oh! Oh, you. Oh, Alba, who's racist now, huh? You thought that was Asian? Mm-hmm.
Alba:	You said "*arigato.*"
Mickey:	Yeah, I mean, for authenticity. And with the utmost respect. There is no one more ancient or mystic than the Chinese.
Alba:	"*Arigato*" is Japanese.
Mickey:	Okay [Stammers] uh, how do you say "good-bye" in Chinese? "*Chow.*"
Alba:	And that is Italian.
Mickey:	Okay, I'm sorry, all right? I'm, I don't know, I'm doing my best here. Okay? I'm sorry. I'm uneducated and I'm ignorant. Excuse me if nobody bothered to teach me stuff. You know this is your fault.
Alba:	What? Ooh.

(Chinn & Sohn, 2018)

In this scene, we notice that Mickey uses the same grammatical features that are used in the episode of *American Dad!* to fake the Asian accent. There are missing articles, prepositions, and copula verbs, for instance. In addition, she adds final vowels to some words (kidnap-a) and some stereotypical honorifics (most honorable policeman). This time, it is Alba who is offended, "Mickey, that was very offensive." Mickey tries to do what Alba did to her earlier, "What are you talking about? That's what you did. I picked an accent and disguised my voice… Oh, Alba, who's racist now, huh? You thought that was Asian?" (Chinn & Sohn, 2018). But Alba points out that Mickey used "*arigato*," which is clearly Japanese, although Mickey does not know this. Here, as in *American Dad!*, we have the conflation of Japanese and Chinese languages. In the end, Mickey simply has to apologize, "I'm sorry. I'm uneducated and I'm ignorant. Excuse me if nobody bothered to teach me stuff." (Chinn & Sohn, 2018).

Why can Alba get away with using what is clearly meant to be an African-American Vernacular English accent but Mickey cannot get away with an Asian one? Perhaps it has to do with Alba being Latinx, while Mickey is white, a member of the majority, privileged race in the U.S., one that has systematically oppressed other races throughout the history of the country. But is the juxtaposition of these two phone calls using two different accents satire? I think it is meant to be. There is an explicit discussion of race at both moments. In the first incident, Alba points out that Mickey's assumption that Alba is using an African-American accent could be built on a false premise. To viewers, it's clear that Alba is representing an African-American accent, but the question to Mickey, and by extension to viewers, calls into question our own assumptions about accent and race. In the second instance, Mickey proffers an explicit apology at the end of the scene in which she uses the Asian accent. This apology seems to recognize that enacting the stereotypical Asian accent that she adopts is inherently racist. The interplay that leads to Mickey's apology comes across as an explicit warning to others who would voice a similar Asian accent—the scene makes it very clear that using a stereotypical Asian accent trades on racial tropes and is wrong. The first scene with Alba using an accent primes the audience to receive this warning against the use of an Asian accent even more powerfully. And, compared to the satirical message in *American Dad!*, which could be misinterpreted, there is no misinterpretation possible in this case.

At the end of the episode, Mickey and Alba leave Dump at the dump. Police find him with a note pinned to his chest. The camera gives the audience a close-up shot of the note. It reads: "We never meant to take the kid. Also, didn't mean to be racist. Next time we'll be more sensitive, but there won't be a next time." (Chinn & Sohn, 2018). The point here is made very clearly. There will be no next time for racist behavior.

Before moving on to some real-world examples of racism against Asians and Asian Americans, let us consider the *Speechless* episode, "S-E—SEOUL B-R— BROTHERS" (Chun & Purple, 2019). In this episode, for reasons not germane to this analysis, patriarch Jimmy begins playing in a Korean wedding band called Seoul Brothers. The band's leader Yoon-Taek is portrayed as a task master. Jimmy is supposed to get $25 a gig plus dinner as payment. However, when Jimmy tries to get dinner during a break in the band's set, Yoon-Taek tells him, "No meat! You messed up the last song" (Chun & Purple, 2019). Later, Jimmy tells his friend Kenneth, "Now I got to go. We're back on soon. And, uh yeah, that signal from Yoon-Taek means I have to go smoke a cigarette while he watches" (Chun & Purple, 2019). Yoon-Taek is depicted as a somewhat sadistic boss, depriving Jimmy of meat after one mistake and forcing Jimmy to smoke while he watches. Why must the Korean character be presented in this negative way? It speaks, once again, to the way Asian characters are treated on television. Yes, there are some aspects of humor in what occurs between Jimmy and his bandleader, but it seems to paint Koreans in a bad light overall.

At the end of the episode, Jimmy and wife Maya "borrow" the band's instruments while they are on a break and sing "I Got You Babe" (1965). Of course, they sing in Korean. Although there are no subtitles, this song is another instance of Anglo characters being depicted as easily able to speak an Asian language. Ultimately, however, in the last moment of the show, when they are discovered by Yoon-Taek (and, unsurprisingly, he yells at them further cementing his negative image), Jimmy says one line in Korean that is subtitled in English. The subtitling reads, "Don't forget to tip your cactus!" (Chun & Purple, 2019). So, maybe he is not as proficient as we were led to believe, but it is still interesting to see that the Anglo characters are loveable and speak Korean, while the Korean character, although he speaks English well, is a mean, sadistic jerk.

In contrast, a more positive portrayal of the Korean community and use of Korean can be found in the season three episode of *This is Us*, "Kamsahamnida" (Herbert & Fortenberry, 2018).[7] In this episode, one of the "big three" main characters, Randall, is running for a city council seat in a Philadelphia neighborhood that is divided between large Black and immigrant Korean/Korean-American populations. At a voter registration event at an outdoor market in the predominantly Korean area, Randall is approached by a young Korean-American man, who accuses Randall of only

---

[7] Interestingly on Amazon Prime Video the title of this episode, the sixth of the third season, has been changed to "Gold Star".

being in their neighborhood because, despite Randall being African-American himself, his African-American competitor has a lock on the Black vote in the divided district. As the man walks away, Randall follows him and admits that he knows very little about the plight of neighborhood residents, but states that he is willing to listen. By this time, the young Korean-American man is standing near his sister and elderly mother or grandmother. His sister begins translating what Randall is saying into Korean. Randall continues speaking and the young woman continues translating, as others in the crowd begin to approach, listening to Randall's impromptu speech.

There are no subtitles in this scene—they don't seem necessary since the conceit is that Randall's speech is the English equivalent of what is being said in Korean. Nonetheless, we are left to assume what Randall is saying is rendered into an appropriate Korean equivalent. At the end of the interaction, Randall tells the gathered crowd, "I, uh, I only know one word in Korean so far. My brother taught it to me. *Kamsahamnida.* Did I say that right?" (Herbert & Fortenberry, 2018). Here, the Korean community is portrayed as diverse (young and old), vibrant, and interested in finding a good representative for themselves. A much more positive depiction than what *Speechless* shows us. Also, Randall demonstrates his own naïveté speaking Korean. He makes it clear that Korean is not a language he knows, indicating that he may have mispronounced the one word he has learned thus far. The young Korean-American man that begins this interaction with Randall eventually ends up becoming his campaign manager.

III. Stereotypes and Discrimination in the Real World

Let's turn, if we might, to a real-world example of discrimination and racism toward Asians in the U.S. In 2014, an independent commission investigated acts of discrimination and racism against Asians and Asian Americans in the National Football League. The firm Paul, Weiss, Rifkind, Wharton & Garrison LLP produced the Report To The National Football League Concerning Issues Of Workplace Conduct At The Miami Dolphins (Wells et al. 2014), which details the harassment of Jonathan Martin and others by players within the Miami Dolphins organization. In this document, there are also incidents of racist behavior toward an Assistant Trainer who was born in Japan. These incidents were based on his race and his use of English. Here is a brief excerpt:

> We found that the Assistant Trainer, who was born in Japan, was the target of frequent and persistent harassment, including insults relating to his race and national origin. [Richie] Incognito, [John] Jerry and [Mike] Pouncey [three Miami Dolphins players] admitted that they directed racially derogatory words toward him, including "Jap" and "Chinaman."

At times, according to [Johnathan] Martin, they referred to the Assistant Trainer as a "dirty communist" or a "North Korean," made demands such as "give me some water you fucking chink," spoke to him in a phony, mocking Asian accent, including asking for "rubby rubby sucky sucky," and called his mother a "rub and tug masseuse." [...]

On December 7, 2012, the anniversary of the Japanese attack on Pearl Harbor, Incognito, Jerry and Pouncey donned traditional Japanese headbands that featured a rising sun emblem (which the Assistant Trainer had given them) and jokingly threatened to harm the Assistant Trainer physically in retaliation for the Pearl Harbor attack. According to Martin, the Assistant Trainer confided in him that he was upset about the Pearl Harbor comments, finding them derogatory toward his heritage.

Wells et al., 2014, p. 22

Clearly, racist attitudes and beliefs persist in the U.S. Making fun of language, i.e., linguicism, is one way to enact these beliefs, by mocking accents as the football players do to the assistant trainer. Moreover, the wounds of Pearl Harbor surface in this excerpt as well, and are used to justify racist threats of violence. Because of the undercurrent of racism against Asians and Asian Americans, stereotypical television representations, such as in *American Dad!* and *The Millers,* are quite troubling. But also, representations of Anglos and other races capable of speaking Chinese perfectly add to this denigration of Asians and Asian Americans. We can speak their language perfectly, but they simply can't speak ours well. These are classic tactics in the process of language subordination.

Language subordination is a process by which "dominant bloc institutions ... convince whole groups of human beings that they do not fully or adequately possess an appropriate human language" (Lippi-Green, 2012, p. 68). Several tactics are employed, such as language mystification, the claiming of authority, and trivialization of targeted languages to a name a few, by, for instance, educational institutions, judicial and legislative bodies, and mass media to get all speakers to conform to the expectations of the dominant group and a Standard Language Ideology, which asserts "a bias toward an abstracted, idealized, homogeneous spoken language" imposed and maintained by these institutions (Lippi-Green, 2012, p. 67).

Clearly, Asians and Asian Americans are targeted by the representations in these episodes. The characters are depicted as less than their Anglo and African American counterparts. These representations can have pernicious repercussions in real life as evidenced by the football players' actions toward a member of their own training staff. In professional football, where players on the field are only one piece of the organization that supports them, one might expect that such negative attitudes and beliefs as were enumerated in the report would be sublimated for the good of the team and its success, however that was not the case. Depictions such as those cited above can exacerbate racist attitudes and beliefs.

IV. Conclusion

To end this chapter, I would like to mention one more news event from 2014 that seems relevant to this discussion. Leland Yee, a Chinese-born state senator in California representing San Francisco who came to the U.S. as a youngster, went to high school in the U.S. and earned his Ph.D., was under indictment by the FBI for being an alleged mobster. In February 2016, Yee was sentenced to five years in prison after pleading guilty in 2015, as reported in the Los Angeles Times (Dolan & McGreevy, 2016).

The result of the Yee case is less interesting than the reaction in the Chinese American community in San Francisco, which tells us a great deal about the sensitivity of such issues. Sue Lee, executive director of the Chinese Historical Society of America of San Francisco's Chinatown, interviewed by NPR's Richard Gonzales for *Morning Edition* on April 8, 2014, commented about the scandal, "I was shocked. Said, oh my God. It's not a good reflection on our community" (Gonzales, 2014). In his piece, Gonzales points out that it is only in recent decades that the Chinese community in San Francisco has succeeded in exercising political power. Lee highlights that, in early 2014 at the time of the interview, there was a Chinese mayor as well as several Chinese members of the board of supervisors. Lee goes on, "You know, that's never happened before and that's something that is a source of pride for Asian-Americans. So, to have an elected official arrested is harmful" (Gonzales, 2014). The piece continues:

Lee:	Today, Chinatown is still important culturally but more and more people have fewer and fewer connection[s] to the cultural institutions that are there.
Gonzales:	But the scandal, a tale of crime and corruption, fits neatly into a caricature of Chinatown, says Sue Lee of the Chinese Historical Society, as if the neighborhood were still full of gambling houses, opium dens, and brothels.

Lee: You know, makes it sound we're from another world,
                  we're exotic, we're foreign, we're not of this world. And
                  it just serves to, you know, nurture this misperception
                  of Chinatown and Chinese.
(Gonzales, 2014)

Lee's comments about Chinese people sounding as if they are exotic, foreign, *not of this world* are the types of stereotypical beliefs that give us reason for pause. It is exactly this type of dangerous attitude that pervades the American consciousness and leads to the stereotypical portrayals of Asians as other and not truly American (cf. Wu, 2002). To conclude on a positive note, *mittendrin*, an online commenter posted the following reaction to *Morning Edition* story:

At the end of this piece, Sue Lee suggested that this incident might cause people to see Chinese people as "other". I think it might show just the opposite. Humans, no matter what race or culture they're from, can be corrupt (or corrupted), especially when power and money are involved. (Gonzalez, 2014)

It is heartening to think that we might be able to look past long-held ethnic stereotypes to see all people as simply *human.*

Part IV:
Language Attitudes
& Mediation

Chapter 10

From *SNL* to Nashville: Attitudes Toward Learning Spanish in American Pop Culture

I. Introduction

When I first started working on the research that has become this chapter, while driving home one evening in my own community of Warwick, Rhode Island, I came across a pick-up truck with two huge banners spanning the back window of the cab. The upper banner read, in all capital letters, "WELCOME TO AMERICA." The lower banner exhorted, also in all caps, "NOW SPEAK ENGLISH." It's been a number of years since I sighted that pick-up. At the time, President Obama had just taken office and reactionary forces were expressing their resistance, even in what is often perceived as the liberal Northeastern U.S. In the years that followed, although no definitive immigration legislation was passed, President Obama took action by creating the Deferred Action for Childhood Arrivals or DACA Program to regularize the status of undocumented children brought to the U.S. by their parents for renewable periods of two years at a time. With the Trump administration in power since 2017, DACA has been threatened, and attitudes around the U.S. seem far more in tune with the banners I saw a decade ago. I mention the political mood of the country as these forces often provide context for and shape people's views on those who speak languages other than English, or even those with L2 English accents.

Television reflects some of the ways that undocumented immigrants and their families are treated. TV shows us not only recent news broadcasts about detention camps on the Southern border holding children and adult immigrants caught entering the U.S. illegally, but dramatizes what can happen even to those immigrant families well integrated into American society. The *Murphy Brown* episode "Thanksgiving and Taking" (Woody & Lembeck, 2018) explores these issues as the character Miguel, a DACA recipient, deals with Immigration and Customs Enforcement (ICE) deporting his family. In a compelling scene, Murphy Brown and her friends attempt to stop the ICE agents from taking Miguel's parents Maria and Carlos, but they cannot. As his parents are ripped from Miguel's grasp, Murphy's son Avery, also a reporter asks a friend to film as he provides voiceover.

(10.1)

Avery:	[Being filmed] [Miguel's parents being removed in the background] It's Thanksgiving Day here in America. ICE agents, with no paperwork, have shown up to arrest an undocumented couple who have lived in this country for 20 years. They have contributed to their community, and they have no criminal record. They pay their taxes, and they are raising a son who will one day become a lawyer.
Murphy:	You don't have to put handcuffs on them, for God's sakes.
Miguel:	What did they do except give up everything so I could grow up in a country that we thought was the most compassionate place in the world?
Agent:	Sorry, kid. We're just following government orders.[1]

(Woody & Lembeck, 2018)

In the next moment, Miguel's parents say their final goodbye:

Maria:	[Speaking to ICE agents] Can we have a moment with our son?
Carlos:	Miguel…Miguel. We always knew this day might come. We've put some money aside for you.
Miguel:	No. No. I'm going to do something, okay? We have to do something. This can't happen.
Maria:	This is why you need to finish school and become a lawyer.
Phyllis:	**Lo siento. No te preocupo**. I will see to it that **él va etudiar mucho**[2] et-et He will always have a roof over his head - as long as I'm around.
Carlos:	Gracias.

(Woody & Lembeck, 2018)

Phyllis (played by Tyne Daly) makes the effort to speak Spanish as best she can to show solidarity with Carlos and Maria and to reassure them that Miguel will be taken care of in their absence.

---

[1] For languages other than English, the English subtitles have been added when provided onscreen. When no English subtitles were present, speech in a language other than English that is not subtitled has been added by the author whenever possible.
[2] I'm sorry. Don't worry. [I will see to it that] he will study a lot.

With these ideas in mind, let us consider language learning in the U.S. Popular attitudes toward the learning of foreign languages are ever-evolving in the United States. From the earliest immigrants, there have been mixed feelings about maintaining native languages as well as the importance of learning to speak English and only English as immigrant parents fought hard for the assimilation of their children. Today, we are at another moment of reflection as the Anglo-American population contemplates its coming minority status in the face of a growing Latinx population. To exemplify these differing views, I will examine two contemporaneous incidents in our popular culture that reflect the range of reactions toward this realization. Those with a positive valence toward this changing demographic embrace the difference while those who fear this change become protectionist and xenophobic.

In this chapter, I will explore these competing reactions in our popular culture. The *Saturday Night Live* (*SNL*) skit "La Policía Mexicana" (Michaels, 2009) aired within days of a citywide referendum on an English-only law in the city of Nashville, Tennessee in January 2009. *SNL*'s humorous sketch presents two detectives interrogating a suspect. It is presented entirely in Spanish. It underscores the importance of knowing Spanish and presents contextualized learning with great pedagogical value. Meanwhile, as a popular TV series dared to present an all-Spanish skit without translation, the city of Nashville considered banning all languages other than English for official city purposes. What do these two moments in our popular culture, occurring as they did simultaneously, indicate about the American attitude toward linguistic and cultural difference then and now? Have we made strides since then or are we in a repeating cycle of views on the issues raised?

II. Official English and Nashville

Let us begin by considering official English and the climate of this debate. The citizens' action organization, U.S. English, created in 1983 by Californian Senator S. I. Hayakawa to promote official English legislation lists 32 states as having passed some kind of official English laws to date, most recently, West Virginia in 2016 (U.S. English, 2016). Some dispute these numbers as overreaching by the group. For example, Herman (2003) in her study of undergraduate college students' attitudes toward official English legislation considered in Iowa states that, "Hawaii's statute actually declares the state bilingual, whereas Louisiana has no official English policy—to the contrary, its constitution recognizes minority language rights" (p. 83). She goes on to point out that many of the states that did enact official English legislation in the 1980s and 1990s, such as Montana, Wyoming, Indiana, Missouri, North and South Dakota, have by and large ethnically homogeneous, monolingual English populations (p. 84). It is also worth noting that Louisiana's official

English laws date to the beginning of its statehood in 1812,[3] when concern was clearly aimed at the prevalence of French in the newly acquired area. On the other hand, Schildkraut (2003) points out that, at that time, only seven states had not recently considered some kind of official English legislation: Delaware, Michigan, Nevada, New Mexico, Oregon, Texas, and Vermont.

Returning briefly to Iowa, Herman (2003) comes on the heels of the Iowa legislature's defeat of an official English measure in April 1999, voted down by just three votes. It was the first time such a bill had made it out of committee to reach the floor in Iowa (p. 87). But, a highlighted map of states with and without official English in the pages of the newspaper *Human Events* dating from March 2005 indicates that some form of official English was adopted since the 1999 defeat ("Do you live?," p. 3). In fact, the Iowa English Language Reaffirmation Act, passed in 2002, made English the official language of the state. Interestingly, on the map accompanying the *Human Events* article, the states that do not have any official English legislation are shaded in black while those with such legislation are not shaded ("Do you live?," p. 3). If it was not clear from that choice, the prevailing attitude of the accompanying article could be easily discerned from the leading citation by Theodore Roosevelt, "The one absolute certain way of bringing this nation to ruin, or preventing all possibility of its continuing to be a nation at all, would be to permit it to become a tangle of squabbling nationalities. We have but one flag. We must also learn one language and that language is English" (p. 3). The article itself expresses concern that the Pledge of Allegiance was being broadcast in foreign languages at some Maryland high schools (to celebrate Foreign Language Week) and reports on a concomitant push for official English in the state of Maryland, which had thus far remained without. The tone of this article epitomizes the passion felt on both sides of this issue.

Maryland still remains without an official English law, but consider that in less than five years, three more states had been added to that list. These include Idaho and Kansas since 2007, and Arizona since 2006. Almost a decade earlier, in the Spring 1997 Harvard BlackLetter Law Journal, Tamayo catalogues the overturning of an English-only amendment to the Arizona constitution, approved by a majority of just 50.5% of voters in 1988 (p. 2). Maria-Kelley Yniguez, a bilingual state government worker who used both Spanish and English to communicate with clients in her job, brought the case and won in federal district court, a decision that withstood appeal to the Ninth Circuit Court of Appeals. A Pyrrhic victory given that in less than ten years Arizona has gone back on the official English list. Since the addition of

---

[3] The article "Do You Live in an Official English State?" cites this year as 1811.

Arizona, Idaho and Kansas, only West Virginia has been added to the list of official English states. However, in August 2014, the *Washington Post* published a brief article by Hunter Schwarz, their "pop culture meets politics" blogger, that cited four states in addition to West Virginia considering official English legislation at that time. Although only West Virginia followed through, clearly this issue is still prevalent on the legislative landscape at the state level.

Reporting on the 2001 United States Supreme Court case *Alexander, et al. v. Sandoval*, Carroll (2001) cites the decision in favor of Alexander and the Alabama Department of Public Safety as potentially giving "impetus to official English laws" (p. 36). In this case, the court ruled in a 5-4 decision that the state of Alabama was not required to provide a Spanish-language version of the state driver's license exam to Martha Sandoval, a Mexican immigrant with limited English proficiency. The reason: an official English amendment to the Alabama constitution dating from 1990. In the same article, Carroll notes that 11 states offer the test in more than ten languages, including, ironically, Massachusetts, which does have an official English law on the books since 1975 (U.S. English website) and offers the test in 25 languages. Moreover, the website for the Massachusetts Registry of Motor Vehicles is available in 12 languages. Thus, even with official English laws on the books, what such a law means in practice is not wholly clear.

With this backdrop, let us consider the official English law proposed in 2009 in the city of Nashville, Tennessee, the state's capital. The law was indeed defeated in a citywide referendum by roughly 10,000 votes in the winter of 2009 (Harris, 2009), but had it passed, Nashville would have been the largest U.S. city to enact such a measure (Harris, 2009). Those who supported the measure claimed that meetings in English only "would have encouraged immigrants to learn English and saved an estimated $150,000 yearly on translation services" (Harris, 2009, ¶9). Such specious goals as encouraging the learning of English by immigrants, improving communication, harmony, and unity in the workplace and in society are often cited by supporters of such initiatives (Herman, 2003; Schildkraut, 2003; English as the Official Language, 2006). It was the third time that such a measure was considered in Nashville (Harris, 2009). Meanwhile, in the U.S. Congress, official English measures have passed in the House, but the Senate chose not to act on them (U.S. English, 2016). U.S. English reports on its website, "The 'English Language Unity Act' has been reintroduced in the U.S. House of Representatives (H.R. 997) and the U.S. Senate (S. 678) for the 115th Congress" (2016).

III. SNL's "La Policía Mexicana"

While this official English movement is taking root, one municipality at a time, state by state, trends in popular American culture tell a different story.

The entirely Spanish-language *SNL* skit "La Policía Mexicana" broadcast days before the Nashville vote demonstrates a current running counter the official English trend. As I mentioned earlier, in this skit two police detectives, Carols Ruiz (a.k.a., Rafael) and Isabella Lopez (a.k.a., Carmen) played by Fred Armisen and Rosario Dawson respectively, question a suspect, Miguel played by Bobby Moynihan, in an interrogation room. Eventually, the police chief, Roberto Gonzalez (a.k.a., El Jefe), played by Bill Hader, enters the scene. The actors present the sketch with no subtitles or translation. It highlights two critical concerns: the value of knowing Spanish and the importance of context for language learning. Below is the transcript of the skit.

(10.2)

[Opens with a shot of Mexico City. Action theme music plays.]

Announcer:	La Policia Mejicana! Con Carlos Ruiz (Carlos poses, big bushy mustache) Isabella Lopez (exotic posing) y Roberto Gonzalez como "El Jefe" (tall man with mustache) La Policia Mejicana! (trio poses with the Mexican flag in the background) Tonight´s episode is written by Ms. Larkin´s fourth grade Spanish class. (A photo of Ms. Larkin surrounded in her desk by six 4th graders)

(Interrogation room. Man in red coat sits in front of table. Isabella and Carlos enter the room)

Rafael:	Hola.(Hi)
Carmen:	Hola.(Hi)
Miguel:	Hola. (Hi)
Rafael:	Me llamo Rafael. (My name is Rafael)
Carmen:	Y me llamo Carmen. (And my name is Carmen)
Rafael:	Mas una vez, me llamo Rafael. (One more time, my name is Rafael)
Carmen:	Y me llamo Carmen. Como te llamas? (And my name is Carmen. What is your name?)
Miguel:	Me llamo Miguel. (My name is Miguel)
Rafael and Carmen:	Hola Miguel. (Hi Miguel)
Carmen:	Miguel, que color es su pelo? (Miguel, what color is your hair?)
Miguel:	Mi pelo es marron. (My hair is brown)
Carmen:	Que color son sus ojos? (What color are your eyes?)
Miguel:	Mis ojos son verdes. (My eyes are green)
Carmen:	Que color es su abrigo? (What color is your coat?)

Miguel:	Mi abrigo es rojo. (My coat is red)
Carmen:	Donde esta la bomba? (Where is the bomb?)
Miguel:	No se. (I don´t know)
Carmen:	No se?! No se?! Donde esta la bomba?!(Don´t know? Don´t know? Where is the bomb?)(grabs Miguel´s arm)
Rafael:	(pulls her away) Mira, mira, mira, mira. Espera. Que pasa? (Look, look, look, look. Wait. What´s happening?)
Carmen:	Tu eres el policia bueno. Y yo soy la policia mala. Tu comprendes? (You´re good cop. I´m bad cop. You understand?)
Rafael:	Si, yo comprendo. (Yes, I understand)
Carmen:	Muy bueno. (Very good)

(Detective Rafael sits with Miguel)

Rafael:	Ok, muy bien. Miguel, quieres agua? (Ok, good Miguel. You want water?)

(shot of a jug of water)

Miguel:	No.
Rafael:	Quieres una hamburguesa? (You want a hamburger?)

(shot of a hamburger)

Miguel:	No.
Rafael:	Quieres una piña? (You want a pineapple?)

(shot of a pineapple)

Miguel:	No, no. Gracias. (No, no. Thank you)
Rafael:	Miguel, yo soy tu amigo. (Miguel, I am your friend) Tu eres mi amigo. (You are my friend) Ella es su amiga. (She is your friend) Nosotros somos amigos. (We are friends) Miguel, donde esta la bomba? (Miguel, where is the bomb?) Esta la bomba en el aeropuerto? (Is it at the airport?) (shows a drawing of an airport) Esta la bomba en el supermercado? (Is the bomb at the supermarket?) (drawing of a supermarket), esta la bomba en la biblioteca?(Is the bomb at the library?) (drawing of a library) (Miguel looks worried) Ah!, la bomba esta en la biblioteca! (Ah!, the bomb is at the library!)
Miguel:	Can I go to the bathroom?
Rafael:	Ah, ah. En español. (Ah, ah. In spanish)
Miguel:	Puedo…ir…al baño? (Can I go to the bathroom?)

Rafael:	No. Esta biblioteca es una biblioteca grande, una bliblioteca mediano o una biblioteca pequeño? (Is this library a big library, a medium library or a small library?)
Miguel:	No se. (I don't know)
Carmen:	Grande o pequeño? (Big or small?)

(Roberto Gonzalez aka El Jefe comes into the room)

El Jefe:	Silencio! Por favor! (Silence! Please!)
Rafael and	
Carmen:	Hola Jefe. (Hi Boss)
El Jefe:	Carmen, que hora es? (Carmen, what time is it?)

(Isabella looks at the clock on the wall)

Carmen:	Son las dos y cuarto. (Its two fifteen)
El Jefe:	Bueno, gracias. (Good, thanks) (leaves)
Rafael:	Ahora Miguel… (Now Miguel…)

(Miguel is gone from the interrogation room)

Carmen:	Ah, donde esta el criminal? (Ah, where is the criminal?)
Rafael:	El criminal no esta aqui! (The criminal is not here!)
Rafael and	
Carmen:	Que lastima! (What a shame!)

(Cut to photo of Ms.Larkin's 4th graders with their fists up in the air)

4th graders:	Yay!!!!!!

(Cheers and applause)

(fade)[4]

(Michaels, 2009)

We can see in "La Policía Mexicana" efforts to create a highly contextualized Spanish language class. At the beginning of the sketch, we observe a ritual we can find in any beginning-level Spanish class: introductions. The characters say hello and introduce themselves to each other using *me llamo*. To do so, the police detectives, who function in the role of the teacher, use the same exaggerated manner that a Spanish instructor might, pronouncing words carefully and distinctly, over-enunciating, and repeating twice. The male detective goes out of his way to indicate that he is repeating, saying "*más una vez*" 'one more time.'

---

[4] Submitted by: Waldo San Miguel on https://snltranscripts.jt.org/08/08mpolicia.phtml. Transcript posted without accents, which have not been added.

After this introduction, the sketch moves on to the faux-interrogation about the location of a bomb. Before passing to direct questions about the bomb, however, the female detective engages in some simple questions about colors, like a warm-up for students in a Spanish class to make them feel comfortable. One might take similar action with a suspect on a police drama. This highly ritualized interaction that can be seen in the vast number of police procedurals on TV in recent years, from *Law & Order* (Wolf et al., 1990) to *CSI: Crime Scene Investigation* (Zuiker et al., 2000) to shows like *The Mentalist* (Heller, 2008) and *Castle* (Marlowe et al., 2009), leaves this exchange an open book, easily interpreted even by those who don't speak Spanish. Moreover, the similarity of the words *color* and *bomba* to English 'color' and 'bomb' adds to this accessibility.

When the suspect refuses to reveal the location of the bomb, the female detective gets angry and is pulled away by her male counterpart. She explains that she is "*la policía mala*" ('the bad cop') and that he is "*el policía bueno*" ('the good cop'). Once more, the good cop/bad cop trope is well known and easily understood. In this exchange, there is also a comprehension check, '*tú comprendes?*' highly reminiscent of the Spanish language classroom (Michaels, 2009).

The next phase of the skit involves props as Rafael, *el policía bueno*, asks the suspect if he would like several items. As each item is offered, *quieres agua?* ('do you want water?'), *quieres una hamburguesa?* ('do you want a hamburger?'), and *quieres una piña?* ('do you want a pineapple?') (Michaels, 2009), the camera focuses on a pitcher of water, a hamburger, and a pineapple, to indicate the item being proffered, much as a good Spanish instructor would indicate the food or drink being offered to create context. Following the suspect's refusal of all things presented to him, the male detective takes another tack. He attempts to create solidarity by stating that the detectives are the suspect's friends: "*Yo soy su amigo. Tu eres mi amigo. Ella es su amiga. Nosotros somos amigos*"[5] (Michaels, 2009). Again, he seeks to create understanding by repeating the word *amigo/amiga* and by employing hand gestures before he returns to queries about the location of the bomb.

In this segment, he asks if the bomb is in specific locations using the verb *estar* and showing a picture of each location with the word written out in Spanish underneath when he asks. For example, while showing a picture of

[5] The mismatch between formal and informal in this exchange is not the only linguistic error that occurs in this scene. Slight errors in pronunciation and verb morphology, mostly from the clearly non-Spanish-speaking actor playing the suspect (or student, as the case may be) also occur.

the airport, he asks *"Está la bomba en el aeropuerto?"* ('Is the bomb at the airport?') (Michaels, 2009). Notably, this is a prototypical use of the verb *estar*, to indicate location, which one would find in any beginning Spanish course. Finally, as the detective determines the bomb's location in the library, the suspect asks, in English, "Can I go to the bathroom?" This question can be found both in the interrogation room and in the language classroom. The detective responds as any Spanish instructor might, *"En español."* Once the suspect haltingly produces the correct Spanish phrase, as any language learner would, his request is refused, as it might be both in the classroom and during an interrogation.

Instead, the interrogation continues with questions about the size of the library, *grande, mediano,* or *pequeño.*[6] At this point, *El Jefe* ('the Chief') enters the room. His entrance can best be characterized as serious as he calls the detectives by name, but the tone quickly changes to comical as he asks *"¿Qué hora es?"* ('What time is it?') with exaggerated inflection. Once more the audience is presented with a typical exchange that one finds in a beginning Spanish class. After this question is answered and *El Jefe* leaves the room, the detectives turn their attention back to the suspect only to find he has escaped. This provides one last occasion for the use of *estar. --Donde está el criminal? --El criminal no está aquí!* And, finally, the coup de grâce, both detectives utter that most recognizable expression of Spanish regret, *"¡Qué lastima!"* ('What a shame!') (Michaels, 2009).

The humor in this episode is created by the conflation of these two very different types of interaction. The typical suspect interrogation as filtered through the Spanish language classroom experience. Moreover, the sketch is preceded by a picture of the alleged writers of the scene, a group of children surrounding their teacher, as the audience is informed, "Tonight's episode, written by Ms. Larkin's fourth grade class" (Michaels, 209). The detectives' manner and exaggerated language use accentuate the classroom experience while the incongruous setting of the cinderblock interrogation room with rusty metal furniture and barred windows for the classroom heightens the improbability of such language use in this type of situation, raising the humor quotient even more. Moreover, some learners probably do equate the language classroom with a prison of sorts, adding to the levity of the scene.

In fact, around the time of this skit's airing on *SNL,* the Spanish language classroom had become ubiquitous in the popular imagination. Shows on Fox

---

[6] Again, another morphological error as these adjectives should agree with the feminine noun *biblioteca,* instead they are uttered several times in their masculine forms.

and NBC were featuring Spanish teachers and the learning of Spanish. The Fox dramedy *Glee* (Murphy et al., 2009), ostensibly about a high school glee club, featured a glee club director who taught Spanish by day. Although in the course of the series relatively few scenes took place in his classroom, one episode from the first season included a short scene presenting a lesson on the *por/para* distinction. Meanwhile, the first season of the NBC sitcom *Community* (Foster et al., 2009) centered around students in a beginning-level Spanish course at a community college who form a study group. Like *Glee*, few scenes took place in the classroom, but the mere inclusion of that space on major network television raised the profile of the Spanish learning environment. These shows, along with *SNL*'s "La Policía Mexicana" sketch, highlight both the Spanish classroom and by extension the utility of learning Spanish in the present-day United States. In the years since a number of shows have made use of Spanish, some quite extensively like FX's *The Bridge* (Stiehm et al., 2013) but perhaps these examples represent the vanguard of this movement.

In addition to these examples, other trends countervailing the official English movement do exist. The 2009 revival of a bilingual version of *West Side Story* at the Palace Theater on Broadway (Laurents, 2009) provides a great example. In this version, the Puerto Rican gang members communicate with each other in Spanish. Songs originally written and performed in English, such as 'I Feel Pretty' and 'A Boy Like That' were transformed into '*Siento Hermosa*' and '*Un Hombre Así*' with translations by Lin-Manuel Miranda. Arthur Laurents, who wrote the original book for the musical, supported these changes, "It gives the Sharks[7] more weight than they ever had" (Cohen, 2009, p. 6). Moreover, he pushed for only Latinx actors to play those roles (Cohen, 2009). Initially, Laurents insisted that the Spanish used could not be "high school Spanish" but after previews where subtitles were tried and quickly eliminated, more strategic use of English was necessary to allow non-Spanish speakers to follow the action in Spanish-only interactions (Cohen, 2009). John Lahr, in his review for *The New Yorker* (2009), praises the choice to update the language used by the Latino characters, "Fifty years on, in a multicultural America, this decision makes the production feel fresh" (p. 60).

IV. Conclusion

So where does this leave us? Our popular culture, most notably in the performing arts, on television and on stage, seems to be re-examining the utility of learning another language and having engagement with another

---

[7] The Sharks are the Puerto Rican gang in the musical.

culture. Simultaneously, victories continue for those who believe in official English, easily confused with English only which calls to mind divisive identity politics. As Schmidt opined in 2002:

> One of the most contentious issues in the recent U.S. culture wars involves the charge of *racism* leveled against efforts to establish an English-only language policy. Reverberating through controversies over bilingual education, linguistic access to political and civil rights, and over campaigns to make English the sole official language, this accusation has provoked unusually heated denials and denunciations by English-only advocates. (p. 141; italics in original)

The clearly charged, polemic nature of this debate continues and seems unlikely to be resolved in near future as this division is emblematic of the many ways in which the U.S. has shown itself to be fractured in the recent past, with strong opinions on both sides and little room for compromise. One need only look to the state of our political discourse today and the contentious nature of such issues as immigration policy, the status of Dreamers, and detained asylum seekers and border crossers to realize how the related issue of language policy, inextricably linked to these issues, remains a locus of considerable uncertainty. This issue touches many others, such as education and our identity as a nation (Schildkraut, 2003), for which we are still seeking direction in this turbulent and disruptive moment in our nation's history.

I will close with something I found ironic. In the same issue of the *N.Y. Times* in which the story appeared lauding the new bilingual production of *West Side Story,* a series of related articles presented as "Remade in America" looked at school-age immigrants who speak languages other than English and the ways in which our educational system leaves them underserved and far below the achievement levels of their English-speaking peers (Thompson, 2009). This coincidence (Was it a coincidence?) highlights the interconnectedness of these issues and the need for increased awareness of our non-English speaking communities and the roles that second languages play in our "official English" society.

Chapter 11

Repeating History: Immigrant and First-Gen Children Mediate America on TV

I. Introduction

Since the founding of the United States, families with little or no command of the English language have come seeking a better life. Immigrant and first-generation children have had the responsibility of interpreting conversations and translating documents from English into their native tongues for their non- and limited-English-speaking parents. This process continually repeats itself as new waves of immigrant parents with some or little English make their ways to America, bringing with them young children who are educated in English-language schools, make English-language friends, and adapt linguistically and culturally to the English-speaking environment around them. These children simultaneously maintain their first language as the principal means of communicating with their parents. Thus, they are ever in the middle and become responsible for bridging the gap between their parents' language and culture and that of the U.S. They become child language brokers.

II. Background Research

In the edited volume *Points and Counterpoints: Controversial relationship and family issues in the 21st century*, Coleman and Ganong (2003) point out:

> Almost 20 percent of children in the United States speak a language other than English at home (http://www.census.gov). [...] In 2000, foreign-born Americans made up about 11 percent of the U.S. population, only slightly less than the 15 percent that was foreign-born in 1900. North America has been and continues to be racially, ethnically, and linguistically diverse, which means that Child Language Brokering...will be an issue for years to come. (p. 153)

Halgunseth (2003) provides a basic definition of language brokering: "when a third party (i.e., a bilingual child) mediates communication between two different linguistic/cultural agents" (p. 154). McQuillan and Tse (1995) provide additional perspective:

Language brokers are distinct from formal translators and interpreters in two important respects: first, brokers are usually involved in informal negotiation for one or both of the parties for which they serve as a liaison, mediating communication rather than merely transmitting it; and second, there exists an unequal power relationship between the broker and the agents, usually one in which the broker (a child) is normally under then authority or supervision of one of the beneficiaries. (p. 195)

Research on child language brokering has indicated that child language brokers tend to have mixed feelings about that role when looking back on it from late adolescence or adulthood. Santiago (2003) discussing her own personal participation in language brokering as a child describes it as "a very mixed experience" (p. 161). Current research, most of which relies on interviews or surveys of child language brokers looking back on the incidents of their youth, presents both positive and negative effects of the experience. Many child language brokers report that the process of language brokering enhanced their L1 and L2 acquisition; enabled them maintain their L1; increased their independence, maturity and interpersonal skills; and helped them to learn more about both their native and American cultures (Acoach & Webb, 2004; Halgunseth, 2003; Hall & Sham, 2007; McQuillan & Tse, 1995; Tse 1996). Particularly, engaging in adult-level problem solving and decision making helped child language brokers develop skills beyond the linguistic domain (McQuillan & Tse, 1995). Moreover, as Malakoff and Hakuta (1991) (cited in McQuillan & Tse, 1995) document, translation is not simply decoding a message from one language and encoding it into another, but rather a series of complex linguistic manipulations requiring metalinguistic skill and knowledge (p. 197).

Despite these positive effects of language brokering as a child, child language brokers do cite negative outcomes of the experience as well. Researchers report that some child language brokers felt added stress and/or burden, increased anxiety, and resentment from the reversal of the typical parent-child relationship since the child is often in the role of having to maintain and care for the parent's best interests in all types of interactions (e.g., at school, at the bank, at the doctor's office, etc.) (Hall & Sham, 2004; Jones & Trickett, 2005; McQuillan & Tse, 1995; Rainey et al., 2014; Umaña-Taylor, 2003).

Rainey et al. (2014) compared bilingual college students who had engaged in language brokering with bilingual counterparts who had not been language brokers for their families. They found that the language broker group had higher levels of anxiety and depression than the non-brokering bilinguals:

Overall, the language brokers had higher levels of anxiety and depression as emerging adults than their non-brokering bilingual peers, which indicates that brokers are at higher risk for these disorders. Although positive cognitive developments and academic growth may come from language brokering (e.g., Dorner, Orellana, and Li-Grining 2007; Orellana 2003), psychological health may be compromised. (p. 473)

Rainey et al. also considered the onset of language brokering as a factor, categorizing participants into three different onset groups: 4-8 years old, 9-13 years old, and 14-18 years old. They found that those bilinguals who began language brokering at 9-13 years old reported the most elevated levels of depression or anxiety. They believe that this may bear some relationship to the development of literacy, but that discussion is beyond the scope of this chapter. Of more interest for the purposes of this chapter, is that many child language brokers in the study viewed brokering as a "family duty" (p. 464).

On the other hand, Tse (1996) found the language brokers had an overall positive view of the brokering experience. She surveyed 64 language minority high school students (Chinese- and Vietnamese-Americans), 90% of whom had brokered, mostly for parents (92%) but also for friends, other relatives and siblings as well as neighbors, school officials, and teachers to varying degrees. She reports that:

Over half of the students believed that brokering helped them learn more of their L1 and L2 (56% and 58% respectively) and about a third believed that it helped them learn more about their first (Chinese or Vietnamese) and second (American) cultures. Nearly half of the subjects felt proud to broker, while a fewer number of subjects reported feeling embarrassed (11%) or burdened (17%). Over half of the subjects liked brokering (52%), with only 15% reporting disliking it. Nearly half of the subjects (45%) indicated that brokering caused them to be more independent and mature. (p. 491)

The full picture of the effect of language brokering is likely most in keeping with Santiago's (2003) description of it as "a very mixed experience" (p. 161).

III. Data

As with many aspects of immigrant life, the process of language brokering finds artistic representation on American television. In the television shows *The Knick* (Jacobs et al., 2014) and *The Mindy Project* (Kaling et al., 2012) children are depicted helping their parents negotiate medical situations with doctors and healthcare workers. Often these children do not merely translate or interpret but rather mediate these interactions and gain language proficiency themselves in keeping with the research cited above.

I'll begin by discussing the pilot episode of the Cinemax show *The Knick*, called "Method and Madness" (Amiel et al., 2014). There are two scenes of child language brokering involving the same child, Yetta. In the first scene, we see the health inspector prowling New York City tenements at the turn of the 20th century in search of suspected tuberculosis sufferers in an effort to prevent a citywide outbreak. He knocks on the door of an immigrant family in search of the family matriarch, who has been reported to the authorities for her illness.

(11.1)

Inspector:	Health Inspector. Health Inspector. Open the door, please. [Enters apartment] Hmm. Mrs. Krawetz? We're here to take you to the hospital. Do you understand? Hospital. Hos hospital. [Addressing husband of women] She has a disease. She must be taken out of here.
Husband:	[Speaking native language; calls for daughter]
Inspector:	Christ alive, it's the Tower of Babel in these shitholes. Never the same language twice. [Yetta arrives from other room] Hospital!
Yetta:	My father says he doesn't want you taking my mother.
Officer:	Well, I'm Officer Sears of the New York Police Department and there is a law that says we have to take her someplace that'll make her well so she doesn't get you sick, too.
Yetta:	[Translates for father; Father responds in native language; Yetta translates] My--my father says they took our neighbor and he never came back.
Officer:	Oh, she'll be back and fit as a fiddle. You watch.[1]

(Amiel et al., 2014)

The health inspector barges into the room and tries to speak directly with the sick woman on the bed. Her husband enters trying to communicate but must

---

[1] For languages other than English, the English subtitles have been added when provided onscreen. When no English subtitles were present, speech in a language other than English that is not subtitled has been added by the author whenever possible.

immediately call in his daughter, Yetta, to broker the interaction. The young girl must not only interpret the language for her father but must also broker the complex emotions of her father's fear at having his wife taken away and the rigid demands of the city inspector and police officer's laws. Yetta remains calm throughout and demonstrates maturity beyond her years. Recall that maturity is a positive side effect associated with the language brokering experience.

In the second part of this storyline, the girl must interpret for her mother in the hospital.

(11.2)

Doctor:	I honestly don't think she'll make it through the week.
Robertson:	Does she know?
Doctor:	She doesn't speak English. Her daughter has been interpreting for me.
Robertson:	I see.
Doctor:	Responsibility is to the patient, but there's no rule that says we have to—
Robertson:	Hello. May I ask your name?
Yetta:	Yetta.
Robertson:	Yetta. A beautiful name. Yetta, my name is Miss Robertson. I'm from the social welfare office of the hospital. I need your help right now to explain something to your mother. All right? [Yetta nods] Please tell your mother that the doctor says her disease has made her very sick.
Yetta:	[Translates into native language]
Robertson:	She will not get better.
Yetta:	[Translates into native language]
Robertson:	She will only get worse. But the hospital will do all it can to make her as comfortable as possible.
Yetta:	[Translates into native language]
Robertson:	If there is anything she or your family needs, we are here to help you. Does she understand?
Yetta:	[Translates into native language; mother nods] She understands.
Robertson:	I'm so sorry.
Mother:	[Speaking native language]
Yetta:	[Translating] My mother wants to know what time it is.
Doctor:	It's 4:30.
Yetta:	[Translates into native language]
Mother:	[Speaking native language]

Yetta: [Translating] My mother says I should go or else I'll
                  be late for my shift.
(Amiel et al., 2014)

In this scene, we see how Yetta is given the horrible news that her mother will
not recover and how she must tell her mother this news. We do not have
subtitles (and I do not speak the language being depicted), so we can only
assume that she is conveying what is being said as exactly as possible. However,
there are indications that some mediation might be occurring. In the two close-
up shots of Yetta facing her mother while translating, Yetta pauses to think. We
see her eyes dart upward as she searches for the best way to explain the
situation. Again, there is no emotion on her part and she maintains an almost
professional distance from the message she is delivering, emphasizing her
adultness in this impossible situation. Moreover, when her mother reminds her
that she will be late for her 4:30 shift and sends her away (the next scene is Yetta
getting in a carriage), she dutifully translates this message to the hospital social
worker and accepts it. The fact that this language brokering depiction coincides
with additional commentary on child labor further emphasizes Yetta's adult role
in this world, despite her being a child.

In the pilot episode of *The Mindy Project* (Kaling & McDougall, 2012), a
young boy, Max, translates an interaction with the main character Dr. Mindy
Lahiri, an obstetrician, while searching for a doctor for his mother who is nine
months pregnant. At the recommendation of his aunt and uncle, Max has
taken his mother to see if they can secure Dr. Lahiri's services.

(11.3)
Dr. Lahiri: Nasreen, you are nine months pregnant, and you
                  don't have health insurance. I'm sorry, I just I can't
                  take you on as a patient.
Max: But my aunt and uncle said you were the person to
                  go to.
Dr. Lahiri: I was. And I really, really want to help you. It's just that
                  I'm at this point in my life where I can't just do what I
                  want to do. You know, I have to do things that really
                  move my life forward. Like, like spinning. Do you guys
                  know what that is?
Max: We won't tell anybody.
Dr. Lahiri: Still, people could find out.
Max: How?

Dr. Lahiri:	Um, let's see, I talk a lot. You know, like in my sleep, on a date. I drink a lot. So I just, I can't control it.
Max:	[Translates to Persian for mother]
Dr. Lahiri:	Okay, okay, okay, look, look. I will take you on as a patient, but you just need to look me in the eye and promise me that you will have health insurance by the time she delivers.
Max:	But I can't promise it. I don't know if it's true.
Dr. Lahiri:	It doesn't have to be true. I just need to hear it. I do this with guys all the time.
Max:	I promise we will have insurance.
Dr. Lahiri:	Great, thank you.
Max:	Welcome.

(Kaling & McDougall, 2012)

In this interaction on three very clear occasions, the boy is mediating the interaction for his mother, not even bothering to translate for her. First, Dr. Lahiri says that she cannot take the mother on as a patient, to which Max replies, "We won't tell anybody" (Kaling & McDougall, 2012). Here he does not translate anything, but is already aware of his mother's dire need for a doctor and feels licensed to offer a solution. When Dr. Lahiri says that people will find out, the boy does not hesitate in asking, "How?" It is clear that he is truly mediating this interaction, attempting to convince the doctor to take on his mother and questioning any impediments to his goal. Later in the conversation, Dr. Lahiri offers to take the mother on as a patient if there is a promise that she will have health insurance by the time of the baby's birth. Here again, the language brokering child merely looks at his mother and responds with a truthful answer, "But, I can't promise it. I don't know if it's true" (Kaling & McDougall, 2012). This use of the first-person pronoun is telling. The *I* would seem to indicate that the child is taking on the responsibility of getting insurance for his mother and acknowledging that he cannot guarantee that he will succeed. In the literature there are examples in which child language brokers are entrusted with the role of making adult decisions, related mostly to schooling:

Nearly all of the informants noted that their parents generally entrusted them with handling school matters independently or with minimal parental involvement, resulting in them sometimes taking sole responsibility for making educational decisions. [...] Both Kim and Jennifer [two participants in the study] said that their relationships with their parents were unlike those of their peers because they were entrusted to make vital decisions and perform important day to day [sic] duties. (McQuillan & Tse, 1995, p. 205)

Although these decisions were mostly related to schooling, two participants in McQuillan and Tse's (1995) study were making "vital decisions," just as the young Persian-speaking boy appears to be doing in this scene.

In addition to the examples above where the child translates the language of the majority culture into his/her parents' native language, there is also another type of child language brokering that American television has depicted. This brokering involves English-speaking children familiar with the language of an immigrant character or community interpreting spoken and written language for English-only family members. On the first season of the CBS series *Life in Pieces* (Adler et al., 2015), a daughter's ability to mediate interaction in a Mexican grocery store between her father and the storeowner results in a successful exchange beneficial to both parties instead of a communication stalemate.

In the episode "Godparent Turkey Corn Farts" (Mull & Lowe, 2015), it is Thanksgiving Day and we see Tim, a father, and Sophia, his daughter, trying to get a turkey at the last minute. Because of a Thanksgiving parade, the route to their normal grocery store is blocked so Sophia suggests they try the Mexican market that they happen to be stopped next to, where her grandfather gets his margarita salt. She correctly translates the sign in Spanish that says, "MERCADO CARNICERIA; PRODUCTOS DE MEXICO Y CENTRO AMERICA" (Mull & Lowe, 2015) and is thus able to offer this suggestion to her father.

They do indeed decide to search for a turkey in the Mexican Market. While in the store, Sophia intervenes in a series of interactions to interpret key ideas for her father from Spanish into English.

(11.4)
Tim:	Oh! Check out these cherry boots! What are these for?
Clerk:	Botas tribaleras.
Tim:	Huh?
Clerk:	Para que bailes. [Pantomimes dancing]
Sophia:	**Dancing shoes.**
Tim:	Oh. Yeah.
Sophia:	[Sees father holding a machete] That isn't on the list.
Tim:	Well, we need something to carve the turkey.
Store Owner:	Hola. How can I helping you?
Tim:	Uh, yeah, I need turkey.
Sophia:	And enough candy to fill our jirafa piñata.

Owner:	Aquí está.
Tim:	Uh, no, no, a turkey.
Owner:	Es un pavo chico.
Sophia:	**He says it's a little turkey.**
Owner:	[Losing his balance] Oh. Oh, Oh, oh.
Tim:	Are you okay?
Clerk:	He loses his balance a lot.
Tim:	Well, you know, I'm a I'm a doctor. Uh, El doctor-o.
Sophia:	**Médico.**
Tim:	Médico. Yeah, ear, nose, and throat.
Clerk:	Ah. Little doctor.
Owner:	Ay.
Tim:	Beg to differ. Okay, I think I see the problem here. Sir, would you mind lying down on your back, please?
Clerk:	Tu espalda.
Owner:	Uh-huh.
Tim:	I'm going to do a procedure. I'm going to roll your head, and it's gonna loosen the crystals in your ear canal. You have, uh How do you say "vertigo"?
Clerk:	Vértigo.
Tim:	Really?
Clerk:	Sí.
Tim:	I speak Spanish. Okay, rotate your head the other way.
[Sophia and Tim leave the store]	
Sophia:	Daddy, I like that you can help people.
Tim:	Aw, thanks, sweetie. **You know, you helped, too. You translated.** Ooh, don't touch that machete. Yours is the little one.

(Mull & Lowe, 2015)

In the scene, Sophia makes clear that the boots are for dancing, that the chicken-sized package the owner hands to her father is indeed a "little turkey," and successfully interprets English "doctor" to Spanish "*médico*". In the scene, we are also exposed to a fair amount of cultural tourism and stereotyping—the dancing shoes, the machete, the piñata, a Mexican flag in the background. Plus, given their English, it seems unlikely that the owners of the market would need such intervention, notwithstanding the doubts that exist about Sophia's Spanish language skills. But, looking past these criticisms, it is an interesting sequence. Sophia does display enough linguistic and cultural knowledge of the Mexican community in California to mediate the interaction. Particularly important is the translation of the word "doctor", for it creates the opportunity for her father to truly aid the store owner and, by extension, his family, by helping cure the vertigo (or *vértigo*) he has been suffering from. Her father even points out how important her role as translator was in this storyline.

IV. Discussion

Coleman and Ganong (2003) ask us to consider the following: "How would it feel to be a *language broker*? How would it feel to know personal information about one's parents that most children do not know? How would you have reacted to the responsibility of relaying correct health information and diagnostic information between your parents and physicians?" (p. 153). Imagine the two medical scenes we observed, *The Knick* hospital scene and the scene in Dr. Lahiri's office. In the first, a young girl must tell her own mother that she is dying. In the second, a young boy must accompany his mother in the search for an obstetrician. In both cases, we can imagine incredible stress and anxiety. Rainey et al. (2014) summarize: "Language brokers may be prone to experiencing anxiety and depression symptoms that are related to constant contextual stressors such as heightened family conflict and challenges related to maintaining adult-like responsibilities" (p. 473). I can imagine no more adult-like responsibility than conveying to your mother that she will die or than fighting to find your mother a doctor who can care for her in a time of need. In the second example, there is the added stressor of embarrassment, such as that reported by 11% of Tse's (1996) high school subjects. In both of these examples, it is clear that language brokering can be a high stakes concern for children to be involved with.

The *Life in Pieces* example (Mull & Lowe, 2015) differs in a significant way from the other examples of child language brokering. In the scene, it does not appear that the marketplace interaction causes much stress for Sophia. If anything, she seems to enjoy her ability to understand and interpret for her father. For this second type of language brokering, I would propose that intercultural competence and some linguistic competence is a positive effect of children growing up in contact with different cultural and linguistic communities. Sophia and the store owners also demonstrate a translanguaging approach (Otheguy et al., 2015) to effective communication. Parties on both sides of the interaction use the linguistic resources available to them in both languages to achieve a series of successful interactions.

One could argue that this is merely linguistic exhibitionism (Pandey, 2016)—an attempt to imbue what would be a monolingual interaction in English with a bit of Spanish-language flair. This criticism is valid, perhaps, but the fact that this type of brokering is depicted on television seems to indicate an understanding of the need for English speakers to recognize the linguistic diversity in the United States and to be willing to make efforts, if possible, to communicate across barriers of language and culture. The fact that a child brokers this exchange sends a clear message to the young about the importance of accepting different cultures and being willing to communicate with each other in spite of differences, linguistic or otherwise.

V. Conclusion

I would like to end this chapter by considering the eras depicted in the examples from *The Knick* and *The Mindy Project*. The former represents a period of time roughly a century ago while the latter portrays the present day. The fact that these examples depict vastly different eras of the American experience indicates that this process of bilingual children mediating interactions for their parents is an ongoing, continually renewing facet of the American experience. Recall the citation with which I began this chapter:

> In 2000, foreign-born Americans made up about 11 percent of the U.S. population, only slightly less than the 15 percent that was foreign-born in 1900. North America has been and continues to be racially, ethnically, and linguistically diverse, which means that Child Language Brokering...will be an issue for years to come.
> (Coleman & Ganong, 2003, p. 153)

Not only will this be an issue for years to come, it has been an issue for as long as the United States, a nation of immigrants, has been in existence.

Chapter 12

Mockery and Moxie:
Resisting Condescension toward
Non-Standard Dialects of English on TV

I. Introduction

Language, including regional or L2 accent, is intimately connected to one's sense of identity. Because of dialectal differences, speakers of non-standard varieties of English are often mocked, belittled, and marginalized by speakers of standard English. Lippi-Green (2012) contends that discrimination on the basis of language persists as a proxy for other more socially stigmatized forms of discrimination in the United States (p. 67). In this chapter, I will build on work I've done previously (Mitchell 2010 [see Chapter 8]; Mitchell 2015), in which I look at the ways in which speakers of English with regional or L2 accents on television are treated as intellectually or morally inferior by their standard-speaking peers. I examine how these tropes continue in the first revival season of the sitcom *Will & Grace* (Mutchnick et al., 2017) and in *The Goldbergs* (Goldberg et al., 2013).

II. Background research

In this volume (Chapter 8), I discuss the appearance of Enrique Iglesias playing Gael, the L2 English speaking boyfriend of Robin, one of the main characters on *How I Met Your Mother* (Harris & Fryman, 2007). I discuss a scene that begins with a conversation between the native English-speaking main characters on the show. The conversation concerns the relationship between Gael and Robin. Gael speaks accented English, but his English is also fluent and free of grammatical errors. In the conversation, Robin's friend Barney says negative things about Robin's relationship with Gael. When Gael shows up, everyone assumes that he will not understand if "big words" are used. They make this preposterous assumption despite Gael's strong abilities in English. Parts of the conversation are repeated using "big words" to prevent Gael from understanding Barney's negative comments about his relationship with Robin. In Chapter 8, I showed why I believe this idea of using "big words" is meant to be satire. But I also point out how this depiction of Gael raises questions about television portrayals of L2 speakers. He comes across as a rube, instead of as a thoughtful character who happens to speak another language in addition to English. Previous research on language attitudes (e.g. Dobrow & Gidney, 1998; Durkin & Judge, 2001; Lindemann, 2005; Mastro et al., 2008) coupled with other television portrayals of L2 English speakers convince me that viewers could easily misinterpret this interaction of Gael with Robin and her friends negatively. Viewers could perceive L2 English speakers as unable to understand and to communicate in English merely because they have an accent.

In related research from 2015, I examined several depictions of Southern dialects on television. Here I will briefly discuss my findings regarding an episode of the show *Bones* (Hanson et al., 2005), in which a Southern dialect speaker suffers discrimination at the hands of a colleague who speaks the standard dialect. The episode includes pointed metalinguistic discourse about dialect differences in the U.S. and prescriptive standards. In "The Hot Dog in the Competition" (Peterson & Little, 2011), Finn Abernathy joins Dr. Temperance Brennan, a.k.a. Bones, and her band of scientists at the Jeffersonian as a brilliant, teenage ex-con who has mended his ways to become a promising young forensic anthropologist. Unfortunately for him, he speaks in a strongly marked dialect that is meant to represent a stereotypical variety of Southern American English. Abernathy's dialect causes friction with Dr. Jack Hodgins (the senior scientist on the *Bones* team). Hodgins criticizes Abernathy's dialect, clearly displaying linguistic prejudice and his belief that Abernathy must speak Standard American English to be taken seriously. Abernathy and the dialect he speaks represents the Southern stereotype of the Country Bumpkin found in film and on television. These characters are often made fun of for their ignorance of the ways of the world beyond their hometowns (Shuttlesworth 2007, p. 196). Thus the paradox of Abernathy's character: he is a brilliant scientist, but he speaks a stigmatized dialect associated with a rural or working-class milieu. From this episode of *Bones* in addition to other depictions, I conclude that Southern dialects are definitely stigmatized, and their speakers often discriminated against by speakers of other regional dialects, which lead to feelings of insecurity and inferiority among these dialect speakers.

After taking Hodgins' abusive attitude for some time, Abernathy eventually stands up for himself and the way he speaks. He points out how no one else at the Jeffersonian seems to be bothered by the way he talks, and speculates that Hodgins is simply making an issue of Abernathy's dialectal speech in order to make him feel bad because he is different. Hodgins has no reply to this spot-on accusation.

Abernathy's resistance to Hodgins prejudice is reminiscent of something that occurs in the foreign language classroom, called foreign language resistance. Worth (2006, 2008) details the ways in which university-level elementary L2 Italian learners resist learning Italian in the classroom, such as by codeswitching into English or by feigning incompetence or lack of knowledge. I believe that this notion of foreign language resistance can be adapted to apply to speakers of stigmatized dialects. *Language resistance* in the context of the power dynamic between standard dialect and stigmatized dialect speakers (be they native or non-native speakers) involves the speaker of the stigmatized dialect rejecting the critiques of the standard dialect speaker, either overtly or covertly. Language resistance occurs when an individual engages in an "act of identity" (Le Page 1985, cited in Meyerhoff 2011, p. 273), staking a claim in the linguistic space for their dialect (or idiolect) and thereby refusing to accept attempts at language subordination by one or more speakers of the "standard" or majority dialect. In other words, Abernathy is exhibiting language resistance in an overt way by taking Hodgins to task for his linguistic prejudice and covertly by refusing to change how he speaks English.

With this idea of language resistance in mind, along with the portrayals from *How I Met Your Mother* and *Bones*, let us consider some additional data.

III. Data and Discussion

In the third episode of the first season of the revival of the series *Will & Grace*, entitled "Emergency Contact" (Pedrad & Burrows, 2017), Grace must undergo an emergency biopsy at the hospital. After the procedure, the hospital calls her emergency contact to pick her up. Grace wakes up to find Leo, her ex-husband (played by Harry Connick Jr.), has come to get her because he is still listed as her emergency contact. He takes her home and they engage in an interesting language-focused discussion in the elevator on the way up to her apartment.

(12.1)

Grace:	Look, thank you for bringing me home. Obviously, I'm going to change my emergency contact.
Leo:	S'awight. It ain't nothin'.
Grace:	I forgot you did that.
Leo:	What?
Grace:	When you want to defuse tension, you turn *up the Cajun spices*. [spaːces] [Southern accent] "Why I'm just a handsome po' boy from N'Orleans. I'm just eatin' my bowl o' zydego."

Leo:	So, a po' boy is a sandwich, and zydeco is a form of music. and I am from Baton Rouge, which is a completely different accent, which I lost years ago.
Grace:	[Speaking like Foghorn Leghorn] I say, I say, yes, you did.
Leo:	I am not Foghorn Leghorn, but I'm gonna give you pass 'cause I know that you're worried about your test results.
Grace:	I'm not worried. Everything's gonna be fine.
Leo:	Y'know, it's okay if you tell me, Grace.
Grace:	Seriously, I'm not worried about it. I'm fine. You could go now, Leo. One of the good things about being single is you learn how to get through a crisis alone.

(Pedrad & Burrows, 2017)

Here we can see again how a speaker of a Southern dialect is criticized for his use of that dialect. Notice again how "ain't" is involved in the initial impetus for Grace's critique of her ex-husband. Ain't serves as a similar flashpoint in the friction between Abernathy and Hodgins (Mitchell 2015). In this example, Grace, who speaks standard English, uses what Bourdieu (1991) has termed "strategies of condescension" to appropriate "the subordinated language for a short period of time in order to exploit it" (Lippi-Green, 2012, p. 223). "Shifting speaking styles can be a powerful performative action, and speakers frequently use shifting their speech as a primary method for doing all kinds of performative work" (Queen, 2015, pp. 196-97). In this case, Grace mocks her ex-'s non-standard accent and lexicon. For example, she says, "you turn *up the Cajun spices* [spaːces]" (Pedrad & Burrows, 2017) and goes on to include cultural items associated with Louisiana in that mockery, e.g., po' boy, N'Orleans, zydeco (which she pronounces zyde**go**). Of course, she also displays her ignorance as Leo corrects her, "a po' boy is a sandwich, and zydeco is a form of music. and I am from Baton Rouge, which is a completely different accent, which I lost years ago" (Pedrad & Burrows, 2017). Leo is demonstrating language resistance. He is overtly rejecting Grace's characterization of his accent and explicitly corrects her lack of cultural knowledge. She continues by again intoning an accent that is not hers to compare her ex-husband to Foghorn Leghorn, an animated rooster from Warner Bros.' cartoons who speaks with an exaggerated Southern accent. Although Leo overtly resists the comparison to a caricature of a Southerner by saying that he is not Foghorn Leghorn, because of Grace's recent health scare he does not dwell on the insult.

The mockery in this scene calls to mind Foucault's (1984) "disciplining of discourse," by which non-standard speakers are silenced, understanding the message that their language is inferior. In fact, we see this in two ways in this particular interaction. First, Leo refuses to engage further in a discussion of the way he speaks. After disagreeing with Grace comparing him to Foghorn Leghorn, he moves on to a new topic. More interesting is what he says in the middle of their exchange about his own accent: "I am from Baton Rouge, which is a completely different accent, which I lost years ago" (Pedrad & Burrows, 2017). Why does he feel it necessary to claim that he lost his accent years ago? Would it be so bad if he did have a stronger accent? Leo clearly displays his own linguistic insecurity—he got the message somewhere along the line that he needed to lose his accent. In fact, I would argue that this line is the writers disciplining the discourse of all non-standard dialect speakers who watch this episode. The message is clear: If you want to be successful like the character of Leo on this show, lose your accent. More broadly, despite Leo's language resistance, this entire scene seems to convey that having an accent can only be a source of mockery that others will exploit. Lippi-Green (2012) has termed this defense of the standard language Standard Language Ideology, which she defines as:

> a bias toward an abstracted, idealized, homogenous spoken language which is imposed and maintained by dominant bloc institutions and which names as its model the written language, but which is drawn primarily from the spoken language of the upper middle class (p. 67)

We see in this dialogue, Bednarek's (2018) thematic message/ideological function, conveying the standard language ideology of the writers even as they imbue the scene with the vaneer of resistance. This message is pretty strong subtext for what on the surface appears to be only a comic interlude in the storyline.

In the second example from the first revival season of *Will & Grace*, in the episode, called "A Gay Olde Christmas" (Quaintance & Burrows, 2017), we see an interaction between Grace and an L2 English speaker. Here Grace approaches the host/hostess stand to request a table and the L2-English speaking character who also appears to be transgender says, "45 minutes," with a pronunciation of the word minutes that is clearly non-native-like.

(12.2)
Grace: Excuse me, do you think--?
Host/ess: 45 "min-oohs."
Grace: Minutes?
Host/ess: "Yus."
Grace: [Returning to friends] It's gonna be a while.
[Later in the scene]

Host/ess: A quick "oop-date," your table will be ready in 51
                 "min-oohs."
Grace: That's more "min-oohs" than before.
Host/ess: That's "race-oost."[1]
(Quaintance & Burrows, 2017)

Grace returns to her friends to say that it will be a long wait. The hostess returns at the end of the scene to give the group an *"oop-date"* (update) saying that the amount of the wait has increased to 51 minutes. Grace complains, "That's more *min-oohs* (minutes) than before!" The other character retorts, "That's *race-oost*," (That's racist) and turns on heal to walk away (Quaintance & Burrows, 2017).

Here the non-standard English-speaking character demonstrates unexpected language resistance to Grace's attempt to discipline their[2] discourse using the strategy of condescension of adopting the way they say minutes. This contrasts with Harry Connick, Jr.'s Leo who feels that he must make explicit that he "lost" his accent. The L2 English character displays language resistance, engaging in an "act of identity" (Le Page 1985, cited in Meyerhoff 2011, p. 273), refusing to give up their identity as a non-native speaker to try to conform to native speakers' expectations. In fact, it goes beyond that, because the character also tells Grace directly that her mockery of their accent is racist. Le Page ascribes rational choice as an underlying component of why speakers choose to use certain linguistic features or a certain way of speaking in certain situations. Perhaps, in this case, the L2 character realized that they could communicate effectively in English with their accent and that achieving a native English pronunciation would be nigh impossible—they embraced their communicative competence and non-native English-speaking identity proudly, choosing to resist Grace's attempted imposition of a more standard English dialect.

In *The Goldbergs* episode "Our Perfect Strangers" (Sikowitz & Smith, 2019), cousin Gleb comes to visit from The Old Country (supposedly Russia, although he flew in from Kiev) in the 1980s. The teenage children of the family, Erica, Barry, and Adam are asked by their grandfather, Al, to show Gleb around Philadelphia, the biggest city near their home. The kids are not very

---

[1] For languages other than English, the English subtitles have been added when provided onscreen. When no English subtitles were present, speech in a language other than English that is not subtitled has been added by the author whenever possible.
[2] I am deliberately using a gender-neutral pronoun here to respect the transgender appearance of the character.

happy about this responsibility, but Barry, upon seeing an episode of the 80s sitcom *Perfect Strangers* playing on TV, gets the idea to use Gleb to do all the adult things he can't yet.

(12.3)

Erica:	Why are we stuck babysitting a complete stranger?
Barry:	[Gasps] Stranger. That's it! [Cut to TV where the opening credits of 80s sitcom *Perfect Strangers* is playing]
Adult Adam:	[v/o][3] Yep, Barry's brilliant plan was inspired by this '80s gem.
Barry:	Cheggit! Looks like we got our very own Balki Bartokomous.
Erica:	The lovable foreign guy from "Perfect Strangers"?
Barry:	Oh, yes. And that makes the three of us Coe-sin [cousin] Larry.
Adult Adam:	[v/o] Crazy as it seems, this was 100% true. Just like the classic sitcom, we had a kooky cousin from the Old Country living with us. Only one question remained.
Adam:	But what do we need a Balki for?
Barry:	Hello? We got a dude who will do whatever we say 'cause he's trusting and unfamiliar with our ways.
Erica:	Do what, exactly? He's an adult man. That means he can buy us beer and rent us cars and co-sign loans. The sky's the limit.
Adam:	Come on. Gleb won't just blindly do whatever we say.
Barry:	Really? For the past ten minutes, he's been listening to that special cassette that cleans the tape deck.
Erica:	Dude, using our childlike foreign relative for our own selfish gain is crossing a line.
Adam:	Not to mention, "Perfect Strangers" is built on the flimsiest of premises.
Barry:	You both make good points that are hard to ignore. And yet, I will.
Adult Adam:	[v/o] And so Barry proceeded to "Perfect Stranger" our cousin Gleb.

(Sikowitz & Smith, 2019)

---

[3] [v/o] = voiceover.

In this excerpt, Barry characterizes Gleb as "trusting" and "unfamiliar with our ways" and Erica later calls Gleb "childlike". These descriptions ignore the fact that Gleb is an adult man, who has managed to travel to a foreign country on his own (and get to the Goldbergs' house on his own). In addition, Gleb speaks functional, if accented English.

As the *Perfect Strangers* theme song plays in the background, there is a montage of all the activities Barry mentioned and then some. Barry has Gleb co-sign a loan, rent a red sports car, accompany him to buy a crossbow and adult magazines. He even makes Gleb stand with an apple on his head in the house as he prepares to fire the crossbow at him like William Tell. Erica and Adam see the fun Barry is having using Gleb to do all the adult things that he cannot and they decide to take advantage also. The *Perfect Strangers* theme song begins again as a new montage shows Erica and Adam getting credit cards at the bank and buying wine coolers and fireworks with Gleb. In the last scene in this montage, the three kids and Gleb enter a building with a revolving door and Gleb gets stuck revolving around in circles screaming (Sikowitz & Smith, 2019).

The way Gleb is portrayed, as naïve and malleable does seem to lend itself to the adjectives the children use earlier in the episode (trusting, unfamiliar, childlike). However, those notions are soon dispelled when Al checks in.

(12.4)	
Adult Adam:	[v/o] We had "Perfect Stranger"-ed our distant cousin Gleb, and it was all working out perfectly. At least, we thought it was.
Al:	So, how's it going with your cousin?
Barry:	Aces.
Erica:	So great.
Adam:	We've been having a blast showing Gleb around. Like yesterday, he was dying to drive me to the Starlog Convention in Jersey.
Erica:	Oh, and today, he insisted on renting me a shore house for the summer. He's the coolest barely-cousin I've ever had.
Gleb:	**No! Is lies! They treat me like idiot and use me for your personal gain. The sweaty boy make me buy crossbow.**
Al:	Crossbow? You can't have that!
Barry:	Ah, according to this license, I can.

Gleb:	**Lady sister make me rent beach house so can party like NBA star. And tiny one make me drive him to American virgin space festival.**
Adam:	I'm just gonna assume there's something lost in translation here.
Gleb:	**You raise spoiled children who make me be Balki Bartokomous from "Perfect Stranger" TV show.**
Adam:	You get "Perfect Strangers" in the Old Country?
Gleb:	**Nyet! You play it in front of me and say your plan out loud, like fools!**
Erica:	That, we did.
Al:	What is wrong with you? You were supposed to get to know him.
Erica:	In our defense, our time together was packed with kooky misadventures and we had very little time to dig in.
Al:	Oh, my God. He came all this way to America. Show him America.

(Sikowitz & Smith, 2019)

Gleb demonstrates his language resistance, by claiming his voice, "They treat me like idiot and use me for your personal gain" (Sikowitz & Smith, 2019). He makes it clear that he is neither naïve nor stupid nor incapable of understanding. In fact, he points out that it's the children who are "fools". He reminds them that they watched *Perfect Strangers* in front of him while talking about their plan.

Despite Al's request the kids still fail to show Cousin Gleb around. Instead, they take him to *Rocky IV* (1985) at the movies and show him Yakov Smirnoff's comedy. Gleb is offended and calls them "people of garbage" (Sikowitz & Smith, 2019). Al agrees and, in a subsequent scene, he threatens to take away every gift he had ever given each grandchild so that Gleb could have it. After this second intervention by Al, they realize how selfish they were being and, with the *Perfect Strangers* theme playing over another montage, bring Gleb to a Phillies game and other places such that "Gleb ended up having the best trip of his life" (Sikowitz & Smith, 2019).

IV. Conclusion

If we compare what happens in this episode of *The Goldbergs* with what we saw in the *How I Met Your Mother* episode from Chapter 8, we find a few differences. First, Gael never demonstrates any language resistance. He leaves the audience believing that big words befuddle him. In contrast, Gleb makes it clear that he understands English just fine. It seems as though he were simply indulging his American cousins in the first part of the episode before he realizes he must resist by telling Al what the teenagers have been making him do. In the same way, the host/ess character resists Grace. Both claim their own equality to native-speaking characters despite having an L2 accent.

Abernathy resists critiques of the way he speaks and the linguistic prejudice that Hodgins displays. Similarly, the L2 English character on *Will & Grace*, rejects Grace's mockery of their accent and calls her out for her prejudice. Gleb on *The Goldbergs* shows the audience and his cousins that he is not "trusting" and "childlike", as they called him. Rather, he understands their plans and recognizes their insincerity. Even Leo won't accept Grace's mockery of his culture and her exaggeration of his Southern dialect, despite his own seemingly internalized negativity toward it. All in all, the resistance shown by these non-standard dialect speaking characters demonstrates that, in some measure, even on television where dialect difference is emphasized for laughs, recognition and acceptance of different dialects is increasing. These examples may represent the beginning of a new paradigm where language difference is celebrated, not disparaged.

Conclusion

In the preceding chapters, we have seen various ways in which L2 language use and L2 language speakers have been employed on television. We looked at a range of contexts: L1 English speakers using a language other than English, L2 English speakers speaking English with an accent, and even L2 English speakers using their native languages. We reviewed a series of issues that these depictions raise, even as for many viewers they go unexamined.

In the first section of this book, we considered the role that L2 use and L2 speakers play in humor, including how that humor can result in more serious commentary on our society. We also looked at how the structure of American TV genres have been influenced by other forms, such as the *telenovela*, and reflected on the use that language can play in that transformation. Finally, we considered how writers employ L2 knowledge, either of the spoken or written language, in the solving of crimes, a trope with a long history finding new life in our own multilingual and globalized context.

We examined language learning in the second part of this book. We considered how a cartoon targeted to children can have positive effects on language learning. We reviewed differences in child and adult language acquisition. And, we explored myths about language learning and loss, discovering that many times the ways in which characters learn a language on TV harkens back to earlier grammar-translation or audiolingual notions of language learning.

In part three, we endeavored to understand the role that stereotypes play in our understanding of L2 speakers and L2 use. We saw how, as in the case of Italian, L2 language use is inextricably linked with the stereotypes we have about people who come from a given place, or even whose ancestors came from that place generations ago. Moreover, we analyzed how the use of faux dialects and accents can racialize the portrayal of a given ethnic or linguistic group; sometimes meant as satire, these depictions can easily cross the line to become demeaning parodies. Evidence demonstrated the ways in which subtitles can be used to reinforce these sometimes negative, prejudiced perspectives on L2 speakers and communities.

We considered the ways in which television reflects repeating patterns as well as ruptures in those patterns in section four. We catalogued the way in which comedy was used to highlight the increasing importance of Spanish in the U.S. against the backdrop of the defeat of an English Only law in Nashville, Tennessee. We examined the role of children functioning as interpreters and mediators of America for their non-English-speaking parents, who immigrate to the U.S. in search of opportunity and a better life. We observed how television reflects the repeating cycle of this process as new waves of immigrants come to our shores and new generations of children are pressed into service. Finally, we embraced the rupture of non-standard dialect and L2 English speakers resisting the hegemony of the "standard" language and its speakers.

In the introduction to this work, I discussed the power of television to create a sense of solidarity—*they* are just like *us*—but I also pointed out that negative portrayals associated with L2 speakers or L2 use can do great damage by emphasizing the differences between *us* and *them* in the collective American psyche. Some of the portrayals we have analyzed were positive, while others leave us to question if their creators considered the potential negative impact of their work. Whether intended or not, we must consider the ideological messages that these examples carry (cf. Bednarek's (2018) functions of dialogue).

We must interrogate the reasons behind the depictions of L2 speakers and L2 use. When we see a character speaking their native language (e.g., Gloria's use of Spanish on *Modern Family*), we must ask ourselves, is this Pandey's (2016) linguistic exhibitionism or is this usage more deeply discoursal? Subtitles, or the lack thereof, can provide some clues. Often, the lack of subtitles is a good indication that the foreign (i.e., not English) language use goes beyond merely exhibitionistic usage. It also usually indicates that the "other" language is fundamental to the character (think of Gloria's unsubtitled use of Spanish in "A Year of Birthdays" from Chapter 1 or David Hodges' Italian fiancée from Chapter 7). L2 usage can also tell us something about the U.S. We discussed how bilingual children mediate a new country for their non-English-speaking parents in a process that continues to repeat itself even today (Chapter 11). We examined how a popular American program like *Saturday Night Live* can show a full skit in Spanish without subtitling (Chapter 10). These last examples indicate that the U.S. is not as monolingual as we might believe, nor has it ever been.

What about when L1 English characters use other languages? When done so poorly, inherent in these scenes seems to be an underlying critique of American monolingualism (e.g., Ted's poor Spanish with Professor Rodriguez from Chapter 1). When English-speaking characters deploy an L2 with aplomb, we need to examine the context more closely. In the crime genre, detectives show their chops as speakers of languages other than English to catch criminals (Chapter 3). They often deploy such language in a communicative way that goes beyond linguistic exhibitionism. Meanwhile, the example of Maya speaking flawless, unsubtitled French in *Speechless* most closely resembles the example of Gloria speaking Spanish—it seems to valorize the knowledge of another language and exceed mere linguistic exhibitionism. However, scenes such as the one from *Rules of Engagement* where Timmy throws Russell under the bus in Italian (Chapter 1, Chapter 7) and the one from *The Simpsons* in which Selma enters into a sham marriage as the *goomar* (Chapter 7) give us pause as it could cause native-speakers of English to feel uncomfortable or fearful of those who speak another language, which Queen (2015) also suggests.

When English is spoken with an accent by non-native speakers (and by speakers of non-standard dialects) other ideologies are at play, even as it is sometimes difficult to ascribe the motives behind such portrayals to writers and producers. Some viewers will understand the satirical if stereotypical use of "broken" English (e.g., Mah Mah from *American Dad!* in Chapter 9) as a critique of such linguistic stereotypes and linguicism more generally. While others will simply take the attempted humor at face value, using the depiction as evidence of the truth of such stereotypes. This reading could have pernicious consequences for the groups being portrayed. In some instances, like *The Millers* episode from Chapter 9, we are led toward this latter interpretation— here, again, subtitling plays a role. In others, such as *The Mick* episode (Chapter 9), the audience is provided explicit guideposts (i.e., the characters' commentary and the letter at the end of the episode) that undermine the racist reading and make it clear that satire was at play. The trouble is, even with that subversive intention made clear, I'm not sure that the overt racism portrayed can be redeemed. Without doubt, some depictions like Gloria's missed metaphors, parsing, and pronunciation difficulties (Chapter 1), played for humor in the episode, are designed to help the audience build empathy and understanding with those who speak English as a second language.

In addition to uses of second languages in simulated real-life communication, language learning itself and the L2 classroom also find representation on television. Based on the portrayals we observed (Chapters 4, 5, and 6), what trends can we discern? First, people believe that learning a language is not easy—Coach Mellor expresses this view in Chapter 6—and perhaps he has a point, at least for adult learners, as evidenced by Daniel (Chapter 5). At the very least, there appears to be a definite distinction between child and adult learners (Daniel and his son in Chapter 5), supported by research in second language acquisition. Television represents the L2 classroom (unfortunately, only in French) as an unforgiving place (cf. Katie the *American Housewife*'s experience in Chapter 6) with teachers who dislike their job (cf. Maya's attack on JJ's French teacher, also Chapter 6). Moreover, out-of-date methodologies for language learning, such as the Grammar-Translation and Audiolingual Methods, hold sway in the popular imagination over more contemporary language pedagogies focused on communication. More positively, in the cartoon world, children are invited to explore language learning (e.g., *Xiaolin Showdown* in Chapter 4 and *Ben 10: Ultimate Alien* in Chapter 6) and develop empathy for L2 speakers (e.g., *Xiaolin Showdown*). Perhaps there is yet hope for better representations of language teaching and learning on the small screen once the children who watched these programs are making the content.

Certainly, the instances that I outline in this work only scratch the surface of the complex and growing phenomenon of L2 speakers and L2 usage on TV. Every television season sees new shows and new stories representing L2 speakers and L2 use. We have only to look to the most recent slate of new network shows from the 2019-2020 season to find shows like *Bob Hearts Abishola* (Lorre et al., 2019) on CBS and *Awkwafina is Nora from Queens* (Awkwafina et al., 2020) on Comedy Central. In the former, the West African language Yoruba and Yoruba-speakers feature prominently, while languages like Mandarin and Spanish, among others, are represented in the latter. As new and different voices continue to make their way into writers' rooms eager to see their own experiences and that of their friends and families represented on the small screen, there is little doubt that the polyphonous diversity of the American experience will expand how languages other than English and how those who speak them, or who speak English with an accent, will come to be depicted.

Appendix

Table A.1: Television Episodes Cited.

TV Series (Network)	Year	Episode Number	Episode Name
10 Things I Hate About You (ABC Family)	2009	1	Pilot
	2009	2	I Want You to Want Me
30 Rock (NBC)	2012	113	Alexis Goodlooking and the Case of the Missing Whiskey
Alcatraz (Fox)	2012	6	Paxton Petty
American Dad! (Fox)	2013	157	Kung Pao Turkey
American Housewife (ABC)	2017	18	The Otto Motto
A.P. Bio (NBC)	2018	4	Overachieving Virgins
Ben 10: Ultimate Alien (Cartoon Network)	2011	29	It's Not Easy Being Gwen
	2017	229	The Cognitive Regeneration
The Big Bang Theory (CBS)	2018	243	The Matrimonial Metric
	2018	249	The Gates Excitation
	2010	95	The X in the File
Bones (Fox)	2011	131	The Hot Dog in the Competition
	2012	143	The Future in the Past
Brooklyn Nine-Nine (Fox)[1]	2017	93	Kicks
Brothers & Sisters (ABC)	2011	101	The One That Got Away
Castle (ABC)	2010	25	Suicide Squeeze
Champions (NBC)	2018	6	Grandma Dearest
The Closer (TNT)	2009	71	The Life

---

[1] This episode of Brooklyn Nine-Nine aired on Fox, although Fox canceled the show after season 5. Subsequent seasons have aired on NBC, which picked up the show.

Cougar Town (ABC)	2011	43	Damaged by Love
CSI: Crime Scene Investigation (CBS)	2013	285	Double Fault
Elementary (CBS)	2013	17	Possibility Two
Family Guy (Fox)	2011	161	Tiegs for Two
The Goldbergs (ABC)	2019	134	Our Perfect Strangers
Go On (NBC)	2013	13	Gooooaaaallll Doll!
Great News (NBC)	2017	19	Love Is Dead
Happy Endings (ABC)	2011	5	Like Father, Like Gun
How I Met Your Mother (CBS)	2007	46	We're Not From Here
	2011	132	The Exploding Meatball Sub
	2013	181	Romeward Bound
Intelligence (CBS)	2014	3	Mei Chen Returns
The Knick (Cinemax)	2014	1	Methods and Madness
Law & Order (NBC)	2009	429	Promote This!
Law & Order: Criminal Intent (NBC)	2009	171	Revolution
Law & Order: Special Victims Unit (NBC)	2009	230	Spooked
Life in Pieces (CBS)	2015	8	Godparent Turkey Corn Farts
	2019	79	Reverse Burden District Germany
Lost (ABC)	2010	113	The Package
The Mentalist (CBS)	2013	108	Red in Tooth and Claw
The Mick (Fox)	2018	30	The Dump
The Middle (ABC)	2016	173	Roadkill
The Millers (CBS)	2013	10	Carol's Parents Are Coming to Town
The Mindy Project (Fox)	2012	1	Pilot
Modern Family (ABC)	2010	30	Halloween
	2011	46	Good Cop, Bad Dog

	2011	47	See You Next Fall
	2011	58	Express Christmas
	2012	64	Virgin Territory
	2013	91	The Future Dunphys
	2017	186	All Things Being Equal
	2019	222	Blasts from the Past
	2019	232	A Year of Birthdays
Monday Mornings (TNT)	2013	1	Pilot
Monk (USA)	2009	111	Mr. Monk and the Foreign Man
Murphy Brown (revival) (CBS)	2018	256 (9)*	Thanksgiving and Taking
New Girl (Fox)	2013	54	The Box
One Tree Hill (CW)	2010	162	Lists, Plans
Partners (CBS)	2012	4	The Key
Pretty Little Liars (ABC Family)	2011	16	Je Suis Une Amie
Raising Hope (Fox)	2013	65	Burt Mitzvah-The Musical
Rules of Engagement (CBS)	2011	66	Anniversary Chicken
Saturday Night Live (NBC)	2009	649	Skit: La Policía Mexicana
Schooled (ABC)	2019	12	CB Likes Lainey
The Simpsons (Fox)	1990	11	The Crepes of Wrath
	2011	483	The Real Housewives of Fat Tony
Single Parents (ABC)	2019	11	That Elusive Zazz
	2019	13	Graham D'Amato: Hot Lunch Mentalist
Speechless (ABC)	2018	36	D-i-Dimeo A-c-Academy
	2019	59	S-e-Seoul B-r-Brothers
Suburgatory (ABC)	2014	56	Les Lucioles
Superstore (NBC)	2018	51	Local Vendors Day
This Is Us (NBC)	2018	42	Kamsahamnida

Trophy Wife (ABC)	2013	3	The Social Network
	2014	21	Back to School
Ugly Betty (ABC)	2008	42	The Manhattan Project
	2008	43	Filing For the Enemy
White Collar (USA)	2009	6	All In
Will & Grace (revival) (NBC)	2017	197 (3)*	Emergency Contact
	2017	201 (7)*	A Gay Olde Christmas
Xiaolin Showdown (WB)[2]	2003-2004	1-13	Season One

*Episode numbers in parentheses indicate the number of the episode since the series was rebooted.

---

[2] The WB Network became the CW in January 2006.

Chapter 1: Lyrics to *Rápido* from *Great News*, "Love is Dead" (2017)

Rápido, rápido
mejor nos damos prisa
tenemos que hacerlo rápido
porque eres mi madrastra
Vámonos, vámonos,
a hacer un triple beso
en trío, contigo
y con tu perro que está enfermo
Rápido, rápido,
estoy desesperado
Por favor, por favor,
cuando estés en el baño
disimulemos los sonidos
para que (something) baño
Rápido, rápido,
tengo el hombro dislocado,
solamente con tus senos
tú puedes arreglarlo
Hay ratas, hay ratas
en el rincón teniendo sexo,
sería una fiesta sexual,
si nos venimos al mismo tiempo, mami
(roguecit, 2018)

Source: The post entitled, "I need the lyrics to Rapido..." from the subreddit /r/Great NewsTV (roguecit, 2018).

Chapter 8: Scene from *How I Met Your Mother*, "We're Not From Here" (2007)

Robin:	And here I am in the drum circle.
Barney:	Woah, are you topless? Ted, check this out!
Ted:	(*not looking up from his menu*) Seen 'em.
Lily:	Wow, it seems like a great trip.
Robin:	Oh, it was. I feel like the Robin who left is not the same Robin who came back, you know?
Lily:	Wow! There's a lot of nude people in here!
Barney:	You haven't changed Scherbatsky! You're a sophisticated, scotch-swilling, cigar-smoking, red-meat-eating, gun-toting New Yorker.
Lily:	Just a shirt and shoes—that's a look.
Barney:	What you are not is a massage-giving, wind-surfing, bongo-playing, teetotaling, vegan, peacenik hippie like your soon-to-be ex-boyfriend, Gael. Back me up here, Ted!
Ted:	Just happy Robin's happy.
Robin:	Thank you.
Lily:	Man, this is like the "Where's Waldo?" of exposed genitalia except that it's really easy to find Waldo (*chuckles*).
Robin:	I have evolved! And I'm enjoying living my life a little bit closer to the way Gael and I did in Argentina.
Barney:	Please. Vacation romances have an expiration date. Gael's got a "best-if-banged-by" sticker on him, and once your romance starts to stink, you'll dump his ass down the drain like sour milk and go back to being "unevolved Robin," the one we actually like. Back me up here, Ted!
Ted:	(*automatically*) I'm just happy Robin's happy.
Barney:	I'm telling you, within three days—
Lily:	Oh, here he comes! Switch to big words.
Barney:	(*without missing a beat, getting up to let Gael sit next to Robin*) Within a triad of solar periods, you'll recognize your dearth of compatibility with your paramour, and conclude your association.
Robin:	My journey was transformative, and I reassert my commitment to both the aforementioned paramour and the philosophies he espouses.
Gael:	(*enthusiastic*) What are we talking of? Baseball?
Barney:	(*smiles, slapping Gael on the back while addressing Robin*) This is all gonna return to masticate you in the gluteals [sic]. Support my hypothesis, Ted!

Ted: *(automatically)* I'm just jubilant my former paramour is jubilant.
(Mitchell, 2010, pp. 238-39)

References

Abrams, J.J., Burk, B., Kurtzman, A., Orci, R., Wyman, J.H., Pinkner, J., & Chapelle, J. (Executive Producers). (2008). *Fringe* [Television series]. Burbank, CA: Warner Bros. Television Distribution.

Abrams, J.J., Lindelof, D., Burk, B., Cuse, C., Bender, J., Pinkner, J., Williams, S., Kitsis, E., Horowitz, A., Higgins, J., & Sarnoff, E. (Executive Producers). (2004). *Lost* [Television series]. Santa Monica, CA: Bad Robot Productions.

Acoach, C.L., & Webb, L.M. (2004). The influence of language brokering on Hispanic teenagers' acculturation, academic performance, and nonverbal decoding skills: A preliminary study. *The Howard Journal of Communications, 15*, 1-19.

Adler, A., Kaplan, A., Morton, J., Winer, J., Copeland, B., & Adler, B. (Executive Producers). (2015). *Life in Pieces* [Television series]. Los Angeles, CA: 20th Century Fox Television.

Adler, B. (Writer), & Reid, A. (Director). (2019). Reverse burden district Germany [Television series episode]. In Adler, A., Kaplan, A., Morton, J., Winer, J., Copeland, B., & Adler, B. (Executive Producers), *Life in Pieces*. Los Angeles, CA: 20th Century Fox Television.

Amiel, J., & Begler, M. (Writers) & Soderbergh, S. (Director). (2014). Methods and madness [Television series episode]. In Jacobs, G., Soderbergh, S., Amiel, J., Begler, M., Sugar, M., & Owen, C. (Executive Producers), *The Knick*. Culver City, CA: Anonymous Content.

Awkwafina, Dornetto, K., Aniello, L., Hsaio, T., Reiss, I., & Principato, P. (Executive Producers). (2020). *Awkwafina is Nora From Queens* [Television series]. Bevery Hills, CA: Artists First.

Baldwin, H., & Coveny, J. (Writers), & Robin, S. (Director). (2009). The life [Television series episode]. In The Shephard/Robin Company (Producers), *The Closer*. Burbank, CA: Warner Bros. Television Distribution.

Barman, A., Chatterjee, A., & Bhide, R. (2016). Cognitive impairment and rehabilitation strategies after traumatic brain injury. *Indian Journal of Psychological Medicine, 38*(3), 172-181.

Barnes, R., & Marimow, A.E. (2019, June 27). Supreme Court puts census citizenship question on hold. *The Washington Post*, Retrieved from http://www.washingtonpost.com

Bednarek, M. (2018). *A Linguistic Approach to TV Dialogue*. Cambridge: Cambridge University Press.

Bemelmens, L. (1939). *Madeline*. New York: Simon & Schuster, Inc.

Bemelmens, L. (1985). *Madeleine*. Paris: Lutin Poche de l'École des Loisirs.

Berman, A. (Writer), & Shakman, M. (Director). (2008a). Lights, camera…homicidio [DVD]. In Franks, S., Henz, C., Kulchak, K., Damaski, M., & Callahan, B. (Executive Producers), *Psych, The Complete Second Season*. Universal City, CA: Universal Studios.

Berman, A. (Writer), & Shakman, M. (Director). (2008b). Lights, camera...homicidio [Television series episode]. In Franks, S., Henz, C., Kulchak, K., Damaski, M., & Callahan, B. (Executive Producers), *Psych*. Universal City, CA: NBCUniversal Television Distribution.

Biasucci, D. (Writer), & Kramer, L. (Director). (2011). The real housewives of Fat Tony [Television series episode]. In Brooks, J.L., Groening, M., Jean, A., Selman, M., Frink, J., & Maxtone-Graham, I. (Executive Producers), *The Simpsons*. Los Angeles, CA: 20th Century Fox Television.

Bielby, D.D., & Harrington, C.L. (2005). Opening America?: The telenovela-ization of U.S. soap operas. *Television & New Media, 6*, 383-99.

Bleichenbacher, L. (2008). *Multilingualism in the Movies: Hollywood characters and their language choices*. Tübingen: Narr Francke Attempto Verlag.

Bleichenbacher, L. (2012). Linguicism in Hollywood movies? Representations of, and audience reactions to multilingualism in mainstream movie dialogues. *Multilingua, 31*, 155-176.

Blickstead, J., & Kollmer, T. (Writers), & Robinson, J.A. (Director). (2018). Overachieving Virgins [Television series episode]. In Meyers, S., O'Brien, M., Michaels, L., Singer, A., & Shoemaker, M. (Executive Producers), *A.P. Bio*. New York, NY: NBCUniversal Television Distribution.

Bourdieu, P. (1991). *Language and Symbolic Power*. Cambridge, MA: Harvard University Press.

Bowman, B. (Writer), & Burrows, J. (Director). (2013). Carol's parents are coming to town [Television series episode]. In Garcia, G., & Burrows, J. (Executive Producers), *The Millers*. Santa Monica, CA: CBS Television Distribution.

Breckman, D., & Brenneman, J. (Writers), & Grossman, D. (Director). (2009). Mr. Monk and the foreign man [Television series episode]. In Breckman, A., Hoberman, D., Shalhoub, T., Scharpling, T., & Thompson, R. (Executive Producers), *Monk*. Universal City, CA: NBCUniversal Television Distribution.

Brown, R. (Writer), & Chemel, L.S. (Director). (2016). Roadkill [Television series episode]. In Heline, D., & Heisler, E. (Executive Producers), *The Middle*. Burbank, CA: Warner Bros. Television Distribution.

Byer, M.R., & Hancock, T. (Writers), & Tanenbaum, B. (Director). (2013). Double Fault [Television series episode]. In Zuiker, A.E., Petersen, W., Bruckheimer, J., Donahue, A., Fink, K., Shankar, N., & Cannon, D. (Executive Producers), *CSI: Crime Scene Investigation*. Los Angeles, CA: King World Productions.

Campolongo, J., & Henderson, J. (Writers), & Kretchmer, J. (Director). (2009). All in [Television series episode]. In Eastin, J., King, J., Goffman, M., & Thiel, N. (Executive Producers), *White Collar*. Los Angeles, CA: 20th Century Fox Television.

Carlock, R., & Means, S. (Writers), & McCarthy-Miller, B. (Director). (2017). Love is dead [Television series episode]. In Fey, T., Carlock. R., Wigfield, T., Miner, D., & McCarthy-Miller, B. (Executive Producers), *Great News*. Universal City, CA: Universal Television.

Carlson, J. (2007, October 2). How I met your mother. Episode recap: We're not from Here [webpage]. Retrieved from http://community.tvguide.com/blog-entry/TV-Show-Blog/Met-Mother/Episode-Recap/800023440

Carroll, J. (2001, June/July). Court OKs official English. *State Government News, 44* (6), 36.

Cathcart, R. (1986). Situational differences and the sampling of young children's school language. In R. Day (Ed.), *Talking to Learn: Conversation and Second-Language Acquisition* (pp. 118-140). Rowley, MA: Newbury House.

Chandrasekaran, V., & Lloyd, S. (Writers), & Savage, F. (Director). (2019). Blasts from the past [Television series episode]. In Levitan, S., & Lloyd, C. (Executive Producers), *Modern Family.* Los Angeles, CA: 20th Century Fox Television.

Chase, D., Gray, B., Green, R., Burgess, M., Landress, I.S., Winter, T., & Weiner, M. (Executive Producers). (1999). *The Sopranos* [Television series]. New York City, NY: HBO Entertainment.

Chernuchin, M.S. (Writer), & Coles, J.D. (Director). (2009). Revolution [Television series episode]. In Wolf, D., Jankowski, P., Barba, N., & Coles, J.D. (Executive Producers), *Law & Order: Criminal Intent.* Universal City, CA: NBCUniversal Television Distribution.

Cherry, M., Spezialy, T., Edelstein, M., Keenan, J., Perkins, G.W., Daily, B., Pardee, J., & Murphy, J. (Executive Producers). (2004). *Desperate Housewives* [Television series]. Burbank, CA: Disney-ABC Domestic Television.

Chinn, L. (Writer), & Sohn, M. (Director). (2018). The dump [Television series episode]. In Olson, K., Chernin, J., Chernin, D., Frenkel, N., Obst, O., & Einhorn, R. (Executive Producers), *The Mick.* Los Angeles, CA: 20th Century Fox Television.

Chun, D. (Writer), & Moore, J. (Director). (2013). The Social Network [Television series episode]. In Halpern, E., Haskins, S., Eisenberg, L., & Stupnitsky, G. (Executive Producers), *Trophy Wife.* Burbank, CA: ABC Studios.

Chun, D. (Writers), & Purple, B. (Director). (2019). S-e-Seoul B-r-brothers [Television series episode]. In Gernan, C., Kasdan, J., Mar, M., & Silveri, S. (Executive Producers), *Speechless.* Los Angeles, CA: 20th Century Fox Television.

Chun, D., & Roller, M. (Writers), & Shapeero, T. (Director). (2018). D-i-Dimeo A-c-Academy [Television series episode]. In Gernan, C., Kasdan, J., Mar, M., & Silveri, S. (Executive Producers), *Speechless.* Los Angeles, CA: 20th Century Fox Television.

Chupack, C. (Writer), & Spiller, M. (Director). (2011). Express Christmas [Television series episode]. In Levitan, S. & Lloyd, C. (Executive Producers), *Modern Family.* Los Angeles, CA: 20th Century Fox Television.

Cohen, P. (2009, March 15). Same city, new story. *The New York Times* (Arts & Leisure), pp. 1, 6.

Coleman, M., & Ganong, L. (2003). 'Mama, He Says...': Children as Language Brokers for their parents. In M. Coleman & L.H. Ganong (Eds.), *Points & Counterpoints: Controversial Relationship and Family issues in the 21st Century, An Anthology* (p. 153). Oxford: Oxford University Press.

Cooper, T.C. (1999). Processing of idioms by L2 learners of English. *TESOL Quarterly, 33*, 233-62.

Covington, C. (Writer), & Junger, G. (Director). (2009a). Pilot [Television series episode]. In Covington, C., Ziffren, J., & Schiff, R. (Executive Producers), *10 Things I Hate About You*. Burbank, CA: Disney-ABC Domestic Television.

Covington, C. (Writer), & Junger, G. (Director). (2009b). I want you to want me [Television series episode]. In Covington, C., Ziffren, J., & Schiff, R. (Executive Producers), *10 Things I Hate About You*. Burbank, CA: Disney-ABC Domestic Television.

Covington, C., Ziffren, J., & Schiff, R. (Executive Producers). (2009). *10 Things I Hate About You* [Television series]. Burbank, CA: Disney-ABC Domestic Television.

Danesi, M. (1992). Metaphorical competence in second language acquisition and second language teaching: The neglected dimension. In J. E. Alatis (Ed.), *Georgetown University Round Table on Languages and Linguistics 1992* (pp. 489-500). Washington, DC: Georgetown University Press.

Darren Starr Productions & HBO Original Productions (Production Companies). (1998). *Sex & the City* [Television series]. Burbank, CA: Warner Bros. Television Distribution.

De Cunha D. (1991). *Metaphor comprehension and second language acquisition*. Toronto: University of Toronto Press.

Deggans, E. (2005a, September). Freddie Prinze, Jr.: Taking back his father's name. *Hispanic*, 16-20.

Deggans, E. (2005b, September). The story behind television's Latin star. *Hispanic*, 22-24.

Dickerson, C., & Kanno-Youngs, Z. (2019, July 11). U.S. prepares to arrest thousands of immigrant family members. *The New York Times*, Retrieved from http://www.nytimes.com/

Diefenbach, R.T., Haselton, V., D'Agostino, L., Fraenkel, J., Kahangi, O., Self, C., Cohen, A., Gamboa Meyers, T., Kohn, A., Neslage, L., Markoff, D., Toran, D., Sebastian, J., Hochman, J., & Volonakis, V. (Executive Producers). (2009). *The Real Housewives of New Jersey* [Television series]. Silver Spring, MD: Sirens Media.

Di Loreto, D., Adler, A., & Murphy, R. (Executive Producers). (2012). *The New Normal* [Television series]. Los Angeles, CA: 20th Century Fox Television.

Dobrow, J.R. & Gidney, C.L. (1998). The good, the bad, and the foreign: The use of dialect in children's animated television. *Annals of the American Academy of Political and Social Science, 557*, 105-119.

Dolan, M., & McGreevy, P. (2016, February 24). Ex-state Sen. Leland Yee gets 5 years in prison in corruption case. *Los Angeles Times*, Retrieved from http://www.latimes.com/

Donovan, B., & Herro, E. (Writers), & Traill, P. (Director). (2017). The Otto motto [Television series episode]. In Dunn, S., Kaplan, A., Schwartz, K., Wiener, R., & Fleischer, R. (Executive Producers), *American Housewife*. Burbank, CA: Disney-ABC Domestic Television.

Do you live in an Official English state?. (2005, March 25). *Human Events, 61*(11), 3.

Duff, P.A. (2000). Repetition in foreign language classroom interaction. In J.K. Hall & L.S. Verplaeste (Eds.), *Second and Foreign Language Learning Through Classroom Interaction* (pp. 109-138). New York, NY: Routledge.

Duffer, M., Duffer, R., Levy, S., Cohen, D., Holland, C., Wright, B., Thunell, M., Gajdusek, K., & Paterson, I. (Executive Producers). (2019). *Stranger Things (season 3)* [Television series]. Los Angeles, CA: 21 Laps Entertainment.

Durkin, K., & Judge, J. (2001). Effects of language and social behaviour on children's reactions to foreign people in television. *British Journal of Developmental Psychology, 19,* 597-612.

Ellis, N.C. (1996). Sequencing in SLA: Phonological memory, chunking, and points of order. *Studies in Second Language Acquisition, 18,* 91-126.

Ellis, R. (1982). The origins of interlanguage. *Applied Linguistics, 3,* 207-23.

Ellis, R. (1984). Formulaic speech in early classroom second-language development. In J. Handscombe, R. Orem, & B. Taylor (Eds.), *On TESOL '83: The question of control* (pp. 53-65). Washington, DC: TESOL.

Ellis, R. (2006). *The Study of Second Language Acquisition, second edition.* Oxford: Oxford University Press.

English as the Official Language: Hearing before the Subcommittee on Education Reform of the Committee on Education and the Workforce, U.S. House of Representatives, 109th Cong. 1 (2006).

Ervin-Tripp, S. (1974). Is second-language learning like the first?. *TESOL Quarterly, 8,* 111-27.

Ferrari, M., Hernandez, T., Howe, J., Holland, S., Kaplan, E., & Gordon, A. (Writers), & Cendrowski, M. (Director). (2018). The matrimonial metric [Television series episode]. In Lorre, C., Molaro, S., Prady, B., & Kaplan, E. (Executive Producers), *The Big Bang Theory.* Burbank, CA: Warner Bros. Television.

Fez (That '70s Show). (n.d.). Retrieved from http://en.wikipedia.org/wiki/Fez_%28That_%2770s_Show%29

Fields, J. (Writer), & Spiller, M. (Director). (2008). Filing for the enemy [Televeision series episode]. In Hayek, S., Horta, S., Goldstick, S., Silverman, B., Tamez, J., & Fields, J. (Executive Producers), *Ugly Betty.* Burbank, CA: Disney-ABC Domestic Television.

Foster, G., Krasnoff, R., Harmon, D., Russo, A., Goldman, N., Donovan, G., Guarascio, D., Port, M., Shapeero, T., McKenna, C., and Schrab, R. (Executive Producers). (2009). *Community (season one)* [Television series]. Culver City, CA: Sony Pictures Television.

Foucault, M. (1984). The Order of Discourse. In M.J. Shapiro (Ed.), *Language and Politics.* Oxford: Oxford University Press.

Fred. (2007, October 3). How I met your mother: We're not from here. Retrieved from http://tvoholic.com/episode-reviews/how-i-met-your-mother-were-not-from-here/

Freddie. (2005, October). *People, 67,* 44.

Gardner, R. (1985). *Social Psychology and Second Language Learning: The Role of Attitude and Motivation.* London: Edward Arnold.

Geary, A., & Steiner, B. (Writers), & Spiller, M. (Director). (2018). Grandma Dearest [Television series episode]. In Kaling, M., Grandy, C., Klein, H.,

Spiller, M., & Warburton, M. (Executive Producers), *Champions*. Universal City, CA: Universal Television.

Gliatto, T. (2008). Ugly Betty. *People, 69*(20), 43.

Goffman, M. (Writer), & Mann, S. (Director). (2013). Possibility Two [Television series episode]. In Doherty, R., Timberman, S., Beverly, C., Coles, J., Polson, J., & Tracey, J. (Executive Producers), *Elementary*. Santa Monica, CA: CBS Television Distribution.

Goldberg, A.F., Robinson, D., Gordon, S., Barnow, A., Firek, M., Guarascio, D., & Katzenberg, D. (Executive Producers). (2013). *The Goldbergs* [Television series]. Culver City, CA: Sony Pictures Television.

Gonzales, R. (2014, April 8). San Francisco's Chinatown Hurt By Yee Scandal. *NPR*, Retrieved from http://www.npr.org/

Greene, J. (Writer), & Leto, P. (Director). (2009). Spooked [Television series episode]. In Wolf, D., & Jankowski, P. (Executive Producers), *Law & Order: Special Victims Unit*. Universal City, CA: NBCUniversal Television Distribution.

Guest, A. (Writer), & Appel, E. (Director). (2017). Kicks [Television series episode]. In Goor, D., Schur, M., Miner, D., Lord, P., Miller, C., & Del Tredici, L. (Executive Producers), *Brooklyn Nine-Nine*. Universal City, CA: NBCUniversal Television Distribution.

Guiora, A.Z., Beit-Hallahmi, B., Brannon, R.C.L., Dull, C.Y., & Scovel, T. (1972). The effects of experimentally induced changes in ego states on pronunciation ability in second language: An exploratory study. *Comprehensive Psychiatry, 13*(5), 421-28.

Hakuta, K. (1976). A case study of a Japanese child learning English as a second language. *Language Learning, 26*, 321-51.

Halgunseth, L. (2003). Language Brokering: Positive Developmental Outcomes. In M. Coleman & L.H. Ganong (Eds.), *Points & Counterpoints: Controversial Relationship and Family issues in the 21st Century, An Anthology* (pp. 154-156). Oxford: Oxford UP.

Hall, N., & Sham, S. (2007). Language brokering as young people's work: Evidence from Chinese adolescents in England. *Language and Education, 21*(1), 16-30.

Halpern, E., Haskins, S., Eisenberg, L., & Stupnitsky, G. (Executive Producers). (2013). *Trophy Wife* [Television series]. Burbank, CA: ABC Studios.

Hanson, H., Josephson, B., Stephen, N., Toynton, I., Kettner, C., Collier, J., Peterson, M., & Zisk, R. (Executive Producers). (2005). *Bones* [Television series]. Los Angeles, CA: 20th Century Fox Television.

Hanson, H., & Nathan, S. (Writers), & Toynton, T. (Director). (2012). The Future in the Past [Television series episode]. In Hanson, H., Josephson, B., Stephen, N., Toynton, I., Kettner, C., Collier, J., Peterson, M., & Zisk, R. (Executive Producers), *Bones*. Los Angeles, CA: 20th Century Fox Television.

Harper, J. (Writer), & Zisk, R. (Director). (2013). Red in Tooth and Claw. [Television series episode]. In Heller, B., Long, C.., Cerone, D., & Szentgyorgyi, T. (Executive Producers), *The Mentalist*. Burbank, CA: Warner Bros. Television Distribution.

Harris, C. (Writer), & Fryman, P. (Director). (2007). We're not from here [Television series episode]. In Bay, C., & Thomas, C. (Executive Producers), *How I met your mother*. Los Angeles, CA: 20ᵗʰ Century Fox Television.

Harris, P. (2009). City of Nashville rejects English-only law. *Reuters*, Retrieved from http://www.reuters.com/

Haukom, M. (Writer), & Mancuso, G. (Director). (2011). Anniversary chicken [Television series episode]. In Tanimura, C., Giarraputo, J., Hertz, T., Stoll, B., McCarthy, V., Robinson, D., & Sandler, A. (Executive Producers), *Rules of Engagement*. Culver City, CA: Sony Pictures Television.

Hayek, S., Horta, S., Goldstick, S., Silverman, B., Tamez, J., & Fields, J. (Executive Producers). (2006). *Ugly Betty* [Television series]. Burbank, CA: Disney-ABC Domestic Television.

Helford, B., Oppenheimer, D., Bullock, S., Borden, R., Caplan, D., Torgrove, M., Kaplan, P.A., & Lopez, G. (Executive Producers). (2002). *George Lopez* [Television series]. Burbank, CA: Warner Bros. Domestic Television Distribution.

Heller, B. (Executive Producer). (2008). *The Mentalist* [Television series]. Burbank, CA: Warner Bros. Domestic Television Distribution.

Herbert, V. (Writers), & Fortenberry, J. (Director). (2018). Kamsahamnida [Television series episode]. In Fogelman, D., Rosenthal, J., Todd, D., Olin, K., Gogolak, C., Requa, J., Ficarra, G., Aptaker, I., Berger, E., & Oyegun, K. (Executive Producers), *This Is Us*. Los Angeles, CA: 20ᵗʰ Century Fox Television.

Herman, D.M. (2003). Iowa College Students' Attitudes Toward Official English Legislation: An exploratory study. *Journal of Language, Identity & Education, 2*(2), 83-103.

Higginbotham, A., & Richman, J. (Writers), & Savage, F. (Director). (2011). Good cop, bad dog [Television series episode]. In Levitan, S., & Lloyd, C. (Executive Producers), *Modern Family*. Los Angeles, CA: 20ᵗʰ Century Fox Television.

Hill, J.H. (1998). Language, race, and white public space. *American Anthropologist, 100*(3), 680-689.

Ho, A. (Writer), & McDonald, M. (Director). (2011). Damaged by Love [Television series episode]. In Lawrence, B., Cox, C., Arquette, D., Swartzlander, R., McCormick, B., & Winston, R.K. (Executive Producers), *Cougar Town*. Burbank, CA: Disney-ABC Domestic Television.

Holdman, B.M. (Writer), & Grismer, C. (Director). (2011). Je suis une amie [Television series episode]. In King, I.M., Craig, C., Goldstick, O., Dougherty, J., Morgenstein, L., & Levy, B. (Executive Producers), *Pretty Little Liars*. Burbank, CA: Warner Bros. Television Distribution.

Holland, S., Hernandez, T., Howe, J., Goetsch, D., Kaplan, E., & Reynolds, J. (Writers), & Cendrowski, M. (Director). (2017). The cognitive regeneration [Television series episode]. In Lorre, C., Molaro, S., Prady, B., & Kaplan, E. (Executive Producers), *The Big Bang Theory*. Burbank, CA: Warner Bros. Television.

Horta, S. (Writer), & Nelli, V. Jr. (Director). (2008). The Manhattan project [Television series episode]. In Hayek, S., Horta, S., Goldstick, S., Silverman,

B., Tamez, J., & Fields, J. (Executive Producers), *Ugly Betty*. Burbank, CA: Disney-ABC Domestic Television.

Howard, J., & Dirksen, P. (Writers), & Chandrasekhar, J. (Director). (2019). CB likes Lainey [Television series episode]. In Firek, M., Robinson, D., Goldberg, A.F., Katzenberg, D., Guarascio, D., & Secunda, A. (Executive Producers), *Schooled*. Culver City, CA: Sony Pictures Television.

Irujo, S. (1986). Don't put your leg in your mouth: Transfer in the acquisition of idioms in a second language. *TESOL Quarterly, 20*, 287-304.

Itoh, H., & Hatch, E. (1978). Second language acquisition: A case study. In E. Hatch (Ed.), *Second Language Acquisition* (pp. 76-90). Rowley, MA: Newbury House.

Jacobs, G., Soderbergh, S., Amiel, J., Begler, M., Sugar, M., & Owen, C. (Executive Producers). (2014). *The Knick* [Television series]. Culver City, CA: Anonymous Content.

Jones, C.J., & Trickett, E.J. (2005). Immigrant adolescents behaving as culture brokers: A study of families from the former Soviet Union. *The Journal of Social Psychology, 145*(4), 405-427.

Jordan, J. (1999, June). Talking with…Wilmer Valderrama. *People, 51*(23), 33.

Kaling, M., Klein, H., Burditt, J., Warburton, M., Grandy, C., Spiller, M., Wigfield, T., Tucker, C., Novak, B.J., & McDougall, C. (Executive Producers). (2012). *The Mindy Project* [Television series]. Universal City, CA: NBCUniversal Television Distribution.

Kaling, M. (Writer), & McDougall, C. (Director). (2012). Pilot [Television series episode]. In Kaling, M., Klein, H., Burditt, J., Warburton, M., Grandy, C., Spiller, M., Wigfield, T., Tucker, C., Novak, B.J., & McDougall, C. (Executive Producers), *The Mindy Project*. Universal City, CA: NBCUniversal Television Distribution.

Kaplan, E., Ferrari, M., Gordon, A., Holland, S., Hernandez, T., & Howe, J. (Writers), & Cendrowski, M. (Director). (2018). The Gates Excitation [Television series episode]. In Lorre, C., Molaro, S., Prady, B., & Kaplan, E. (Executive Producers), *The Big Bang Theory*. Burbank, CA: Warner Bros. Television Distribution.

Kaplan, P.A., & Torgove, M. (Writers), & Gordin, E. (Director). (2013). Burt Mitzvah-the musical [Television series episode]. In Garcia, G.T., Mariano, M., Gutierrez, J., & Stegemann, M. (Executive Producers), *Raising Hope*. Los Angeles, CA: 20th Television.

Kapnek, E. (Writer), & Hardcastle, A. (Director). (2014). Les Lucioles [Television series episode]. In Kapnek, E., & Fresco, M. (Executive Producers), *Suburgatory*. Burbank, CA: Warner Bros. Television Distribution.

Keller, Joel. (2007, October 1). How I met your mother: We're not from here [Review of television series episode]. Retrieved from http://www.tvsquad.com/2007/10/01/how-i-met-your-mother-were-not-from-here/

Kellerman, E. (1979). Transfer and non-transfer: Where we are now. *Studies in Second Language Acquisition, 2*, 37-57.

Kelley, D.E. (Writer), & D'Elia, B. (Director). (2013). Pilot [Television series episode]. In D'Elia, B., Gupta, S., & Kelley, D.E. (Executive Producers), *Monday Mornings*. Atlanta, GA: TNT Original Productions.

Ko, E. (Writer), & Case, R. (Director). (2013). The Future Dunphys [Television series episode]. In Levitan, S., & Lloyd, C. (Executive Producers), *Modern Family*. Los Angeles, CA: 20th Century Fox Television.

Ko, E. (Writer), & Winer, J. (Director). (2012). Virgin territory [Television series episode]. In Levitan, S., & Lloyd, C. (Executive Producers), *Modern Family*. Los Angeles, CA: 20th Century Fox Television.

Kohan, D., & Mutchnick, M. (Writers), & Burrows, J. (Director). (2012). The Key [Television series episode]. In Kohan, D., & Mutchnick, M. (Executive Producers), *Partners*. Burbank, CA: Warner Bros. Television Distribution.

Krashen, S. (1982). *Principles and Practice in Second Language Acquisition*. Oxford: Pergamon.

Krause, Staci. (2007, October 2). How I met your mother: We're not from here [Review of television series episode]. Retrieved from http://tv.ign.com/articles/824/824455p1.html

Kring, T., Hammer, D., Arkush, A., Beerman, G., Shakman, M., Elkoff, P., & Middleton, J. (Executive Producers). (2006). *Heroes* [Television series]. Universal City, CA: NBCUniversal Television Distribution.

Lahr, J. (2009, March). Turf wars. *The New Yorker, 85*(7), 60-62.

Laurents, A. (Writer & Director). (2009). *West Side Story*. Palace Theater, New York, NY.

Leone-Pizzighella, A. (2016). Enregistering *Inglaliano* via parodic metacommentary. *Working Papers in Urban Language and Literacies, WP196*, 2-22.

Levitan, S. (Writer & Director). (2019). A year of birthdays [Television series episode]. In Levitan, S., & Lloyd, C. (Executive Producers), *Modern Family*. Los Angeles, CA: 20th Century Fox Television.

Levitan, S., & Lloyd, C. (Executive Producers). (2009). *Modern Family* [Television series]. Los Angeles, CA: 20th Century Fox Television.

Li, F.T. (2003). *The Acquisition of Metaphorical Expressions, Idioms, and Proverbs by Chinese Learners of English: A Conceptual Metaphor and Image Schema Based Approach* [Unpublished doctoral dissertation]. The Chinese University of Hong Kong, Hong Kong, China.

Libman, D., & Libman, M. (Writers), & Shapeero, T. (Director). (2011). Like father, like gun [Television series episode]. In Caspe, D., Groff, J., Bycel, J., Tarses, J., Russo, A., & Russo, J. (Executive Producers), *Happy Endings*. Culver City, CA: Sony Pictures Television.

Lilien, S., Wynbrandt, B., Hull, R., & Johnson, J. (Writers), & Edwards, P. (Director). (2012). Paxton Petty [Television series episode]. In Abrams, J.J., Bender, J., Burk, B., Johnson, J., & Pyne, D. (Executive Producers), *Alcatraz*. Burbank, CA: Warner Bros. Television.

Lin, J. (Writer), & Liddi-Brown, A. (Director). (2010). The X in the file [Television series episode]. In Hanson, H., Josephson, B., Stephen, N., Toynton, I., Kettner, C., Collier, J., Peterson M., & Zisk, R. (Executive Producers), *Bones*. Los Angeles, CA: 20th Century Fox Television.

Lindemann, Stephanie. (2005). Who speaks "broken English"? US undergraduates' perceptions of non-native English. *International Journal of Applied Linguistics, 15*(2), 187-212.

Lippi-Green, R. (1997). *English with an Accent: Language, ideology and discrimination in the United States.* New York: Routledge.

Lippi-Green, R. (2012). *English with an Accent: Language, ideology and discrimination in the United States, second edition.* New York: Routledge.

Lloyd, S. (Writer), & Fryman, P. (Director). (2011). The exploding meatball sub [Television series episode]. In Bay, C., & Thomas, C. (Executive Producers), *How I Met Your Mother.* Los Angeles, CA: 20th Century Fox Television.

Long, M. (1981). Input, interaction and second-language acquisition. In H. Winitz (Ed.) *Native Language and Foreign Language Acquisition. Annals of the New York Academy of Sciences, Volume 379* (pp. 259-278). New York, NY: The New York Academy of Sciences, Publications Department.

Long, M. (1983a). Native speaker/non-native speaker conversation and the negotiation of comprehensible input. *Applied Linguistics, 4,* 126-41.

Long, M. (1983b). Native speaker/non-native speaker conversation in the second-language classroom. In M. Clark and J. Handscombe (Eds.) *On TESOL '82* (pp. 94-120). Washington, DC: TESOL.

Lopez, Q., & Bucholtz, M. (2017). "How my hair look?" Linguistic authenticity and racialized gender and sexuality on *The Wire. Journal of Language and Sexuality, 6*(1), 1-29.

Lorre, C., Gorodetsky, E., Higgins, A., & Yashere, G. (Executive Producers). (2019). *Bob Hearts Abishola* [Television series]. Burbank, CA: Warner Bros. Television.

Madon, S., Guyll, M., Aboufadel, K., Montiel, E., Smith, A., Palumbo, P., & Jussim, L. (2001). Ethnic and national stereotypes: the Princeton trilogy revisited and revised. *Personality and Social Psychology Bulletin, 27*(8), 996-1010.

Malmuth, J. (Writer), & Patel, G.V. (Director). (2018). Local Vendors Day [Television series episode]. In Spitzer, J., Fleischer, R., Bernad, D., Miller, G., Green, J., & Clarke, J. (Executive Producers), *Superstore.* Universal City, CA: NBCUniversal Television Distribution.

Mandabach, C., Carsey, M., & Werner, T. (Executive Producers). (1998). *That '70s Show* [Television series]. Encino, CA: Carsey-Werner Distribution.

Markert, John. (2004-2007). The George Lopez show: The same old hispano? *Bilingual Review, 28*(2), 148-165.

Marlowe, A., Bowman, R., Bernstein, A., Zaks, L., Schindel, B., Echevarria, R., Amann, D., Grae, D., Hanning, R., Miller, T.E., Winter, T.P., & Hawley, A. (Executive Producers). (2009). *Castle* [Television series]. Burbank, CA: Disney-ABC Domestic Television.

Mastro, D.E., Behm-Morawitz, E., & Kopacz, M.A. (2008). Exposure to television portrayals of Latinos: The implications of aversive *racism* and social *identity* theory. *Human Communication Research, 34*(10), 1-27.

McCormick, B. (Writer), & O'Malley, E. (Director). (2019). Graham D'Amato: hot lunch mentalist [Television series episode]. In Meriwether, E., Pope, K.,

Philbin, J.J., & Winer, J. (Executive Producers), *Single Parents*. Los Angeles, CA: 20th Century Fox Television.

McQuillan, J., & Tse, L. (1995). Child language brokering in linguistic minority communities: Effects on cultural interaction, cognition, and literacy. *Language and Education, 9*(3), 195-215.

Meyer, G., Simon, S., Swartzwelder, J., & Vitti, J. (Writers), & Archer, W., & Gray, M. (Directors). (1990). The crepes of wrath [Television series episode]. In Brooks, J.L., Groening, M., & Simon, S. (Executive Producers), *The Simpsons*. Los Angeles, CA: 20th Century Fox Television.

Meyerhoff, M. (2011). *Introducing Sociolinguistics, second edition*. New York: Routledge.

Michaels, L. (Executive Producer). La policía mexicana (2009, January 17). *Saturday night live* [Television broadcast]. New York: NBC.

Mike. (2007, October 2). How I met your mother. Epidosde recap: We're not from here [Review of television series episode]. Retrieved from http://channelguidemag.wordpress.com/2007/10/02/how-i-met-your-mother-recap-were-not-from-here/

Mintz, L.E. (1996). Humor and ethnic stereotypes in Vaudeville and Burlesque. *MELUS, 21*(4), 19-28.

Mitchell, J.G. (2010). *How I Met Your* foreign boyfriend: what primetime TV tells us about popular attitudes toward L2 English speakers. In Donaher, P (Ed.), *Barbarians at the Gate: Studies in Language Attitudes*. Newcastle upon Tyne: Cambridge Scholars Publishing.

Mitchell, J.G. (2015). Ain't no *Bones* about it: dialect discrimination in prime time. In P. Donaher & S. Katz (Eds.), *Ain'thology: The History and Life of a Taboo Word*. Newcastle upon Tyne: Cambridge Scholars Publishing.

Molina, J. (Writer), & Barrett, D. (Director). (2010). Suicide Squeeze [Television series episode]. In Marlowe, A., Bowman, R., Bernstein, A., Zaks, L., Schindel, B., Echevarria, R., Amann, D., Grae, D., Hanning, R., Miller, T.E., Winter, T.P., & Hawley, A. (Executive Producers), *Castle*. Burbank, CA: Disney-ABC Domestic Television.

Monreal, G. L., & Babcock, D. (Writers), & Morris, M. (Director). (2011). The one that got away [Television series episode]. In Baitz, J.R., Berlanti, G., & Olin, K. (Executive Producers), *Brothers & Sisters*. Burbank, CA: ABC Studios.

Motz, B., Roth, B., & Schwartz, S. (Executive Producers). (2003). *Xiaolin Showdown* (season one) [Television Series]. Burbank, CA: Warner Bros. Television Distribution.

Mull, M. (Writer), & Lowe, C. (Director). (2015). Godparent turkey corn farts [Television series episode]. In Adler, A., Kaplan, A., Morton, J., Winer, J., Copeland, B., & Adler, B. (Executive Producers), *Life in Pieces*. Los Angeles, CA: 20th Century Fox Television.

Murphy, R., Falchuk, B., Di Loreto, D., Brennan, I., Friend, R., Lerner, G., & Buecker, B. (Executive Producers). (2009). *Glee* [Television series]. Los Angeles, CA: 20th Century Fox Television.

Mutchnick, M., Kohan, D., & Burrows, J. (Executive Producers). *Will & Grace* [Television series]. Universal City, CA: NBCUniversal Television Distribution.

Nerlich, B., Clarke, D.D., & Todd, Z. (1999). "Mummy, I like being a Sandwich": Metonymy in language acquisition. In K.-U. Panther & G. Radden (Eds.), *Metonymy in language and thought* (pp. 361-383). Amsterdam: John Benjamins Publishing Co.

Newman, M. (2014). *New York City English*. Boston: Walter de Grutyer.

Otheguy, R., García, O., & Reid, W. (2015). Clarifying translanguaging and deconstructing named languages: A perspective from linguistics. *Applied Linguistics Review*, 6(3), 281-307.

Pandey, A. (2016). *Monolingualism and linguistic exhibitionism in fiction*. New York, NY: Palgrave Macmillan.

Pandey, A. (2019, March). *Multilingualism-lite in the age of post structuralism: stylistics, spatiality, and sociolinguistics under scrutiny*. Paper presented at the Forging Linguistic Identities: Language in the Nation, the Region & the World Conference, Towson, MD.

Paz, J. (2017, April). *When the French become German and a "fucking coconut" becomes a "puta idiota": problems in dubbing & subtitling the L3 on TV*. Paper presented at the 47th Annual Popular Culture/American Culture Association National Conference, San Diego, CA.

Paz, J. (2018, March). *"You live in Miami, why you no learn Spanish?": the many uses of multilingualism in U.S. TV series*. Paper presented at the 48th Annual Popular Culture/American Culture Association National Conference, Indianapolis, IN.

Paz, J. (2019, April). *Shit masks and twatting at boys: dubbing multilingual humor in U.S. television series*. Paper presented at the 49th Annual Popular Culture/American Culture Association National Conference, Washington, D.C.

Pearson, R. (2005). Fact or Fiction?: Narrative and Reality in the Mexican Telenovela. *Television & New Media, 6*, 400-06.

Pedrad, N. (Writer), & Burrows, J. (Director). (2017). Emergency contact [Television series episode]. In Mutchnick, M., Kohan, D., & Burrows, J. (Executive Producers), *Will & Grace*. Universal City, CA: NBCUniversal Television Distribution.

Peterson, M. (Writer), & Little, D. (Director). (2011). The hot dog in the competition [Television series episode]. In Hanson, H., Josephson, B., Stephen, N., Toynton, I., Kettner, C., Collier, J., Peterson M., & Zisk, R. (Executive Producers), *Bones*. Los Angeles, CA: 20th Century Fox Television.

Prinze, F. Jr., Rasmussen, B., Oppenheimer, D., & Helford, B. (Executive Producers). (2005). *Freddie* [Television series]. Burbank, CA: Warner Bros. Television Distribution.

Quaintance, J. (Writer), & Burrows, J. (Director). (2017). A gay olde Christmas [Television series episode]. In Mutchnick, M., Kohan, D., & Burrows, J. (Executive Producers), *Will & Grace*. Universal City, CA: NBCUniversal Television Distribution.

Queen, R. (2004). 'Du hast jar keene Ahnung': African American English dubbed into German. *Journal of Sociolinguistics, 8*(4), 515-37.

Queen, R. (2015). *Vox Popular: The Surprising Life of Language in the Media*. Malden, MA: Wiley-Blackwell.

Rainey, V.R., Flores, V., Morrison, R.G., David, E.J.R., & Silton, R.L. (2014). Mental health risk factors associated with childhood language brokering. *Journal of Multilingual and Multicultural Development, 35*(5), 463-478.

Richards, J.C., & Rodgers, T.S. (2001). *Approaches and Methods in Language Teaching, second edition.* Cambridge: Cambridge University Press.

Richards, J.C., & Wilson, O. (2019). On transidentitying. *RELC Journal, 50*(1), 179-187.

Richardson, J. (Writer), & Davola, J. (Director). (2010). Lists, plans [Television series episode]. In Schwahn, M., Tollins, M., Robbins, B., Davola, J., Prange, G., & Perry, M.B. (Executive Producers), *One Tree Hill.* Burbank, CA: Warner Bros. Television Distribution.

Richman, J. (Writer), & Spiller, M. (Director). (2010). Halloween [Television series episode]. In Levitan, S., & Lloyd, C. (Executive Producers), *Modern Family.* Los Angeles, CA: 20th Century Fox Television.

Richter, E. (Writer), & Clouden, R. (Director). (2013). Kung Pao Turkey [Television series episode]. In MacFarlane, S., Barker, M., Weitzman, M., Boyle, B., Wiener, R., Schwartz, K., Goodman, D.A., Zuckerman, D., & Appel, R. (Executive Producers), *American Dad!.* Los Angeles, CA: 20th Century Fox Television.

Riggi, J. (Writer), & Slovis, M. (Director). (2012). Alexis Goodlooking and the case of the missing whiskey [Television series episode]. In Michaels, L., Fey, T., Klein, M., Miner, D., Carlock, R., & Richmond, J. (Executive Producers), *30 Rock.* Universal City, CA: NBCUniversal Television Distribution.

Rogers, K., & Liptak, L. (2019, July 11). Trump turns to executive action to press citizenship question on census. *The New York Times,* Retrieved from http://www.nytimes.com/

roguecit. (2018, February 1). I need the lyrics to Rapido... [Subreddit post]. Retrieved from https://www.reddit.com/r/GreatNewsTV/comments/7t5dkl/i_need_the_lyrics_to_rapido/

Rosell, R. (Writer), & Fleming, A. (Director). (2013). The box [Television series episode]. In Meriwether, E., Kasden, J., Chernin, P., Pope, K., Finkel, D., & Baer, B. (Executive Producers), *New Girl.* Los Angeles, CA: 20th Century Fox Television.

Rosenstock, K., & Tapscott, S. (Writers), & Chadrasekhar, J. (Director). (2019). That elusive zazz [Television series episode]. In Meriwether, E., Pope, K., Philbin, J.J., & Winer, J. (Executive Producers), *Single Parents.* Los Angeles, CA: 20th Century Fox Television.

Sacchetti, M. (2019, July 10). 'Kids in cages': House hearing examines immigration detention as Democrats push for more information. *The Washington Post,* Retrieved from http://www.washingtonpost.com/

Salsano, S., Jeffress, S., & French, J. (Executive Producers). (2009). *Jersey Shore* [Television series]. Seaside Heights, NJ: 495 Productions.

Santiago, S. (2003). Language Brokering: A Personal Experience. In M. Coleman & L.H. Ganong (Eds.), *Points & Counterpoints: Controversial Relationship and Family issues in the 21st Century, An Anthology* (pp. 160-161). Oxford: Oxford UP.

Saville-Troike, M. (1988). Private speech: Evidence for second-language learning strategies during the "silent period." *Journal of Child Language, 15,* 567-90.

Scarcella, R., & Higa, C. (1981). Input, negotiation, and age differences in second-language acquisition. *Language Learning, 31,* 409-37.

Schaefer, R.T. (2011). *Race and Ethnicity in the United States, sixth edition.* Boston, MA: Prentice Hall.

Schildkraut, D.J. (2003). American Identity and Attitudes Toward Official-English Policies. *Political Psychology, 24*(3), 469-99.

Schmidt, R. Sr. (2002). Racialization and language policy: The case of the U.S.A. *Multilingua, 21,* 141-161.

Schwarz, H. (2014, August 12). States where English is the official language [Blog entry]. *The Washington Post,* Retrieved from https://www.washington post.com/blogs/govbeat/wp/2014/08/12/states-where-english-is-the-official-language/?noredirect=on&utm_term=.726a156f9856)

Seidell, S. (Writer), & Sohn, M. (Director). (2014). Back to School [Television series episode]. In Halpern, E., Haskins, S., Eisenberg, L., & Stupnitsky, G. (Executive Producers), *Trophy Wife.* Burbank, CA: ABC Studios.

Shimosawa, S. (Writer), & Williams, S. (Director). (2014). Mei Chen Returns [Television series episode]. In Seitzman, M., Tripp, V., & Schindel, B, (Executive Producers), *Intelligence.* Santa Monica, CA: CBS Television Distribution.

Shin, S.J. (2018). *Bilingualism in Schools and Society, second edition.* New York, NY: Routledge.

Shuttlesworth, C. (2007). Southern English in Television and Film. In M. Montgomery & E. Johnson (Eds.), *The New Encyclopedia of Southern Culture, Volume 5: Language* (pp. 193-197). Chapel Hill: University of North Carolina Press.

Sikowitz, M. (Writer), & Smith, K. (Director). (2019). Our perfect strangers [Television series episode]. In Goldberg, A.F., Robinson, D., Gordon, S., Barnow, A., Firek, M., Guarascio, D., & Katzenberg, D. (Executive Producers), *The Goldbergs.* Culver City, CA: Sony Pictures Television.

Siqueira, M. & Settineri, F.F. (2003). A aquisição da metáfora: Um estudo exploratório. *Letras de Hoje, 38,* 197-204.

Slade, C., & Beckenham, A. (2005). Introduction. Telenovelas and Soap Operas: Negotiating Reality. *Television & New Media, 6,* 337-41.

Snyder Urman, J., Silverman, B., Pearl, G., Granier, J., & Silberling, B. (Executive Producers). (2014). *Jane the Virgin* [Television series]. Burbank, CA: Warner Bros. Television Distribution.

Stiehm, M., Ried, E., Bernstein, C.G., & Blomgren, L. (Executive Producers). (2013). *The Bridge* [Television series]. Los Angeles, CA: 20th Century Television.

Straton, K., & Walls, R. (Writers), & MacLaren, M. (Director). (2017). All things being equal [Television series episode]. In Levitan, S., & Lloyd, C. (Executive Producers), *Modern Family.* Los Angeles, CA: 20th Century Fox Television.

Sweren, R., & Ambrose, C. (Writers), & Watkins, M. (Director). (2009). Promote this! [Television series episode]. In Wolf, D., Balcer, R., Jankowski, P., &

Berner, F. (Executive Producers), *Law & Order*. Universal City, CA: NBCUniversal Television Distribution.

Tamayo, Y.A. (1997). 'Official Language' Legislation: Literal Silencing/Silenciando La Lengua. *Harvard BlackLetter Law Journal, 13*, 107.

Tatham, C. (Writer), & Fryman, P. (Director). (2013). Romeward bound [Television series episode]. In Bay, C., & Thomas, C. (Executive Producers), *How I Met Your Mother*. Los Angeles, CA: 20ᵗʰ Century Fox Television.

Thompson, G. (2009, March 15). Where Education and Assimilation Collide. *The New York Times* (National Section), pp. 1, 16-18.

Tse, L. (1996). Language brokering in linguistic minority communities: The case of Chinese- and Vietnamese-American students. *The Bilingual Research Journal, 20*(3 & 4), 485-498.

Umaña-Taylor, A. J. (2003). Language Brokering as a Stressor for Immigrant Children and Their Families. In M. Coleman & L.H. Ganong (Eds.), *Points & Counterpoints: Controversial Relationship and Family issues in the 21st Century, An Anthology* (pp. 157-159). Oxford: Oxford UP.

U.S. Department of State. (n.d.). Foreign language training [Webpage]. Retrieved from https://www.state.gov/key-topics-foreign-service-institute/foreign-language-training/

U.S. English. (2016). Official English [Webpage]. Retrieved from https://www.usenglish.org/official-english/about-the-issue/

Viener, J. (Writer), & Langford, J. (Director). (2011). Tiegs for Two [Television series episode]. In MacFarlane, S., Goodman, D., Sheridan, C., Smith, D., Hentemann, M., & Callaghan, S. (Executive Producers), *Family Guy*. Los Angeles, CA: 20ᵗʰ Century Fox Television.

Wayne, M. (Writer), & Youngberg, M. (Director). (2011). It's not easy being Gwen [Television series episode]. In Miller, B.A., Pelphrey, J., Wigzell, T., Swartz, R., & Sorcher, R. (Executive Producers), *Ben 10: Ultimate Alien*. Burbank, CA: Warner Bros. Television Distribution.

Webster, L.W. (Writer), & Holland, T. (Director). (2013). Gooooaaaallll doll! [Television series episode]. In Silveri, S., Holland, T., Burke, K., & Pollack, J. (Executive Producers), *Go On*. Universal City, CA: NBCUniversal Television Distribution.

Wells, T.V. Jr., Karp, B.S., Birenboim, B., & Brown, D.W. (2014, February 14). *Report To The National Football League Concerning Issues Of Workplace Conduct At The Miami Dolphins*.

Whedon, J., Solomon, D., & Minear, T. (Executive Producers). (2009). *Dollhouse* [Television series]. Los Angeles, CA: 20ᵗʰ Century Fox Television.

Wilson, S. (2006, March 9). Freddie Prinze Jr. Impact players special report 1: V plus: Latino impact report. *Daily Variety*, A9-10.

Wolf, D., Balcer, R., Jankowski, P., & Berner, F. (Executive Producers). (1990). *Law & Order* [Television series]. Universal City, CA: NBCUniversal Television Distribution.

Woody, R. (Writer) & Lembeck, M. (Director). (2018). Thanksgiving and taking [Television series episode]. In Bergen, C., Saltzman, M., Bragin, R., Diamond, B., Flanagan, M., Shukovsky, J., English, D., Schotz, E., Siamis, K.,

Bowman, J., Dontzig G., & Peterman, S. (Executive Producers), *Murphy Brown*. Burbank, CA: Warner Bros. Television Distribution.

Worth, R.A. (2006). *Learner Resistance in the University Foreign Language Classroom* [Unpublished doctoral dissertation]. University of Wisconsin-Madison, Madison, WI.

Worth, R.A. (2008). Foreign Language Resistance: Discourse analysis of online classroom peer interactions. In S.S. Magnan (Ed.), *Mediating Discourse Online* (pp. 245-271). Amsterdam: John Benjamin Publishing Co.

Wu, F.H. (2002) *Yellow: Race in America Beyond Black and White*. New York: Basic Books.

Zbyszewski, P., & Roland, G. (Writers), & Edwards, P. (Director). (2010). The package [Television series episode]. In Abrams, J.J., Lindelof, D., Burk, B., Cuse, C., Bender, J., Pinkner, J., Williams, S., Kitsis, E., Horowitz, A., Higgins, J., & Sarnoff, E. (Executive Producers), *Lost*. Santa Monica, CA: Bad Robot Productions.

Zuiker, A.E., Petersen, W., Bruckheimer, J., Donahue, A., Fink, K., Shankar, N., & Cannon, D. (Executive Producers). (2000). *CSI: Crime Scene Investigation* [Television series]. Los Angeles, CA: King World Productions.

Zuker, D. (Writer), & Levitan, S. (Director). (2011). See you next fall [Television series episode]. In Levitan, S., & Lloyd, C. (Executive Producers), *Modern Family*. Los Angeles, CA: 20th Century Fox Television.

Index